Georg Cavallar
Kant's Embedded Cosmopolitanism

Kantstudien-Ergänzungshefte

—

Im Auftrag der Kant-Gesellschaft
herausgegeben von
Manfred Baum, Bernd Dörflinger
und Heiner F. Klemme

Band 183

Georg Cavallar
Kant's Embedded Cosmopolitanism

History, Philosophy, and Education for World Citizens

DE GRUYTER

ISBN 978-3-11-055467-0
e-ISBN (PDF) 978-3-11-042940-4
e-ISBN (EPUB) 978-3-11-042945-9
ISSN 0340-6059

Library of Congress Cataloging-in-Publication Data
A CIP catalog record for this book has been applied for at the Library of Congress.

Bibliographic information published by the Deutsche Nationalbibliothek
The Deutsche Nationalbibliothek lists this publication in the Deutsche Nationalbibliografie; detailed bibliographic data are available on the Internet at http://dnb.dnb.de.

© 2017 Walter de Gruyter GmbH, Berlin/Boston
This volume is text- and page-identical with the hardback published in 2015.
Printing and binding: Hubert & Co. GmbH & Co. KG, Göttingen

♾ Printed on acid-free paper
Printed in Germany

www.degruyter.com

Contents

Acknowledgements —— VII

Abbreviations —— IX

1 Introduction —— 1
1.1 Types of cosmopolitanisms —— 4
1.2 The new Kant —— 5
1.3 Was Kant really a cosmopolitan? —— 10
1.4 Kant's embedded and dynamic cosmopolitanism —— 13
1.5 Outline of the book —— 15

2 Cosmopolitanisms in Kant's philosophy —— 21
2.1 Cosmopolitanisms according to Kant —— 23
2.2 The concept of the highest good: immanent or transcendent? —— 30
2.3 Kant's philosophy of history: The manipulation, education or self-education of humankind? —— 40
2.4 The ethical commonwealth: the duty of the human race towards itself —— 44

3 Kant's right of world citizens: a historical interpretation —— 49
3.1 Kant's commercial cosmopolitanism —— 51
3.2 The historical context I: international legal theory —— 55
3.3 The historical context II: the spirit of commerce, the four-stage theory, *doux commerce*, global integration, and mutual self-interest —— 64

4 Educating Émile: Rousseau on embedded cosmopolitanism —— 76
4.1 Rousseau's attack on forms of cosmopolitanism —— 77
4.2 Rousseau's tentative republican cosmopolitanism —— 78
4.3 Rousseau's vision of cosmopolitan education —— 81
4.4 The limitations of Rousseau's approach —— 87

5 Sources of Kant's cosmopolitanism: Basedow, Rousseau, and cosmopolitan education —— 92
5.1 Johann Bernhard Basedow: a cosmopolitan-minded educational reformer —— 94
5.2 Kant's assessment of Basedow's educational theory —— 97

5.3 Rousseau: The split between cosmopolitan *homme* and patriotic *citoyen* —— 102
5.4 Reinterpreting Rousseau: dynamic moral cosmopolitanism —— 105

6 Taking a detour: Kant's theory of moral cosmopolitan formation —— 117
6.1 An outline of moral education according to Kant —— 119
6.2 Education following Kantian principles as cosmopolitan formation —— 124

7 Res publica: Kant on cosmopolitical formation —— 133
7.1 The republican tradition and the Kantian republic —— 134
7.2 Cosmopolitical education according to Kant —— 136
7.3 Kant's vision of progress in a genuine republic —— 140

8 Conclusion: From Kant to the present —— 147
8.1 From cosmopolitanism to nation states in German philosophy: Schiller, Novalis, Fichte, Hegel, Herbart (1795–1835) —— 147
8.2 Kant's cosmopolitanism as a historical phenomenon: metaphysics, history, contingency —— 161
8.3 Kant's legacy and the new cosmopolitanism —— 165
8.4 Kant's didactics, contemporary discourses, and cultural developments —— 174

Bibliography —— 181

Subject index —— 207

Index of names —— 214

Acknowledgements

Kant's is omnipresent in contemporary cosmopolitan discourses. According to a widespread assumption, Kant's philosophy is a key or even *the* major source of contemporary cosmopolitan theories, of what Fine calls the "new cosmopolitanism" (see Fine 2003: 609 and 2007: 7). In this book, I claim that the interpretation of Kant as the key founding father of the new cosmopolitanism is largely unfounded. Without any doubt, there is some overlap (for instance, in terms of normative individualism or the focus on the normative basis of cosmopolitanism), but he differs in many respects from contemporary approaches. The problem is that many contemporary interpretations tend to offer a homogenised view of the past; they use a very broad brush to see continuity from Kant to the present. They very often wind up with an anachronistic and Whiggish interpretation. The Kant presented on these pages is therefore not (only) the founding father of present cosmopolitan discourses but above all a challenge to them. My interpretation sides with those contemporary Kant scholars who tend to emphasize the difference rather than the continuity with the present (which does not imply that we have to deny the latter out of hand). The authors who have influenced me in this respect are, among others, Katrin Flikschuh, Georg Geismann, Norbert Hinske, Lutz Koch and Rudolf Langthaler.

Several conferences and personal contacts were indispensable in writing this book: my special thanks go to Sorin Baiasu, Gideon Baker, Garrett Brown, Lorena Cebolla, Lutz Koch, Chris Laursen, Rudolf Langthaler, Rebecca Lettevall, Robert Louden, Herlinde Pauer-Studer, Hans Schelkshorn, Howard Williams, and Sandra Zakutna. I have begun to understand Kant's claim that, even if philosophy is about thinking for oneself or *Selberdenken*, we need others to *learn* to think for ourselves. I am also indebted to the editors of the *Kantstudien-Ergänzungshefte*, Heiner Klemme and Bernd Dörflinger, and Gertrud Grünkorn and Johanna Wange from De Gruyter for invaluable support.

Several chapters are based on previous articles and papers. The second chapter, "Cosmopolitanisms in Kant's philosophy", is a revised version of an article of the same title, printed by *Ethics and Global Politics*, 5 (2012), 95–118. Chapter three on Kant's famous *Weltbürgerrecht* was first published in Rebecka Lettevall and Kristian Petrov, eds., *Critique of Cosmopolitan Reason: Timing and Spacing the Concept of World Citizenship* (Oxford: Peter Lang 2014), 141–79. The fourth chapter is very different from its first version, printed as "Educating Émile: Jean-Jacques Rousseau on Cosmopolitanism" in *European Legacy*, 17, 4 (2012), 485–99, see www.tandfonline.com, as I have revised my Rousseau and Kant interpretation since then. The fifth chapter was my first foray into a field that I call "cosmopolitan formation" in this book. "Sources of Kant's cosmopolitanism: Rousseau, Basedow and cosmopolitan education" was published in *Studies in Philosophy and Education*, 33, 4 (2014), 369–389. The sixth chapter is a modified version of "Taking a detour: Kant's theory of moral cosmopolitan education", part of a volume edited by Tom Bailey and Garrett W. Brown, *Publicity and Cosmopolitics* (Edinburgh: Edinburgh University Press 2015). The seventh chapter grew out of a paper presented at the Kant conference at the Faculty of Arts, University of Prešov, Slovakia, in May 2014, and was subsequently printed as "Res publica: Kant on cosmopolitical formation (*Bildung*)" in *Studia Philosophica Kantiana*, 5, 1, (2014), 3–22. The "Introduction" and the "Conclusion" are original contributions. I want to thank all the publishers for the permission to use previous material.

My greatest debts are to my family, to my wife Angelika and our three children Clemens, Valentina and Antonia. Writing a book about embedded cosmopolitanism and cosmopolitan education is fairly easy; helping one's own children to develop and cultivate a cosmopolitan disposition is a challenge. Becoming a cosmopolitan oneself is perhaps an impossible task.

Abbreviations

All references to Kant's works are in accordance with the *Akademie-Edition* Vol. 1–29 of *Kant's Gesammelte Schriften*, Berlin/Leipzig, 1902-. References to the *Critique of Pure Reason* follow the customary pagination of the first (A) and second (B) edition. The English translations are from the *Cambridge Edition of the Works of Immanuel Kant,* New York: Cambridge University Press, 1992-. The following abbreviations are used:

Anthropology	= *Anthropologie in Pragmatischer Hinsicht* (1798), *Anthropology from a Pragmatic Standpoint*
Beginning	= "Muthmaßlicher Anfang der Menschengeschichte" (1786), "Conjectural beginning of human history"
Collins	= Collins, *From the Lectures of Professor Kant* (1784–5)
Conflict	= *Streit der Fakultäten* (1798), *Conflict of the Faculties*
End	= "Das Ende aller Dinge" (1794), "The End of All Things"
Enlightenment	= "Beantwortung der Frage: Was ist Aufklärung?" (1784), "An Answer to the Question: What is Enlightenment?"
Groundwork	= *Grundlegung zur Metaphysik der Sitten* (1785), *Groundwork of the Metaphysics of Morals*
Herder	= Herder, *Kant's practical philosophhy*
Idea	= "Idee zu einer allgemeinen Geschichte in weltbürgerlicher Absicht" (1784), "Idea toward a Universal History with a Cosmopolitan Aim"
KrV	= *Kritik der reinen Vernunft* (1781, 1787). Cited by A/B pagination, *Critique of Pure Reason*
KpV	= *Kritik der praktischen Vernunft* (1788), *Critique of Practical Reason*
KdU	= *Kritik der Urteilskraft* (1790), *Critique of the Power of Judgment*
Logic	= *Immanuel Kant's Logik* (1800), *Lectures on Logic*
LP	= *Pädagogik* (1803), *Lectures on Pedagogy*
LR	= *Vorlesungen über die philosophische Religionslehre*, *Lectures on the philosophical doctrine of religion*
MM	= *Metaphysik der Sitten* (1797–1798), *Metaphysics of Morals*
Observations	= *Beobachtungen über das Gefühl des Schönen und Erhabenen* (1764), *Observations on the Feeling of the Beautiful and Sublime*
Peace	= *Zum ewigen Frieden: Ein philosophischer Entwurf* (1795), *Toward Perpetual Peace: A Philosophical Project*
Philanthropinum	= "Aufsätze, das Philanthropin betreffend" (1776/1777), "Essays regarding the Philanthropinum"
Principles	= *Über den Gebrauch teleologischer Principien in der Philosophie* (1788), *On the Use of Teleological Principles in Philosophy*
Religion	= *Religion innerhalb der Grenzen der bloßen Vernunft* (1793), *Religion Within the Boundaries of Mere Reason*
Theodicy	= "Über das Misslingen aller philosophischen Versuche in der Theodicee" (1791), "On the miscarriage of all philosophical trials in theodicy"

Thinking	= "Was heißt: Sich im Denken orientieren?" (1786), "What does it mean to orient oneself in thinking?"
Tone	= "Von einem neuerdings erhobenen vornehmen Ton in der Philosophie" (1796), "On a recently prominent tone of superiority in philosophy"
TP	= "Über den Gemeinspruch: Das mag in der Theorie richtig sein, taugt aber nicht für die Praxis" (1793), "On the Common Saying: That May Be Correct in Theory But It Is of No Use in Practice".

1 Introduction

> The final vocation of the human race is moral perfection,
> so far as it is accomplished through human freedom
>
> Collins, 27: 470

"Kant was enough of a child of the eighteenth century to be cosmopolitan, not nationalistic, in his feeling", John Dewey wrote in 1915 (Dewey 1970: 98). With this statement, Dewey reproduces the familiar cliché of the allegedly "cosmopolitan Enlightenment". Yet recent studies emphasize the diversity and complexity of the term "cosmopolitan" in the eighteenth century, stress that many intellectuals just displayed a pro-European attitude, often equated cosmopolitanism with moderate patriotism, and were frequently challenged by critics (see among others Albrecht 2005, Cavallar 2011). Secondly, Dewey dogmatically assumes that Kant's cosmopolitanism was "nothing but" a reflex or mirror of widespread intellectual stances. Dewey's assessment is dogmatic by standards of Kant's critical epistemology (the causal relationship is never proven), and this study will try to show that Kant's theory of cosmopolitanism is the outcome of his own systematically developed practical philosophy, not a mere repetition or copy of widely held Enlightenment beliefs. Third, Dewey does not even attempt to understand Kant's systematic approach, which is not a matter of feeling, but of rational argumentation, not a matter of unthinking copy-and-paste, but of profound reflection, of an analysis of possible alternative positions, and a careful reworking of one's own thoughts over the years (for a full analysis see Kleingeld 2012). Finally, Dewey's attempt to situate Kant historically (as a child of the Enlightenment) in turn invites historical contextualization. The context of Dewey's assessment is the hysteria of the Great War, when one's enemies and their most formidable thinkers were usually perceived as illiberal, militaristic, nationalistic, and politically extremist. German authors in turn offered similar biased judgements of thinkers allegedly belonging to the allied camp; these Germans were apparently even more radical. And they sometimes believed that Kant should not belong to the camp of the "true Germans". It is interesting to note here that some German intellectuals before 1945 almost hated Kant for what they perceived as a cosmopolitan attitude or disposition, and believed he should have become an ardent German nationalist instead (cf. Cavallar 1992: 247–52, 433–5, 445–50).

Roughly one hundred years later, the intellectual climate has considerably changed. For most scholars in the U. S., Germany and elsewhere, the term cosmopolitanism is no longer an insult. Intellectuals outside Germany have started to appreciate Kant's cosmopolitanism, among them politicians, political scientists like Garrett Brown, philosophers like Martha Nussbaum or Kant scholars like Pauline Kleingeld or Robert Louden. Scholars have started to investigate into the ramifications of the concept in Kant's philosophy (see among others Bacin et al. 2013). Theories of cosmopolitanism, widely discussed in recent years, are the background of this new focus (see, among others, Fine 2009, Baker 2013, Brown and Held 2010, Halldenius 2010, Lutz-Bachmann, Niederberger and Schink 2010 and Cavallar 2011). Historical studies of the concept are rare, but Kant is usually seen as one of the founding fathers of contemporary cosmopolitanism (see for instance Cheneval 2002, Brown 2009 and Kleingeld 2012). At roughly the same time, cosmopolitan educational theories have been developed, and vigorously discussed (recent contributions include Hansen 2010, McCarty 2010, Nussbaum 2010, Todd 2009, Waks 2009 and 2010, Zembylas 2010). Finally, there has been a renewed interest in Kant and his educational theory (see Breun 2002, Kauder 1999, Koch 2003, Moran 2009, Surprenant 2010, and Roth and Surprenant 2012 among others). Kant's omnipresence in contemporary cosmopolitan discourses contrasts with the fact that little is known about the historical origins of his cosmopolitan theory.

Kant's Embedded Cosmopolitanism argues that many contemporary interpretations are potentially anachronistic and one-sided. It examines the historical context of Kant's cosmopolitanism, and focuses on its neglected pedagogical and republican dimension. It argues that Kant's cosmopolitanism should be understood as rooted in one's particular community and thus embedded. Inspired by Rousseau, Kant tried to develop a synthesis of republican patriotism and republican as well as thin moral cosmopolitanism. In contrast to static forms of cosmopolitanism prevalent in traditional conceptions, Kant belonged to a generation of Enlightenment reformers who conceived the tensions between embedded, local attachments and cosmopolitan obligations in dynamic terms. Kant in particular posited duties to promote the legal, moral and religious communities, to establish common laws or cosmopolitan institutions, and to develop a cosmopolitan disposition. This is the cornerstone of Kant's cosmopolitanism, and the key concept is the vocation (*Bestimmung*) of the individual as well as of the human species. Since trying to realize or at least approach this vocation was a long-term, arduous and slow process, Kant turned to the pedagogical implications of this "project" and spelled them out in his later writings. Embedding Kant in his proper late eighteenth century context, the book analyses possible influences, in particular the writings of Rousseau and educational reformer

Basedow. In short, rather than jumping to the facile and Whiggish conclusion that Kant's cosmopolitanism merely anticipated contemporary forms of cosmopolitanism, the book emphasizes possible differences and the uniqueness of Kant's cosmopolitan theory, even by late eighteenth-century standards.

Recent years have witnessed a growing interest in the concept and theories of cosmopolitanism and of cosmopolitan educational theories. So far there has been only one comprehensive interpretation of Kant's cosmopolitanism, Pauline Kleingeld, *Kant and Cosmopolitanism. The Philosophical Ideal of World Citizenship* (Cambridge University Press 2012). The main theses of this excellent book are innovative, well argued, and plausible. Yet her book also has a few shortcomings: Rousseau is presented as a critic of cosmopolitanism and is ignored by and large; his possible influence on Kant is not discussed. While Kleingeld's book is very strong in contrasting Kant's views with those of his contemporaries, the author has little to say about the moral and educational dimensions of Kant's cosmopolitan theory. Finally, I claim that Kant's concept of an ethical commonwealth is deeply rooted in his understanding of Christianity and the role the Christian churches (clearly favoured over other religious traditions). In Kleingeld's account, the ethical commonwealth, together with the concept of the highest good, are presented as fully secularized notions.

To my knowledge, only one monograph and one dissertation have so far been published on cosmopolitan education. Sharon Todd's *Toward an Imperfect Education. Facing Humanity, Rethinking Cosmopolitanism* (Boulder and London: Paradigm Publishers 2009) occasionally refers to Kant. Todd bypasses Kant's theory of moral formation and its cosmopolitan dimension, and instead offers a brief interpretation of his cosmopolitan right. Matthew J. Hayden's dissertation *Cosmopolitan Education and Moral Education: Forging Moral Beings Under Conditions of Global Uncertainty* (Dissertation Columbia University 2012) develops a contemporary theory of moral cosmopolitan education based on the "fundamental fact of shared humanity" (p. 18). He is above all inspired by authors such as Arendt, Nagel, Habermas and Mouffe; Kant plays an insignificant role.

Felicitas Munzel's excellent *Kant's Conception of Pedagogy. Toward Education for Freedom* (Evanston, Illinois: Northwestern University Press 2012) sometimes overlaps with what I try to do in this study. Munzel's key claim is that Kant's doctrines of method (*Methodenlehren*) in the three critiques contain a "fourth critique" (cf. XVf., XIX, 232). According to Munzel, critical philosophy is in fact a pedagogical project, "essentially a *paideia*" (XXI), which is the programme of cultivating the mind with the goal of wisdom and fulfilling one's vocation, namely autonomy and inner freedom. "From Kant's perspective, the basic pedagogical task is not the inculcation of a principle (such as the prevalent effort in the eighteenth century to curb the detrimental effects of the workings of self-interest by instilling some variant of 'love thy neighbor'), but rather the task is the preparation of the mind to exercise its inherent principle of freedom" (XX). Although Munzel's monograph and my study sometimes overlap, there are different emphases: Munzel's goal is to assign Kant a place "among the great pedagogical thinkers" (ibid., 83, cf. 181) and to explore his educational theory, whereas I try to investigate into Kant's cosmopolitanism (and its educational ramifications). In the first part of her study, Munzel situates Kant's pedagogy within the divergent educational theories of the 18th century (5–183); my own focus is almost exclusively on Rousseau, Basedow and Spalding. Munzel is interested in inner, moral freedom as the transcendental condition of the possibility of external, political freedom: true political freedom presupposes moral freedom (cf. XVI, 83, 171–9, 233). My own approach looks at the issue from a different angle: external freedom helps humans to cultivate their dispositions and thus also their moral potentials as free moral agents (see chapters 6 and 7). Our respective studies definitely overlap when Munzel develops "Articles for a Cosmopolitan Education" (cf. 285–93).

1.1 Types of cosmopolitanisms

Cosmopolitanism is the belief or the theory that all humans, regardless of race, gender, religion or political affiliation belong to, or should belong to, one single community. Cosmopolitanism's three basic tenets are: its reach is global in scope, all humans belong to it. Second, it includes an element of normative universalism: all humans enjoy equal moral status, and they share certain essential features. The focus is on individuals, not on nations, tribes or peoples. Finally, this global community should be cultivated and promoted, for instance, by trying to understand cultures different from one's own (see Albrecht 2005: 22–61, Benhabib 2004: 133, Hayden 2005: 3, Held 2010, Kleingeld 1999: 505, Kleingeld and Brown 2002).

Implicitly or explicitly, contemporary discourses usually distinguish among different types of cosmopolitanism (see among others Kleingeld 1999 and Hayden 2012: 23–40). The core idea of *human rights* (or *moral*) cosmopolitanism is that there are universal rights and obligations, and these should not be limited in scope, that is, they should be applied to all human beings. *Political* cosmopolitanism usually argues for some sort of global world order based on the rule of international law. Some – but not all – advocate a world federation or world state (Cavallar 2011, Kleingeld 1999, Hansen 2008: 292). *Cultural* cosmopolitanism acknowledges the diversity of cultures across the globe, and claims that "we should recognize different cultures in their particularity" (Kleingeld 1999:

515). In the eighteenth century, *economic* or *commercial* cosmopolitanism held "that the economic market should become a single global sphere of free trade" (Kleingeld 1999: 518). Major representatives were Adam Smith and other intellectuals of the Scottish Enlightenment, but also the German Dietrich Hermann Hegewisch. In recent years, economic exchange unrestricted by state intervention has been attacked as neoliberalism, and classic economic cosmopolitanism has been reformulated in a way that includes elements of moral and political cosmopolitanism (Hansen 2008: 293, Sen 1999). *Epistemological* cosmopolitanism is a way of thinking ("global thinking", according to Ulrich Beck), a cognitive orientation with the key feature of impartiality. It is a disposition which may lead to openness towards others (Beck 2006, Vertovec and Cohen 2002: 13).

Forms of cosmopolitanism can come in thin (moderate, weak) or thick (strong, extreme) versions. Strong moral cosmopolitanism, for instance, claims that loyalties, affiliations and preferences at the local level can *only* be justified "by reference to the interests of all human beings considered as equals." Thin moral cosmopolitanism, on the other hand, claims that the ideal of world citizenship is not the ultimate source of legitimization. This type of cosmopolitanism simply insists "that one's local attachments and affiliations must always be balanced and constrained by considerations of the interests of other people" (Scheffler 2001: 115).

The different forms of cosmopolitanism are not mutually exclusive. In fact, most cosmopolitan theories include elements of various forms. For instance, Martha Nussbaum combines thick and cognitive moral cosmopolitanism with cultural and epistemological cosmopolitanism (Friedman 2000). Kwame Anthony Appiah argues for "rooted cosmopolitanism", which negotiates between legitimate local loyalties and universalism. In contrast to Nussbaum's approach in the 1990ies (which she modified later on), he holds that local affiliations are not derivative. Appiah thus argues for a version of thin moral cosmopolitanism (Appiah 1996 and 2007; see also Hansen 2008: 292–3).

1.2 The new Kant

At the time of John Dewey, a narrow focus on the first Critique, the *Critique of Pure Reason* (1781), was widespread. All too often, Kant's other works, especially his anthropology, his doctrine of right and his philosophy of religion, were seen as a mere appendix, or as contradicting critical philosophy. The standard of "critical" was usually derived from an interpretation of the first Critique. This also applied to most representatives of Neo-Kantianism (cf. Heinz and Krijnen 2007, Alexy 2002). An example of this generic trend is the Austrian legal philosopher

Hans Kelsen (1881–1973), who dismissed the *Rechtslehre* of 1797 as "completely useless" (Kelsen 1992: 58), rejected Kant's alleged "metaphysical dualism" (Kelsen 1928: 349), and claimed that the concept of practical reason was "untenable" (Kelsen 1960: 419; cf. 425) since the categorical imperative was empty (Kelsen 1960: 368–74). Kelsen himself reconstructed a "pure science of law" (*reine Rechtslehre*) from the premises of Kant's epistemology expounded in the first Critique (Kelsen 1960, Haase 2004). Kelsen was influenced by Neo-Kantianism and its particular scientific and positivistic approach to Kant's philosophy (Kelsen 1988, Paulson 2002 and 2006).

Neo-Kantianism came under attack in the 1920ies; the centennial of Kant's birthday in 1924 and the dispute between Ernst Cassirer and Martin Heidegger at Davos in 1929 are usually seen as turning points (Cavallar 1992: 256–7, Mertens 2002). Roughly since the 1970ies, a string of interpretations has moved further away from Neo-Kantianism and conventional interpretive patterns, and argued for a much richer account. In moral philosophy, interpreters have, for instance, investigated into Kant's account of perfection and humility, his conception of human flourishing and happiness, the role of moral and aesthetic feeling and his theory of motivation, and have discussed whether it makes sense to speak of Kantian virtue ethics (Dean 2006, Grenberg 2005, Jost and Wuerth 2011, Munzel 1999, Reath 2006, Recki 2001 and 2012). They have challenged the old and widespread cliché that Kant's approach implies the solipsistic isolation of the transcendental ego and suggest that if there is a reduced account of human agency in the *Groundwork*, then only for methodological reasons. They claim that Kant's mature position is not that of solipsistic, but that of public and communicative reason, and that Kantian morality entails the opening up towards the world, either (only) "in thought" or also (and more importantly) in practice, by checking the validity of our judgements with the help of others (cf. Anthropology, 7: 219; Keienburg 2011, Moran 2012). Judgements are exercised in interaction with others, and the enlarged conduct of thought even *requires* others and their divergent perspectives. Kant's notion of autonomy is social or relational – that is, embedded in the context of the moral agent's relationship to other rational beings – rather than individualist in the sense of an unencumbered, isolated rational agent (cf. Rossi 2005: 30–2, 43–4 and Recki 2006: 111–25).

Critics have often deplored the fact that Kant's ethics seem to lack any social dimension. More recent interpreters tend to emphasize the central role of the ethical commonwealth and of the highest good, and reinterpret his ethics as a "system of ends" (Langthaler 1991 and 2014, Reath 2006: 173–95, Rossi 2005, Moran 2012). As Kate Moran put it, "we must first overcome the tendency to think that Kant's moral philosophy is wholly non-consequential and unconcerned with achieving an end" (Moran 2011: 96). Earlier authors like Lewis White Beck tended to dismiss Kant's doctrine of the highest good. More recently, authors have reassessed these negative judgements and asked whether the juxtaposition of pure moral motivation and autonomy as opposed to teleological morality with eudaimonistic elements is not too narrow. They emphasize that Kant distinguished between "determining ground" and "object" of the will. According to Kant, the moral law, as the ground of moral action, necessarily has an object, the highest good. Some argue that the concept of the highest good might serve as a supplement to Kant's theory of moral motivation, since the moral agent has to believe that attaining the highest good is possible to avoid despair (see the discussion in O'Connell, 2008). Promoting the highest good is not only the task of individuals, but of the whole species working together, a "shared project" (Moran 2011: 95).

Traditionally, Kant's doctrine of radical evil has been seen as an untenable rehearsal of the Christian teaching of original sin, and as incompatible with the principles of autonomy and inner freedom. Others have been worried that nowhere Kant seems to offer a convincing, systematic and coherent proof of his doctrine. Revisionist interpreters have tried to make sense of Kant, attempting to reconstruct Kant's complex arguments and the systematic role of the notion of radical evil within Kant's practical philosophy (see for instance Anderson-Gold and Muchnik 2010, Muchnik 2009, 2010, Kemp 2011). Ryan Kemp, for instance, concludes that Kant's reasoning is coherent if we realize that he moves from the noumenal to the anthropological level, from individuals to the whole species, and that he does not offer an empirical generalization, but a reflective, regulative judgement: "Kant's proclamation concerning the universality of evil is merely regulative – a heuristic posited by reflective judgment" (Kemp 2011: 103). Pablo Muchnik claims that Kant offers in the *Religion* a complex architectonic that mixes empirical and a priori elements in a "moral anthropology" that focuses both on the disposition (*Gesinnung*) and the "heart" of the individual and the propensity (*Hang*) of the whole species. "The traditional deontological picture of Kant, confined to evaluating isolated actions, must give way to a view in which the individual's *Gesinnung* and the collective dimension of the moral enterprise take center stage" (Muchnik 2009: XXV). Interpreters have also "discovered" Kant's concept of pedagogy and his ethical didactics, his unique theory of moral education which has been neglected for almost two hundred years (see chapter 6 for more).

In the 1960ies, Stuart M. Brown summarized a widespread assessment of Kant's legal and political philosophy, asserting that he failed in his attempt at a critical legal theory "and has no philosophy of law" (Brown 1962: 36). Many interpreters since then have moved away from this negative evaluation, investigating into Kant's historical sources (Byrd and Hruschka 2010), arguing that the legal philosophy should be considered part of Kant's overall critical work (Kersting 1993, Flikschuh 2003 and Ripstein 2009), stressing the role of publicity and of public (not solipsistic) reason (Blesenkemper 1987, Gerhardt 1995, Simon 2003, Keienburg 2011), and praising Kant's philosophy of peace and its cosmopolitan dimension, in particular his cosmopolitan right (see chapter 3). In a similar vein, many interpreters have underlined the critical modesty of Kant's tentative and reflective philosophy of history and its innovative methodology, investigated into its roots in Enlightenment philosophy and historiography, and contrasted it with the more daring systems of German idealism (Cohen 2009: 109–142, Rorty 2009, Sommer 2006).

Kant defined pragmatic anthropology as a practical science that helps us to realize our inner freedom and asymptotically approach our moral vocation. Interpreters have usually discussed the systematic status of anthropology vis-à-vis pure philosophy. They debated, for instance, whether Kant's anthropology is fundamental to his moral philosophy or merely supplements it; whether it plays a role in specifying ethical duties or has a pedagogical function, considering the subjective conditions of fulfilling the moral law (for an introduction see Cohen 2009: 35–108, Falduto 2014: 53–126, Jacobs and Kain 2003, Louden 2000, Sturm 2009, Thorndike 2008 and 2011). Recent studies have looked into Kant's complex theory of moral motivation, which includes the feeling of respect for the moral law (Falduto 2014: 204–41, Guyer 2010 and Recki 2012). This contradicts the standard interpretation (or perhaps prejudice) that there is no room for any form of feelings in Kant's ethics. A focus pertaining to this study is the vocation (*Bestimmung*) of the individual and of the human species "*in weltbürgerlicher Bedeutung*" and Kant's cosmopolitan conception of human nature, a type of anthropology that is not empirical but "cosmological" in that it focuses on what human beings "in all times and places share with one another" (Louden 2008: 97) and specifies what they can make of themselves as potentially moral actors (see Brandt 2003, 2009 and the works by Louden).

Kant's pedagogy is usually seen as part of Kant's applied moral philosophy, with strong ties to philosophical, "pragmatic" anthropology. For a long time, Kant's texts about education, in particular moral education and ethical didactics, have been neglected. In the English speaking world, Lewis White Beck offered what might be seen as a typical assessment: Beck claimed in an essay published in the late 1970ies that Kant "does not even seem to see that his strict moral philosophy has, and can have, no place for moral education" (Beck 1979: 201). This standard interpretation is based on the mistaken assumption that morality is an all-or-nothing affair and that autonomy cannot be taught or educated – or more provocatively, that there cannot be a bridge between the phenomenal level (educational endeavours) and the noumenal world (autonomy, freedom of the will). Recent interpretations have challenged this standard interpretation. Perhaps 2003 can be seen as a turning point: in their respective works, Michael Großmann and Lutz Koch claimed that Kant's pedagogy formed an integral part of Kant's critical system, and argued that his concept of ethical didactics or moral formation does not only make sense, but is a unique and extremely innovative phenomenon in the history of moral philosophy (see also Roth and Surprenant 2012 and Munzel 2012).

More recent research has also outlined the overarching philosophical system Kant intended, focusing on the teleological principles outlined in the *Critique of the Power of Judgment* (1790) and revolving around the power of judgment, the concept of the ultimate end and the final end, the sublime, the vocation of the human species, and the highest good. Kant's text is of unmitigated complexity, and culminates in a moral theology (cf. §§ 85–91). The key thesis is that the human species is the ultimate end (*letzter Zweck*) of nature, and that the final end (*Endzweck*) of creation is unconditional and independent of nature, namely the highest moral good approached by noumenal humanity. Nature cannot produce a final end, but can reflectively be interpreted as a "moral facilitator" (Rorty 2009: 40) which promotes the ultimate end with the help of culture. The third Critique outlines ways and methods of mediation (*Vermittlung*) between the phenomenal and the noumenal in a conscious attempt to bridge the gap between the two. Reflective judgement asserts the compatibility of nature and the concept of the highest good. Our vocation is revealed by the sublime, and entails becoming a fully developed human being by controlling one's inner nature and promoting the highest good (Guyer 2003, Höffe 2008; see also Rorty 2009).

A few decades ago, one might have got the impression that Kant wrote only two books: the *Critique of Pure Reason* and the *Groundwork of the metaphysics of morals*. In the latter work, interpreters often focused narrowly on the first sections (especially the famous passage on the good will) and the notorious examples illustrating the categorical imperative. Too often they overlooked that the *Groundwork* as well as the *Critique of Practical Reason* were only intended as foundational works. Nowadays this narrow focus is often abandoned, and the *Metaphysics of Morals* (dismissed for two centuries as the work of a senile scholar, to put it bluntly), the difficult and complex *Critique of the Power of Judgment*, Kant's lectures (especially on moral philosophy, anthropology and physical geography), his preparatory notes, the short essays on history – in the past often dismissed as "minor" or "less important" writings – and his writings on religion are taken into consideration. In terms of ethics, it has been argued, for instance, that there has been a recent "awareness of and appreciation for Kant's views not just on isolated actions but also on the moral agent, character, emotions, and judgment grounded in experience, and the moral importance of actively shaping each of these over time" (Jost and Wuerth 2011: 2–3; cf. Wood 2011: 59 and Wuerth 2011: 147–51, 162–3, Swanton 2011: 259). The overall result is a richer account of Kant's philosophy: Kant is no longer simply seen as a brilliant epistemologist, but in the first place as a moral philosopher and educator: Kant wanted to curtail the assertions of "subtle reasoning" (*Vernünftelei*) and challenge "the omnipotence of theoretical reason" (MM, 6: 378). Epistemology is not an end in itself, but a means to arrive at a new, critical and modest philosophy which offers practical and regulative knowledge about the (moral) vocation of the individual as well as the human species.

I see this book as part and parcel of this new trend of Kant interpretation. The key hermeneutic maxim is to be wary of entrenched patterns of interpretation, and to challenge them whenever there is textual evidence. Kant's first critique is not the infallible standard that defines "critical". Kant's work is seen as dynamic and evolving. There is not just one watershed, namely 1781 (when the first critique was published): in all likelihood there are additional ruptures, breaks and developments (see below). I should not fail to mention a crucial consequence of this new interpretation. It turns Kant into a champion of practical metaphysics, and seems to open the door to the kind of reckless speculation Kant's criticism claims to put an end to (see chapter 8, section 2).

1.3 Was Kant really a cosmopolitan?

An answer to this question depends on how cosmopolitanism is defined. Whenever the issue is raised, two related aspects can be separated: first, there are doubts about the lifestyle of an apparently parochial scholar who never left his home town in a remote province of Prussia. Secondly, there are allegations that Kant was in fact a blatant racist. The first aspect can briefly be dealt with: Kant, who actually left his home town Königsberg when he had to earn his living as a young private tutor working for aristocratic families in the countryside of East Prussia, spent most of his life in a city that was by eighteenth-century standards very cosmopolitan (see Manthey 2005: 95–350).

The second issue is more complex, and I can only briefly comment on the racist statements directed against non-Europeans scattered all over Kant's published writings. For instance, Kant asserts in 1764 that there is an "essential" difference between whites and blacks and that "it seems to be just as great with regard to the capacities of mind as it is with respect to colour" (Observations, 2: 253). Kant seems to be just another White western male whose universalism masks naked Eurocentrism. Most interpreters conclude that Kant's racist statements are incompatible with his normative universalism and moral cosmopolitanism (see for example Bernasconi 2010, Anderson-Gold 2001a: 20–7, Hedrick 2008, 262 and 268, Louden 2000: 102–3, Kleingeld 2007: 575 and 582f and Scrivener 2007: 18–9).

Interpreters have offered various explanations for these tensions (to put it mildly) between Eurocentric and cosmopolitan statements. Authors like Bernasconi tend to argue that Kant's racism is part and parcel of his philosophical system (Bernasconi 2010). A straightforward historical or psychological argument would be that Kant did not manage to overcome the prejudices of his time, and was unable to see the glaring contradiction between his professed cosmopolitan stance and his racist statements. Given Kant's intellectual stature, this assessment is hardly convincing. Some develop what may be termed "independency thesis": Kant's empirical observations about people all over the world based mainly on travel reports are systematically independent from, and thus irrelevant for, his transcendental philosophy based on principled reasoning (see Makino 2013, Terra 2013). Robert Louden asserts that Kant was logically committed to a cosmopolitan approach, but personally prejudiced, and that ultimately Kant's theory with its element of universality is stronger (Louden 2000: 105). Pauline Kleingeld has offered a more lenient interpretation. She claims that Kant dropped his earlier race theory in the 1790s, restricted the role of race, and arrived at a coherent version of moral cosmopolitanism by the time he wrote *Zum ewigen Frieden* in 1795. By then Kant granted full juridical status to non-Europeans like the Hottentots, rejected slavery and criticized European colonialism. He also revised his views concerning migration, asserting that it was Nature's will that all humans, regardless of race, would eventually live everywhere in the world. Finally, the issue of race disappeared almost completely from his writings, for instance in his *Anthropology*, published in 1798 (Kleingeld 2007: 586–9).

This interpretation would let Kant off the hook. He would be the Enlightenment intellectual who, after decades of critical thinking in accordance with, but also against the "spirit of the times", finally got rid of (almost all) prejudices. This favourable interpretation is supported by recent interpreters, who challenge the familiar and widespread distinction between the pre-critical and critical Kant, and favour a more nuanced approach than this blunt binary juxtaposition. They emphasize the evolutionary aspect of Kant's thought, and convincingly show that Kant continuously refined his theories. In other words, the Kant of the early 1780s is very different from the Kant of the late 1790s. For instance, Francis Cheneval illustrates how Kant rethought, rewrote and refined his concept of the highest good in subsequent writings (Cheneval 2002: 440–7 and passim). Eckart Förster outlines how Kant's rational theology changed, also in the years after 1781 (Förster 1998 and 2000: 118–47). Cheneval, Kleingeld, Byrd and Hruschka demonstrate how Kant repeatedly changed his opinion on key issues of international law such as the enforcement problem or the status of hospitality rights (Cheneval 2002: 582–621, Kleingeld 2009: 179–86 and Byrd and Hruschka 2010: 205–11).

Although this fairly lenient interpretation is supported by textual evidence, it is also plausible to argue that Kant endorsed a form of "western-Eurocentric gradualism" (Louden 2000: 178; see also Hedrick 2008: 264–7). Non-Europeans were backward children, but – according to the later Kant – capable of *Bildung* or education and possible future members in good standing in the international community. Finally, Ian Hunter offers a totally different approach. He interprets Kant's cosmopolitan theory as the offspring of a metaphysical and "de facto Protestant" tradition regional within Europe and hostile towards different philosophical cultures (Hunter 2010: 14; see also Hunter 2001: 274–363). Hunter attempts to deconstruct Kant's own effort to construct a theory that transcends historical and cultural particularity (see also below and chapter 8, section 2).

Giving a fully adequate account of this complex issue is beyond the scope of this inquiry. As a historian, I tend to side with the developmental interpretation: the human race was conceived as one community, but subdivided into various races. For most intellectuals of the Enlightenment, there was a hierarchy between races, yet "the issue was no longer whether human beings encountered on other continents were in fact human or not" (Bartelson 2009: 118). Non-Europeans were often – but not always – seen as backward children, but capable of *Bildung* or education. This form of paternalism – which is uncosmopolitan by contemporary academic standards – holds that even children are persons and have rights, and they may eventually grow up; but as long as they are still children they are in need of guardians. In other words: According to Kant, we are not equal in terms of our cultivated prudence, of cultural development, skin colour, talents, perhaps not even in terms of moral capacities. However, we are equal in terms of our humanity or dignity and our moral vocation.

In the following chapters, my focus is on Kant's express cosmopolitan theory, and I attempt a coherent reconstruction. The question whether Kant lived up to his own cosmopolitan ideals is of biographical interest only, and has limited *philosophical* significance. Allen Wood advises contemporary readers to appreciate the complex "relation of important philosophical principles to the historical conditions of their genesis" and not see "a case of simple hypocrisy" (Wood 2008: 9, cf. ibid. 7–12). Philosophical principles may be valid even if they originate in a cultural environment that is hostile to, or diametrically opposed to, these principles, and even if proponents themselves did not always meet the standard of consistency and live up to these principles.

1.4 Kant's embedded and dynamic cosmopolitanism

This study emphasizes three distinct features of Kant's cosmopolitanism: that it is embedded, dynamic and pedagogical. The embedded element can be traced back to Rousseau's influence (see chapters 4 and 5). Kant's juridical and moral cosmopolitanism is compatible with thin forms of patriotism (such as contemporary "constitutional patriotism"). In a manner reminiscent of Rousseau, Kant criticized the indifferent *Weltliebhaber*, "because of too much generality, he scatters his affection and entirely loses any particular personal devotion" (17: 673, translated in Kleingeld 2003: 485). Kant advocated a form of civic and moderate patriotism with citizens enjoying legal freedom and equality and regarding "the commonwealth as the maternal womb" (TP, 8: 291). The commonwealth, where citizens are "authorized to protect its rights by laws of the common will", is the opposite of despotism or a paternalistic government (ibid.). The common bond is formed by republican principles, not an ethnic or national identity, and civic republicanism is therefore compatible with forms of cosmopolitanism. This way Kant offers a form of embedded cosmopolitanism, with people identifying with the local and the embedded, while also conceiving themselves in terms of universal obligations and rights. I argue that this is one neglected aspect of Rousseau's legacy for Kant.

The embedded element is also obvious in Kant's cosmopolitan right. It becomes a political and philosophical issue because of commercial interaction on a day-to-day basis in a world of increasing globalization (see chapter 3). Kant's idealism is not utopian but anticipatory, and contradicts a typical cliché about the Enlightenment in general and Kant's philosophy in particular, namely that it was utopian and only concerned with "pure reason" irrespective of historical contingencies. Kant did not preach the unencumbered self, but reflected upon embedded moral agents of flesh and blood with a capacity for practical reason, but whose moral lives are constantly threatened by temptations and means-end calculations based on prudence.

The second distinct feature this study emphasizes is the dynamic nature of Kant's cosmopolitanism, with the notion of the final vocation (*Bestimmung*) of the human species as its cornerstone. As Robert Louden has pointed out, *Bestimmung* incorporates three meanings (Louden 2013: 6–7): first, Kant sometimes compares humans with animals or even plants, pointing out that they are equipped with certain germs (*Keime*), and they are determined to develop in a certain way. In this context, *Bestimmung* can be rendered as "determination", since it is "merely a matter of proper sowing and planting that these germs develop" (LP, 9: 445). Here humans are part of the natural world subject to its laws. The second meaning relates *Bestimmung* to the concept of indetermination, as a human being, even from the perspective of empirical anthropology, is capable of reflection, deliberation and the freedom of choice, that is, "choosing for himself a way of living and not being bound to a single one" (Beginning, 8: 112). This corresponds with the level of the cultivation of skilfulness and prudence. Finally, as beings with moral predispositions, we are *bestimmt* to cultivate or develop them. "The human being shall make himself better, cultivate himself, and, if he is evil, bring forth morality in himself" (LP, 9: 446). This is the level of moral freedom and of cosmopolitanism, and our *Bestimmung* is a vocation or a calling: humans "feel destined [or called] by nature to [develop] … into a *cosmopolitan society* (*cosmopolitismus*) that is constantly threatened by disunion but generally progresses toward a coalition" (Anthropology, 7: 331). The regulative principle of a cosmopolitan society comes in two versions: one is a political union of the whole human species based on coercive laws that are mutual and "come from themselves" (ibid., see chapters 2 and 3), the other one is the moral commonwealth developed in the *Religion Within the Boundaries of Mere Reason*. Our "moral vocation" is "the ultimate end (*letzter Zweck*) of our existence" (KdU, 5: 431 and 435). Kant contributed a novel idea to the Enlightenment debates about human destiny: he went beyond the focus on the individual typical of Spalding and Mendelssohn and included the species as a whole and its future, without abandoning the individualistic perspective (see Cavallar 2016 for more).

The dynamic element of Kant's cosmopolitanism is clearly expressed in his conception of pedagogy. Education is the key means so that individuals as well as the whole species can reach their vocation, that is, develop their "natural predispositions proportionally and purposively" (LP, 9: 446). Put bluntly, the education of the individual is dealt with in pedagogy; the education of the species is the topic of the philosophies of history and religion (see chapter 2). Kant's interpretation of history is teleological and reflective: Nature has purposes, and "one can assume as a principle that nature wants every creature to reach its destiny through the appropriate development of all predispositions of its nature" (Anthropology, 7: 329). Kant's anthropology "is not merely a descriptive account of human culture. Rather, his aim is to offer the species a moral map that they can use to move toward their collective destiny" (Louden 2000: 106; cf. Louden 2011: 76–77, Louden 2013). This is what distinguishes pragmatic from physiological anthropology (Anthropology, 7: 119). The key teleological assumption is that predispositions and germs are potentials that could and should be developed – it is each individual's task as "an animal endowed with the *capacity of reason* (*animal rationabile*)" to develop this potential and to make oneself "a *rational animal*" (Anthropology, 7: 321; LP, 9: 445). One indispensable means is pedagogy or educational science. Its cornerstone, ethical didactics, cannot make humans rational or moral; but it can help to provide a stimulating environment. The adoption of a morally good disposition can only be done by the agent herself, but pedagogy can shape the conditions where this goal is achieved in a better and faster way (see chapter 6). Kant sees possible progress even in these tools or methods of instruction (cf. LP, 9: 444 and 447). An important step in attempting to reach humanity's vocation will be taken as soon as "the design for a plan of education [is] ... made in a cosmopolitan manner" (LP, 9: 448).

Nowadays Kant scholars frequently refer to Kant's "projects" – usually in connection with his legal philosophy, his concept of Enlightenment (hence the "Enlightenment project") or moral education. This book concludes that Kant's overall practical-metaphysical project is the aesthetic, political, moral and religious formation (*Bildung*) of the human species so that via freedom the "kingdom of God" on earth is asymptotically approached.

1.5 Outline of the book

The second and third chapters offer a systematic interpretation of Kant's cosmopolitanism as part of his practical philosophy. Interpretations usually focus on his legal or political cosmopolitanism, a cluster of concepts revolving around perpetual peace, an international organization, the reform of international law, and what Kant has termed cosmopolitan law or the law of world citizens (*Weltbürgerrecht*). *Toward perpetual peace* (1795) is the essential and famous text in this regard. Other types of cosmopolitanism – moral, cognitive, religious – are often neglected. This is surprising, since Kant develops the idea of a moral commonwealth in the *Religion Within the Boundaries of Mere Reason* (1793), which has a strong religious and theological dimension, and which seems to bring Kant closer to a more traditional form of cosmopolitanism, namely Christian cosmopolitanism. I argue that there are different cosmopolitanisms in Kant. I focus on the relationship among legal/juridical, moral and religious cosmopolitanisms. I claim that these form part of a comprehensive system and are fully compatible with each other, given Kant's framework. The centre of contention is the concept of the highest good, and the heated debate on its proper interpretation is closely related to discussions concerning the role of the philosophies of history and religion within Kant's system. I highlight some problems connected with the tendency to pick out elements of this greater system as if they were independent of it. I divide Kant interpreters rather brutally into three camps, the group of the system thinkers, who believe in the co-existence of the philosophies of history and religion within Kant's system, the secularists, who assert that the philosophy of history should replace the philosophy of religion, and the theologians, who claim the opposite. I side with the first group, offering an exegetical argument how Kant might have understood the compatibility and systematic coherence of legal, moral and religious cosmopolitanisms.

Kant's right of the world citizen (*Weltbürgerrecht*) is sometimes seen as the centrepiece of his cosmopolitanism. The third chapter tries to qualify this assessment, minimizing its systematic role within Kant's overall cosmopolitan theory and offering a historical contextualization. It illustrates how this right relates to other conceptions of hospitality rights developed in international legal theory from Francisco de Vitoria up to Kant's time. I make comparisons and suggest where Kant's originality should be located. In his philosophy of history, Kant understands Nature reflectively and tentatively as a "moral facilitator" of the education of the human species. One section thus focuses on this very philosophy of history, on the role of the "spirit of commerce" to promote more peaceable relations among communities, on the so-called four-stage theory, *doux commerce*, global integration, and mutual self-interest. This chapter argues that Kant's cosmopolitan right is not the blueprint of a cosmopolitan democracy or a global and democratic civil society where individuals are co-legislators building "democratic structures". This is an anachronistic interpretation I try to counter with my historical analysis. Since *commercium* also includes the exchange of ideas, cosmopolitan right indeed "opens up a space" for a thin version of global civil society. Cosmopolitan right has one key function: it is the third segment of the juridical framework, of what Kant terms "a universal *cosmopolitan condition*" (Idea, 8: 28; see also Anthropology, 7: 333) as the basis or "womb" of proper formation or *Bildung* (the other two segments are the republican constitution and the reformed right of nations).

Whereas the second and third chapters primarily offer a systematic interpretation of Kant's cosmopolitanism, the next two look into the eighteenth-century context, in particular relevant educational theories. The fourth chapter focuses on Rousseau, whose philosophy exerted a strong influence on Kant, yet whose ideas on cosmopolitanism, patriotism and nationalism flatly seem to contradict Kant's. Traditionally, the eighteenth century has been seen as a cosmopolitan age before the rise of nationalism. Though this assessment is in need of qualification, many Enlightenment philosophers were in fact more cosmopolitan than representatives of previous or later eras: there was an amount of openness towards and fascination with other cultures, and many intellectuals perceived themselves as members of a transnational "republic of letters". The diversity of attitudes, opinions and theories concerning cosmopolitanism was impressive, yet a common feature of Enlightenment cosmopolitanism was that it tried to strike a tenable balance between patriotism and cosmopolitan obligations. Rousseau was the thinker who tried to go beyond these often easy compromises. In the first place, he emphatically rejected various types of cosmopolitanism as degenerate, deformed and immoral, such as cultural or economic cosmopolitanism. However, this did not turn him into the founding father of modern nationalism, as generations of interpreters up to the present have misleadingly asserted. In fact, as I argue in the second chapter, Rousseau attempted to show that his brand of civic patriotism was compatible with genuine moral cosmopolitanism as well as republican cosmopolitanism. Rousseau ended up with a form of embedded cosmopolitanism which tried to strike a balance between republican patriotism and republican as well as thin moral cosmopolitanism, offering a synthesis through education. A careful reading of *Émile* shows that this is a book about the formation of a moral and cognitive cosmopolitan, who avoids the deformations of a commercial society influenced by processes of globalisation.

The fifth chapter tries to fill a gap: to my knowledge, the possible influence of Johann Bernhard Basedow and Rousseau on Kant's cosmopolitanism and concept of cosmopolitan education has not yet been analysed. Basedow is still a widely unknown figure of the Enlightenment educational reform movement, especially outside Germany. Basedow's *Philanthropinum* institute, which was admired and supported by Kant, practiced a form of non-sectarian and non-denominational education with cosmopolitan overtones. I consider Basedow one of the key authors who influenced Kant's concept of cosmopolitan education. The chapter compares Basedow's ideas with those of Kant, and argues that both defined cosmopolitan education as non-denominational moral formation or *Bildung*, encompassing – in different forms – a thin version of moral religion following the core tenets of Christianity. Kant's encounter with Basedow and the *Philanthropinum* in Dessau also helps to understand the development of Kant's concept of cosmopolitanism and educational theory *"in weltbürgerlicher Absicht"*. Rousseau's role is more complex: he clearly influenced Kant; he is usually considered a precursor of modern nationalism and national education; and some passages seem to suggest a cosmopolitan dimension in his educational programme. How do nationalism – or less anachronistically, civic republicanism – and cosmopolitanism fit together? My focus will be on the systematic status of cosmopolitanism within the wider context of Rousseau's philosophy, its relation to education, and its tensions, and on Kant's attempt to make sense of Rousseau's overall philosophy and its cosmopolitan dimension. According to Rousseau, the dilemma of education is that one has to choose between the cosmopolitan education of the *homme* and the patriotic education of the *citoyen*, who considers all foreigners potential enemies. For Rousseau, avoiding or going beyond this stark alternative is impossible (though many contemporary interpreters try to do just that). Kant's reinterpretation of Rousseau is favourable and creative and has found many followers up to the present, but is misleading, as he ignores Rousseau's dilemma of education and imposes his own conception of cosmopolitanism, of cosmopolitan education and of possible progress in history on Rousseau while claiming that this was actually Rousseau's message.

The last two chapters turn to another neglected topic of Kant studies: Kant and cosmopolitan formation (*Bildung*). Kant frequently invokes the term "cosmopolitan" when referring to what he thinks is the proper educational method. At the beginning of his *Lectures on pedagogy* (1803), Kant deplores that parents usually foster skilfulness and prudence in their children, hoping that they will be successful in the world, whereas princes or rulers often just use their subjects as means to political ends. Both parents and princes are criticized for not caring about moral formation (*Bildung*), which would enable the younger generation to work on behalf of "the best for the world" (*das Weltbeste*). The key claim of this chapter is that Kant's moral educational theory is cosmopolitan in character. Moral self-legislation and self-motivation ultimately aim at a cosmopolitan conduct of thought (*Denkungsart*) and a cosmopolitan comportment of mind or disposition (*Gesinnung*). This is our supreme or highest-order maxim, the "subjective ground" as a deed of our freedom which gives our whole lives an overall orientation. Kant takes a detour: in his moral theory, cosmopolitan values are not simply instilled in pupils. A cosmopolitan disposition is a long-term result of helping adolescents to form their own moral characters. The conclusion briefly hints at differences between Kant's approach and contemporary cosmopolitan educational theories. The key difference is that Kant tries to achieve his cosmopolitan goals by taking a detour: unlike most contemporary approaches, Kant does not simply posit "cosmopolitan values" in an age of globalization and interdependence, but stresses moral formation (*Bildung*) as an end in itself irrespective of its usefulness. It revolves around maxims that can be universalised, the three maxims of understanding, especially the enlarged conduct of thought, a proper comportment of mind and a moral character. In its ideal form, this moral formation coincides with a cosmopolitan formation.

The starting point of the last chapter is Kant's surprising remark that "it is not the case that a good state constitution is to be expected from inner morality; on the contrary, the good moral formation of a people is to be expected from a good state constitution" (Peace, 8: 366). The statement is at odds with the familiar assumption that Kant's philosophy is preoccupied with inner morality rather than external circumstances; that true reform has to start with our inner lives, not with politics. In this chapter, I want to show that Kant's remark is not some odd side note, but part and parcel of a coherent pedagogical theory, whose widely ignored ramifications deserve more attention. In addition, it helps us to rethink Kant's relationship to the republican tradition. A widespread interpretation of Kant as a typical early liberal is an oversimplification. Especially because of Rousseau's influence, Kant is close to the republican tradition, even though he does not share key features. Kant's pedagogy is indeed distinct from the educational theories of the civic republicans: Above all, moral self-legislation and self-motivation ultimately aim at a cosmopolitan conduct of thought (*Denkungsart*) and a cosmopolitan comportment of mind or disposition (*Gesinnung*), thus going beyond civic humanism's focus on one's own republic. Yet Kant shared with civic republicans, especially with Rousseau, the conviction that education was indispensable for morality and virtue; subscribed to their belief in law's educational function; and held that a republic – or rather the republican form of government – was the proper basis of moral formation. A final section outlines Kant's vision of progress in a genuine republic. The conclusion offers a brief sketch of cosmopolitan ideas from Kant to Herbart (1795–1835), and discusses the merits and shortcomings of Kant's theory, while also relating it to contemporary cosmopolitan discourses and educational theories.

I want to finish my introduction with a few remarks on methodology. In one of my previous books, I have subscribed to the methodological approach developed by Mark Bevir in his *The Logic of the History of Ideas* (1999), where he defined the task of the intellectual historian as reconstructing an individual's belief as a reasonably consistent web, developed a concept of weak intentionalism and procedural individualism, and defended a thin concept of rationality (see Cavallar 2002: 37–40; for a useful discussion see O'Neill 2012 with more references). I cannot deal extensively with these issues here, but would like to state where I agree and disagree with Bevir's approach, or rather his subsidiary reflections more than ten years later. I subscribe to Bevir's "post-analytic historicism" which is all in favour of critical genealogies to check whether moral claims just reflect particular traditions, interests or metaphysics rather than universal truths. We should be sceptical of moral claims, but should also keep in mind that "objective ethical knowledge" is not impossible (Bevir 2012: 664). This book is also a historical study of Kant's cosmopolitanism that focuses on its genesis. Yet it avoids the kind of historical relativism that is usually in danger of becoming dogmatic itself. Normative principles may be valid even if they have a specific historical origin, are historically situated, if they originate in a particular cultural environment, and even if proponents themselves fail to meet the standard of consistency (this standard itself is always spelled out in a particular context, but may claim universal validity as a formal principle of thinking). I disagree with Bevir's "radical historicism" which holds that religious perspectives, teleological principles or any belief in "structures and quasi-structures" and comprehensive meanings have to be abandoned as untenable (Ian Hunter's interpretation of Kant mentioned above may be an example of this "radical historicism"). When Bevir claims that there are neither structures nor meanings that redeem activity, he winds up with dogmatic metaphysics: claims of this sort go beyond the realm of experience or the "natural world" he appeals to (Bevir 2012: 665). The term "natural world" is ambiguous: I subscribe to Bevir's view that scientific historiography has to reject "appeals to anything beyond the natural world", but it is not clear whether this world is really devoid of anything general or universal and without any structures. Kant's a priori structures of theoretical and practical reasoning may be a case in point. Thus I want to argue for what I term critical historicism, which is also critical towards historicism's key tenets themselves, and avoids ontological assertions Bevir seems to consider indispensable.

2 Cosmopolitanisms in Kant's philosophy

As mentioned in the introduction, Kant's cosmopolitanism has become the focus of recent interpretations, most of them zooming in on his legal or political cosmopolitanism, a cluster of ideas revolving around perpetual peace, an international organization, the reform of international law, and what Kant has termed cosmopolitan right or the right of world citizens (*Weltbürgerrecht*). *Toward perpetual peace* (1795) is the essential and famous text in this regard. Other types of cosmopolitanism – moral, cognitive, cultural or religious – are usually neglected. This is surprising, since Kant develops the idea of a moral commonwealth in the *Religion within the boundaries of mere reason* (1793), which has a strong religious dimension, and seems to bring Kant close to a more traditional form of cosmopolitanism, namely theological cosmopolitanism.

This chapter offers a systematic analysis. I argue that there are different cosmopolitanisms in Kant. I focus on the relationship among political, legal or juridical, moral and religious cosmopolitanisms. I claim that these form part of a comprehensive system and are fully compatible with each other, given Kant's framework. The centre of contention is the concept of the highest good, and the debate on its proper interpretation is closely related to discussions concerning the role of the philosophies of history and religion within Kant's system. I conclude that it is not self-evident that one can pick out some elements of this greater system as if they were independent of it.

There is a three-part division in Kant's philosophy concerning the highest good and the future of the human race:
1. The highest good in the writings on politics and history is the highest *political* good, namely a global juridical condition (*Rechtszustand*) which approximates world peace (cf. MM, 6: 354–5), "a universal *cosmopolitan condition*" (Idea, 8: 28).
2. the establishment of a global ethical community is the "highest moral (*sittliche*) good" (Religion, 6: 97). This is Kant's moral cosmopolitanism. Kant calls the duty to promote this highest good as a member of this cosmopolitan moral community or "union [...] of well-disposed human beings" (Religion, 6: 98) a duty "*sui generis* [...] of the human race toward itself", since the highest good is a good "common to all" (ibid., 97).
3. the highest good proper coincides with the transcendent kingdom of God, the "supersensible (intelligible) world" (Theodicy, 8: 264) or the "Kingdom of Heaven" (Religion, 6: 134; cf. End, 8: 328–30). As Kant puts it in *The Conflict of Faculties*, "the human being must be destined for two entirely different worlds: for the realm of sense and understanding and so for this terres-

trial world, but also for another world, which we do not know – a moral realm" (Conflict, 7: 70; cf. 28: 301). This is Kant's religious cosmopolitanism.

I think we can press Kant interpreters – rather brutally, I admit – into three camps. The first group – the theologians – consider Kant's moral theology as inherently flawed: Kant, though perhaps a brilliant author, did not grasp the full religious truth contained in the Christian faith (Cassirer 1988, Palmquist 2000, Sala 2004). Along these lines, Kant's final synthesis would be a more or less critically modified religious cosmopolitanism, expressing the idea of a commonwealth of ends or a "kingdom of God" on earth or a transcendent kingdom of Heaven, which ultimately guarantees the harmony of morality and deserved happiness.

Representatives of the second group – the system thinkers – believe in the co-existence of the philosophies of history and religion within Kant's system. An early example was Allen Wood in the 1970ies, who tried to show that Kant's moral theology is "an integral part of the critical philosophy" (Wood 1970: 9), but not at the expense of the philosophy of history. These interpreters keep the basic tenets of Kant, implying that all forms of cosmopolitanisms, especially juridical, moral and theological cosmopolitanisms, harmoniously fit into Kant's overall system. I suppose Georg Geismann is a typical representative of this group (Geismann 2009 and 2010; see also Albrecht 1978, Anderson-Gold 2001a and b, Brandt 2009, Cheneval 2002, Dierksmeier 1998, Flikschuh 2010, Langthaler 1991 and 2014, and Wimmer 1990).

Authors of the third group – the secularists – are diametrically opposed to the first one. They assert that the philosophy of history ought to replace the philosophy of religion, provided that one follows the "spirit" or the "inner logic" of Kant's critical philosophy. For the secularised camp, the concept of the highest good has to be coherently reconstructed as immanent. The moral and/or legal community of the human race is realized in the future without divine assistance. The concept of the highest good proper is dropped as inconsistent or detrimental to human agency (Axinn 1994, Förster 1998 and 2000, Linden 1988, Michalson 1999, Moran 2012, Yovel 1980).

I side with the second group, offering an exegetical argument how Kant might have understood the compatibility and systematic coherence of moral, legal and religious cosmopolitanisms. I start with a clarification of the concept of cosmopolitanism in Kant, and distinguish among its various forms which are related to each other (section 1). Kant's later theory in the 1790s focused on legal, moral and religious cosmopolitanism. There is a three-part division in his philosophy concerning the concept of the highest good and the future of the human race: The foundation of a cosmopolitan condition of perpetual peace, a global legal society of peaceful states, a "*cosmopolitan* whole" (KdU, 5: 432), perhaps a world republic is the highest *political* good. The establishment of a global ethical community is – secondly – the highest *moral* good in this world. Finally, the highest good proper coincides with the transcendent kingdom of God, the intelligible world, the kingdom of Heaven or a moral realm. A secularized concept of the highest good would have to drop the crucial element of a *necessary* connection of morality and appropriate happiness, thus would be an extremely thinned down version of the highest good (section 2). Next I turn to Kant's philosophy of history, in particular his understanding of Nature as a "moral facilitator" of the education of humankind. There is a tension between the human species propelled or instigated by Nature towards moral ends on the one hand and an understanding of human history as a collective learning process, whereby humans are seen as autonomous agents not manipulated by Nature. The fourth section focuses on the ethical commonwealth and its cosmopolitan dimension. God and humans together try to realize it, with humans promoting (*befördern*) and "preparing" this ethical community while God is offering fulfilment (attainment, realization or *Verwirklichung*). I try to reconstruct Kant's arguments in favour of an ethical commonwealth with a religious dimension. The purpose of the chapter is to show that the different cosmopolitanisms form part of a greater system and are compatible with each other, and that contemporary attempts to pick out some elements as if they were independent are quite problematic.

2.1 Cosmopolitanisms according to Kant

It is useful to distinguish among different types of cosmopolitanisms in Kant: epistemological, economic or commercial, moral, religious, political, and cultural (these distinctions partly follow Kleingeld 1999 and 2011; see also Brown 2009: 10–15). *Epistemological* or *cognitive* cosmopolitanism refers to the world citizen who tries to transcend the "egoism of reason", the unwillingness to test one's judgements with the help of the reason of others. The normative ideal is one of the three maxims of common understanding: the "extended way of thinking" (*erweiterte Denkungsart*). "The opposite of egoism can only be *pluralism*, that is, the way of thinking in which one is not concerned with oneself as the whole world, but rather regards and conducts oneself as a mere citizen of the world" (Anthropology, 7: 130; see Häntsch 2008, Kemp 2006 and Wood 2008: 17–20). Anyone who tries to overcome logical egoism will attempt to see things from a different perspective, consider and perhaps adopt "the standpoint of others", and weigh one's judgement against those of others. As in Adam Smith, the figure of impartial spectators is a recurrent theme in Kantian philosophy. They attempt to enlarge their own thinking and aim in their judgements at the universality and consistency which is the hallmark of fairness, justice, and morality. Ideally, the result is a cosmopolitan standpoint and a broad-minded or extended way of thinking where the person "reflects on his own judgment from a *universal standpoint* (which he can only determine by putting himself into the standpoint of others)" (KdU, 5: 295; see also 19: 184–5). Kant makes it clear that this way of thinking is in need of careful instruction and training. One excellent training ground is the field of metaphysics, and Kant advises educators not to hesitate to expose the young to "dangerous propositions" put forth by the enemies of religion and morality (KrV B 782). The young could then realize that the only compelling argument against these "supposed" free-thinkers – humans do not have any theoretical knowledge in the realm beyond experience – equally applies to their own metaphysical assumptions about freedom, immortality, and the existence of God. This is in itself already a fine exercise in cosmopolitan thinking: by putting ourselves into the standpoint of others – in this case, of the unbeliever, freethinker, materialist or atheist – we train our capacity for the extended or enlarged way of thinking. The Socratic way of thinking, that is, accepting our ignorance in speculative metaphysics, is another side-effect of this kind of learning (see KrV B 780–797 and the profound analysis in Munzel 2012: 238–61). There is also a historical dimension here. Kant sees the issue from the perspective of an enlightened Christian who fights against dogmatic atheism and materialism and defends moral theism; this is particularly obvious in his *Lectures on the philosophical doctrine of religion* (LR, 28: 1011–12; on atheism 28: 1010, 1001, 1026; see also Cavallar 2014). A critic might see this as biased. However, this criticism misses the crucial point. Any position is rooted and embedded, yet the nub is one's principled attempt to go beyond one's own perspective; in Kant's case, this was a perspective deeply influenced by Wolff's and Baumgarten's metaphysics. In contemporary discourses, an example might be the dispute between proponents of the intelligent design movement on the one hand and Richard Dawkins and his followers on the other. Both sides could find common ground in the reflective awareness that all participants eventually reach a point when they leave the world of experience and step beyond the "determinate boundaries" of pure theoretical reason "within which all of our cognition of objects is enclosed" (KrV B 789).

One might raise the following question now: what is the connection with cosmopolitanism? The crucial element is formal, the enlarged way of thinking as a certain *Denkungsart* – and ultimately a moral disposition or *Gesinnung* (see chapter 6). Trying to realize this kind of thinking also applies to shedding one's own ethnocentric biases. For example, authors like Locke and Vattel developed the agricultural argument in favour of European colonialism, asserting that ownership was based on settlement and use of the soil. The theory came in handy when dispossessing nomadic aboriginal peoples. Other Europeans like Wolff or Diderot criticized the argument (see Cavallar 2011: 32–5). These criticisms can be read as examples of cognitive cosmopolitanism. Kant himself sided with Wolff and Diderot in these matters, asserting that Europeans may settle in regions adjacent to natives, but "if these people are shepherds or hunters (like the Hottentots, the Tungusi, or most of the American Indian nations) who depend for their sustenance on great open regions, this settlement may not take place by force but only by contract, and indeed by a contract that does not take advantage of the ignorance of those inhabitants with respect to ceding their lands" (MM, 6: 353; additional examples can be found in chapter 6). The enlarged way of thinking is sensitive to context – in this case, it takes into consideration that nomadic peoples have a different way of life compared with agricultural or commercial nations. Yet it also brackets the contingent – European standards of property, statehood and sovereignty – to give top priority to universal principles such as the right of peoples not to be used as mere means in the name of progress, the prohibition of deception or reciprocal rights. Along these lines, if we return to the religious issues mentioned above, the enlightened Muslim believer from Al-Azhar University in Cairo may find a common ground with the secularized scientist from Japan in a debate: it is the *docta ignorantia* of *non liquet* (cf. KrV B 770). "The conflict cultivates reason by the consideration of its object on both sides, and corrects its judgment by thus limiting it' (B 772). Judgements are limited to the sphere of possible experience. Reason is cultivated by deepening the insight into its own boundaries. The problem is looked at from "both sides", not only from one's own preferred perspective.

Kant's first systematic statement on cosmopolitanism comes in the *Critique of pure Reason* (see Cheneval 2002: 403–11, 423–33, Falduto 2014: 69–76). The background is the Greek word *kosmos* for "the world". Philosophy in accordance with a "cosmopolitan concept" (*Philosophie nach dem Weltbegriffe*; KrV B 868) revolves around "the essential ends of human reason" (B 867), the ideas of moral self-legislation of practical reason, of inner freedom and our vocation (*Bestimmung*). The cosmopolitan concept (*conceptus cosmicus*) is distinguished from the scholastic concept of philosophy, which focuses only on the theoretical unity of knowledge (B 866). In other words, at stake here is the practical, systematic unity or totality of the intelligible world or the moral world, the kingdom of ends. The "world concept" of philosophy aims at the "relation of all cognition to the essential purposes of human reason" (B 867). At this point, cognitive cosmopolitanism expands itself towards moral cosmopolitanism, the idea of each person as "legislator of human reason" and the idea of the unity of these persons in one single commonwealth or a moral world (ibid. and below, sections 2 and 4; for a different interpretation see Wilson 2013).

The social and political dimension of cognitive cosmopolitanism will be discussed in the context of republican education (see chapter 7). Suffice it to say here that Kant's main argument is spelling out the implications of the insight that we need others to cultivate our own reason and judgement. The sceptic, for instance, challenges our dogmatic assertions in metaphysics, and helps us to reconsider them. The proponent of the agricultural argument may instigate us to look for a principled counter-argument in favour of the dispossessed natives. Thinking against and in community with others helps us to cultivate our enlarged way of thinking. In his essay on Enlightenment, Kant redefines the boundaries of privacy (Muchnik 2008): the crucial element is communicability, not the capacity to express any kind of vocabulary. As potential *Gelehrte* capable of rational argument, self-reflection and communication, we all form a cosmopolitan – in contrast to a merely local and private – community. "Dare to make your village cosmopolitan" (ibid.: 314).

Kant's *cultural* cosmopolitanism is more hinted at than a fully developed theory (for the following see Muthu 2003: 122–70 and 2006). Kant distinguished "humanity" (*die Menschheit*) as the intelligible, moral element in humans or rational beings in general from the human race (*das Menschengeschlecht*) and a biological concept of the species (Byrd and Hruschka 2010: 286–8, Cheneval 2002: 514 and Wimmer 1990: 124–8). Especially the term "humanity" is often confusing, since in modern German usage *Menschheit* also denotes the human race. The human species is the subject of inquiry in Kant's philosophy of history. Some passages suggest that Kant perceived biological humanity – the middle term between animality and personality – as cultural agency, which is characterized by a certain amount of incommensurability and latitude of judgement, namely in those spheres which go beyond the essence of the human race. Kant hinted at this culturally sensitive and contextualized view when he assessed and tolerated China's and Japan's isolationist policies. The more important passages are those where he defended the ways of life of hunters and pastoralists like the Hottentots (see above, MM, 6: 266 and 353). Kant's antipaternalism, the formal character of the categorical imperative, and his theory of legitimate latitude with respect to cultivating one's capacities allowed him to argue that *some* judgements on forms of societies – hunting in comparison with commercial societies, for instance – are morally neutral. However, there can be no doubt that Kant's cultural cosmopolitanism is only fragmentary. Other passages suggest that the "essence" of biological humanity was closely modelled along European conceptions (see Introduction above, section 3).

Kant is well-known and famous for his *political, contractual, juridical* or *legal* version of cosmopolitanism, and this form is also elaborated in his writings. He distinguished between legal and moral spheres, the former focusing on mutual restrictions of domains of external freedom, the other on the free adoption of ends, and this distinction resulted in a differentiation between legal and moral cosmopolitanism. In *Toward Perpetual Peace*, for instance, Kant claimed that individuals and states "are to be regarded as citizens of a universal state of mankind" (Peace, 8: 349 note). This universal commonwealth is a legal, not a moral community. The quote hints at a small revolution: in contrast to eighteenth- and nineteenth-century international law, Kant's legal theory posits individuals as full juridical persons outside the sphere of their respective domestic jurisdictions – a status that foreshadows contemporary international law and international human rights doctrines. On the other hand, states do not simply disappear in Kant's theory, swallowed up by a future world republic, but form with individuals a legal community which has to reform itself so that a complete juridical state or *Rechtszustand* is approximated (for an introduction see Cavallar 2011: 64–84 and chapter 3 below).

Kant's *commercial* or *economic* cosmopolitanism holds that the economic market will in all likelihood become a single global sphere of trade (this is the proposition of the philosophy of history and a reflective judgement) and should be regulated by right (*Recht*) and its corollary, the principle of external juridical freedom of choice (cf. Kleingeld 1999: 518). This right is couched in juridical terms as the right of hospitality, both in *Perpetual Peace* (1795) and in the *Doctrine of Right* several years later. Kant's cosmopolitan right has acquired a kind of cult status in contemporary debates on cosmopolitanism, but its systematic role within Kant's practical philosophy has remained contested. An extensive historical interpretation is offered in the next chapter.

Kant defends *moral* cosmopolitanism in the 1790s with the claim that all rational beings, irrespective of their race, should be regarded as ends in themselves and as lawgiving members of "the universal kingdom of ends" (Groundwork, 4: 438 and 428; see also 27: 462 and Cheneval 2002: 434–65). Moral cosmopolitanism is expressed in the idea of a "kingdom (or commonwealth) of ends" or ethical community where humans unite freely into a commonwealth based on equality and self-legislation, rational beings are respected as ends in themselves, and a moral whole of all ends is achieved. According to Kant, this moral cosmopolitanism has a basis in the moral predispositions of humans such as moral feeling, conscience or respect (MM, 6: 399–403). An additional predisposition, the love of human beings, is *amor complacentiae*, a delight in moral striving for perfection of oneself and of others (MM, 6: 401–2, Guyer 2010 and Schönecker et al: 2010). Given these shared moral capacities, humans are not isolated islands, but are called to feel compassion and sympathy and take responsibility towards each other. Thus Kant transforms Terence's saying *Homo sum. Nihil humani a me alienum puto* into: "I am a human being; whatever befalls human beings concerns me too" (MM, 6: 460). The ethical commonwealth or community should encompass the entire human race, is distinct from a political community – which governs the external actions of humans -, is based on the moral law, coincides with the invisible church, and is the moral destiny of the human race (see below). Kant couches this commonwealth in theological terms: it is founded by God, the author of its constitution, who also guarantees the harmony of morality and deserved happiness (Groundwork, 4: 433–440, KpV, 5: 128–9, Religion, 6: 97–102 and 121–4). The ethical commonwealth has some similarities with the religious commonwealth of the theologians and Christian philosophers before Kant such as Leibniz (see Cheneval 2002: 51–131), and moral cosmopolitanism, when incorporating the idea of the highest good, merges with a Kantian form of religious cosmopolitanism. The decidedly Kantian and novel element is the frequent reminder on Kant's side that this ethical commonwealth is a matter of *practical* metaphysics and moral *faith*, not of theoretical knowledge.

This distinction between forms of cosmopolitanism is useful because it clarifies Kant's various uses of the term in his philosophy. For instance, in his famous essay "Idea for a universal history with a cosmopolitan aim" (1784), Kant refers to legal cosmopolitanism, not to moral or cultural versions (see below). Kant understands himself in this essay as a philosopher who writes from a cosmopolitan perspective, so Kant implies that he practices a form of epistemological cosmopolitanism. Along these lines, Kant argues for a cosmopolitan historiography, which is based on the maxim that the only relevant perspective or viewpoint is "what nations and governments have accomplished or harmed regarding a cosmopolitan aim" (Idea, 8: 31). The two major cosmopolitan tasks are political in nature, establishing a just civil society and "lawful external relations between states" (ibid. 8: 22 and 24). This new, cosmopolitan historiography is distinct from an older version focusing on courts, the dignity of princes, military campaigns and battles (cf. 15: 610 and 629; Kauder 1999: 170–5). It is also distinct from a nineteenth- and twentieth-century focus on the modern nation-state, one might add. The new historiography and philosophy of history look at historical and political phenomena from a "*cosmopolitan* perspective", which means "a view to the well-being of the *human race* as a whole and insofar as it is conceived as progressing toward its well-being in the series of generations of all future times" (TP, 8: 277; see also ibid.: 307). The distinction between forms of cosmopolitanism thus helps to understand Kant's complex divisions in his systematic philosophy, and avoids confusion and misinterpretation.

Kant divided philosophy into theoretical and practical philosophy (see for instance MM, 6: 217 and KdU, 20: 196). Epistemological cosmopolitanism relates to our cognitive faculties and thus to theoretical reason aiming at knowledge. Moral and juridical cosmopolitanism are situated within the two branches of practical philosophy, the doctrine of virtue (concerned with our inner moral dispositions) and the doctrine of right (governing external relations of humans; cf. MM, 6: 205, 396–7, 406–7; see Geismann 2010: 11–146, Kersting 1984 and 2004 for extensive interpretations). Cultural cosmopolitanism has to be systematically located near political or legal cosmopolitanism, as it reflects upon and evaluates how the universal principle of right manifests itself and is interpreted and applied in cultures and historical epochs. Commercial cosmopolitanism is another branch of legal philosophy. Kant distinguished among three forms of justice in a juridical state (cf. MM, 6: 306). Whereas the *iustitia tutatrix* amounts to positive legislation to make rights possible and the *iustitia distributiva* represents the judiciary (making rights a necessity), the *iustitia commutativa* "represents the public market where people can exercise their rights to external objects of choice by buying and selling them" (Byrd and Hruschka 2010: 69) and makes rights a reality. Cosmopolitan right refers to commutative justice, the public order for the market beyond state borders (cf. ibid.: 72–6 and 205–11 and the next chapter for a full analysis).

The wider issue of Kant's system of philosophy is beyond the scope of this study, and I can only briefly drop a few hints here (useful introductions are Flikschuh 2010, Geismann 2009 and 2012, Guyer 2003, 2005 and 2006, and Langthaler 2014). This philosophy tackles the following problems, among others:
1. The *Critique of the Power of Judgment* is supposed to bridge the gulf between nature and freedom (see KdU, 5: 175–6).
2. Kant argues for "the moral significance of a teleological conception of nature" (Guyer 2006: 539).
3. Kant's goal is critical, but still substantive practical metaphysics, revolving around the concept of an unconditional, non-sensible "final end" of creation (KdU, 5: 434 and 443).

The *Bestimmung* (destiny, vocation) of each individual as well as of the whole human race is, together with the doctrine of the highest good, the core of Kant's critical practical philosophy (Brandt 2003 and 2009, Louden 2000: 37, 53–4 and 101). It is the answer to the question "why it is necessary that human beings exist" (KdU, 5: 378). Kant's answer is that the *Bestimmung* of humans is *Selbstbestimmung* or autonomy, moral freedom (cf. KrV A 464, Groundwork, 4: 396, KdU, 5: 301, 443, 445, Anthropology, 7: 324–5). Picking up elements of Stoic metaphysics, Enlightenment theologians and philosophers such as Johann Joachim Spalding revived the debate about human vocation after 1750. Like some of his contemporaries, and in contrast to Moses Mendelssohn, Kant widens the scope: he moves from the familiar focus on individuals to the species as a whole and its history and future (Beginning, 8: 115, Idea, 8: 18–9, TP, 8: 307–13 and Cavallar 2016). The goal is the complete, proportionate and suitable (*zweckmässig*) development of all natural or original predispositions in the future, including, of course, the moral disposition (see Idea, 8: 18–20 and 29–30, LP, 9: 441–2, 445). It is prepared by the culture of skill in civil society (KdU, 5: 433, LP, 9: 449–51). This can only be achieved by the human species as a whole (LP, 9: 445, KdU, 5: 432, Idea, 8: 18), and humans who have enlightened themselves about their proper vocation – which goes beyond their roles or functions in civil society – and have begun to cultivate their moral disposition are in a position to become citizens of the world. According to Kant, human dignity is not some absolute inner value all humans possess (this is rather the doctrine of more traditional forms of moral cosmopolitanism), but refers to sublimity (*Erhabenheit*), the prerogative of humans over the rest of nature because they are beings capable of self-legislation or "internal lawgiving" and moral freedom, who should respect this potential or capacity in all other rational agents and should develop it in themselves (MM, 6: 436; cf. Sensen 2009 for a full analysis).

I want to finish this section with a brief comparison of Kant's cosmopolitanism with traditional approaches, in order to put Kant into historical perspective (if only superficially). Natural law cosmopolitanism posited a global – and usually morally very thin – *societas humani generis*, a society of the entire human race where members share common features like rationality or compassion for others. This society was conceived as static, and often lacked a legal dimension (Cavallar 2011: 17–36 and 64–84). Kant was different, together with authors like Christian Wolff (Cheneval 2002: 132–213 and Cavallar 2002: 208–21). Founding, cultivating and perfecting juridical and ethical communities are practical tasks and duties, not something already given. They should be promoted by cosmopolitan-minded agents working for a better future. As a philosopher of religion, Kant adds that by doing this, these agents can at the same time be understood reflectively as helping to realize the kingdom of God on earth, the *telos* of history and the ultimate vocation (*Bestimmung*) of the human race.

2.2 The concept of the highest good: immanent or transcendent?

The highest good is the coincidence of virtue and happiness, with the latter "distributed in exact proportion to morality", and an idea of pure practical reason aiming at "unconditioned totality" (KpV, 5: 108–9 and 111 and KdU, 5: 450). The concept has been interpreted in divergent ways, ever since John Silber published his famous article in the late 1950ies (Silber 1959; for an introduction see the discussions in Cheneval 2002: 441–56, Denis 2005, Flikschuh 2010, O'Connell 2008 and Pasternack 2011). Some offer a religious – or transcendent – and personal interpretation: the highest good proper is attainable for individuals only in the afterlife and guaranteed by God. The system thinkers defend the co-existence of the philosophies of history and religion within Kant's system. Others understand the highest good as a worldly or immanent concept, as the ultimate end (*letzter Zweck*) of nature and history and attainable as a collective achievement of humanity. These interpreters – the secularists – usually drop the theological dimension, or Kant's moral religion. Kant's kingdom of ends coincides with a global political – or semi-political/moral – order (see Louden 2000: 161–2, Cheneval 2002: 404, 406–7, 409, 413 and 448; for a discussion see Cheneval 2002: 434–94, Flikschuh, 2010, Geismann 2009: 87–118, Moran 2009: 479–84, Moran 2011 and 2012, and Anderson-Gold 2001b: 8–52). All three "camps" share a core interpretation of the highest good: it is a normative goal, an ideal which cannot be fully realized but approximated by the human species as a whole. Attempting to realize this ideal of reason, and bringing it "ever nearer to a possible greatest perfection" (KrV A 317) is a task humans should set themselves. In Kant's tentative cosmopolitan philosophy of history, world history becomes a learning process, a process of education where humans grasp the meaning of their task, spell out its implications, and eventually try to promote its realization.

There are various reasons why Kant would not merge the philosophies of history and religion (a fairly early criticism of the secularist interpretation can be found in Knippenberg 1991, a recent one in Flikschuh 2010). In the following paragraphs, I try to reconstruct them. The relevant catchwords and phrases are: the distinction between the phenomenal and the noumenal world; the difference between the irreducible spheres of external actions and inner moral dispositions; the moral paradox; human finiteness and wickedness; the *necessary* connection of morality and proportionate happiness.

First, there is the distinction between the phenomenal and the noumenal world. The world of phenomena, the sensible world, is subject to natural laws, and not related to the laws of morality and the idea of the highest good (KpV, 5: 115 and 128–9). "In nature, everything *is:* the question of *ought* does not arise there" (Conflict, 7: 71). This leads to a gulf between morality, freedom and virtue on the one hand and (the laws of) nature on the other: "no necessary connection of happiness with virtue in the world, adequate to the highest good, can be expected from the most meticulous observance of moral laws" (KpV, 5: 113). Unlike legal progress, moral or religious progress is not a topic of historical development (cf. Religion, 6: 124), since it belongs to the noumenal world. From the outside, that is, as far as actions as phenomena are concerned, we humans can never tell the difference between legality where someone "complies with the law according to the *letter*" and is "a human being of good morals" and morality, where she "observes it according to the *spirit*" and is "a morally good human being" (Religion, 6: 31; see also MM, 6: 219). The philosophy of history is exclusively concerned with the former, progress in the realm of legality (compliance with the letter of the moral law), the philosophy of religion with the latter, namely moral progress, which is beyond human cognition and an issue of moral hope only. Some secularist interpreters tend to confound these two perspectives or spheres (cf. Groundwork, 4: 452–3 and 458), which amounts to abandoning the core of Kant's critical enterprise.

In terms of the philosophy of history, the results are fairly meagre: The belief that moral progress is an intrinsic part of social life is unfounded (against Kleingeld 2012: 173), there can be no certainty that "moral agency" is "expected to increase" (165), or that eventually a "genuine moral transformation" would take place (162). What can be found in Kant's last text on the issue, in the *Conflict of Faculties* (1798), are two related and explicit claims: first, that we cannot have any clear-cut theoretical knowledge whatsoever of (the development of) our own moral disposition, that of others, or indeed that of the human race as a whole. Secondly, if progess takes place, this concerns progress in moral legality, that is, "in dutiful actions whatever their motives" (Conflict, 7: 91).

These distinctions are – and this is the second argument – closely connected with the difference between the irreducible spheres of external actions of the human species and individual, inner morality (see for instance MM, 6: 220 and 231). The philosophy of history only focuses on actions as phenomena, no matter whether these were caused by practical reason or natural impulses, by the spirit or the letter of the moral law. Therefore Kant constructs the history of humankind in "Idea for a universal history" as a development based on *natural* causes such as unsocial sociability or the cunning of nature. The final end (*Endzweck*) of creation is thus not an issue of the philosophy of history (see below).

Third, there is the moral paradox: the idea of collective progress towards the highest political good does not solve the issue of deserved happiness for the individual. Humans do not know the moral status of other humans – or their own, to be precise (cf. Groundwork, 4: 407). Therefore, they are in no position to assess if others deserve happiness – only an omniscient, omnipotent and just being could do that (cf. KdU, 5: 444). In addition, progress in history does not answer the problem of individual happiness. A purely immanent interpretation of the highest good is unable to solve the moral paradox, the discrepancy between morality and deserved happiness. The concept of the highest good devoid of any transcendent dimension, often coinciding with the highest political good, keeps the dialectic of practical reason unsolved (cf. KpV, 5: 107–13). Kant himself points out that it is odd that ancient philosophers like Epicurus or the Stoics believed that the highest good could be found in our sensible world (KpV, 5: 115). Experience contradicts this belief. Virtue does not necessarily produce happiness on earth. Thus "we find ourselves compelled" to postulate "an intelligible world" where the highest good as an unconditioned totality is possible or thinkable (ibid.; see Albrecht 1978: 58–101, Denis 2005, Langthaler 2014: vol. 1, 424–33, vol. 2, 26–363, Pasternack 2011, Wood 1970: 125–9). In the words of one interpreter, we are justified in believing in God and immortality "*because* we need them to explain how the Highest Good is possible" (Pasternack 2011: 315). This idea of an omnipotent, transcendent and omniscient moral being compensating a moral disposition or virtue with happiness is of course beyond possible human experience (cf. KdU, 5: 444). There is an additional problem mentioned in the third proposition of Kant's "Idea for a universal history". Kant states that it is "strange" that according to the philosophical reconstruction of history, only the later generations will enjoy the "good fortune" the previous ones might also have deserved (cf. Idea, 8: 20). It is significant that Kant does *not* use the word "happiness" here, which would relate to the highest good proper. In the philosophy of history, the issue is *not* the highest good proper, but the highest political good; the realm of experience or phenomena, and thus also of history, can never relate to the intelligible world of the highest good proper.

Kant's fourth argument is human finiteness and wickedness. One standard theme of Kant's critical philosophy is the fact of limited human faculties in cognitive and moral terms. The spheres of human agency and those of nature are separated by a wide gulf. "[T]he acting rational being in the world is [...] not also the cause of the world and of nature itself" (KpV, 5: 124); in fact, there is no necessary connection between rational agency and nature. Finite human beings are not in a position to reward virtue with the appropriate amount of happiness, as they do not have the necessary amount of insight, good will, or power (Religion, 6: 7 note). As Kant puts it, "the moral law in fact transfers us, in idea (*der Idee nach*), into a nature in which pure reason, if it were accompanied with suitable physical power, would produce the highest good" (KpV, 5: 44). However, this "suitable power" of human reason is in fact missing. Humans do manage, though, to improve their external, legal arrangements and institutions, as Kant's assessment of European history suggests. This legal progress can be confirmed by empirical evidence (cf. Idea, 8: 29–30 and section 3 below). Moral progress, by contrast, becomes very unlikely – though remains a possibility – due to radical evil (Religion, 6: 57–9). This is the conscious and deliberate subordination of the moral law under a disposition (*Gesinnung*) that gives the "subjective principle of self-love" priority (Religion, 6: 36). Interpreters have not failed to emphasize that Kant's doctrine of evil is close to, and shares some similarities with, the Christian doctrine of *peccatum originarium*, or original sin, though there are also profound differences (cf. Religion, 6: 31; see for instance Horn 2011: 43 and 64 and Forschner 2011: 83–9). The doctrine does not deny moral predispositions and a "germ of goodness" (ibid.: 45) within each individual, even criminals; but Kant holds that we should also acknowledge the will's tendency to subordinate the incentives stimulating morality or the rational commands of duty to the incentives of self-love (cf. Religion, 6: 32–9).

The secularist interpretation faces an additional challenge (this is argument number five). It has to abandon the element that Kant found central to the highest good, namely a *necessary* connection of morality and proportionate happiness "as ground and consequent" (KpV, 5: 111), the idea of "just deserts" – that virtue ought to be rewarded by happiness (O'Connell 2012: 258). The secularized interpretation has to water down Kant's idea of happiness, defined as "an absolute whole, a maximum of well-being in my present condition and in every future condition" (Groundwork, 4: 418; cf. KrV B 834, MM, 6: 387). As Hare has pointed out, *Glückseligkeit* in Kant's holistic understanding is not simply a happy holiday or a moment of bliss; it relates to "lives as wholes" and to us as rational, but also finite beings with sensuous needs and desires (Hare 1996: 72). The secularists tend to drop Kant's definition of the highest good as happiness proportionate to virtue, and replace this proportionality thesis by the weaker maximization thesis – that the highest good is nothing but the maximization of happiness and virtue (a succinct criticism of the maximization thesis is offered by O'Connell, 2012). However, this interpretation does not solve the antinomy of practical reason or the moral paradox: according to Kant, the Epicureans and the Stoics made the mistake of trying to find "happiness in precise proportion to virtue already in *this life* (in the sensible world)" (KpV, 5: 115). They understood the relationship as analytical; in fact, it is synthetic, and a matter of cause (virtue) and effect (happiness). However, no "necessary connection of happiness with virtue" can be found or expected in this world; it can only be a matter of coincidence (ibid.: 113). Practical reason thus demands the "combination (*Verbindung*)" of two distinct realms, of the realms of freedom and of nature, and our cognitive faculties can think if this combination only if we assume "a higher, moral, most holy, and omnipotent being" who unites the two (Religion, 6: 5). Without the postulate of God's existence, I would in all likelihood either deceive myself concerning my powers or those of the species or reduce the moral demand, degrading the moral law "from its *holiness* by making it out to be *lenient* (indulgent) and thus conformed to our convenience" (KpV, 5: 122).

Finally, the interpretation of the secularists is anachronistic. They usually try to play this world off against the afterlife, earth against heaven. Gordon Michalson's interpretation is a case in point: in the *Religion*, so he argues, "the concept of the ethical commonwealth in fact displaces Kant's postulate of the immortality of the soul in the depiction of moral perfection" and "heaven is absorbed by earth" (Michalson 1999: 100–1; see also ibid.: 90–1, 105, 109 and Förster 1998: 346, 348, 351). The contrast is constructed as binary, as a stark "either-or". Kant does indeed distinguish between the "people of God" on earth (Religion, 6: 100) or the ethical community on the one hand and the transcendent kingdom of God beyond history where "nature and morals come into a harmony" (KpV, 5: 128) on the other, a harmony which is impossible on this earth. Kant never abandons this distinction. However, following Christian tradition, Kant also goes beyond a simple juxtaposition of this versus the next world or the afterlife: Both legal and moral commonwealths are preliminary steps in the true goal of world history, which lies beyond history and is a cosmopolitan "visible Kingdom of God *on earth*" (Religion, 6: 134, my emphasis; cf. KdU, 5: 442–50, refl. 1396 and 1397, 15: 608–9). Kant hopes that gradually the true religious faith, natural religion or the pure faith of moral reason will spread across the globe; he sees his own century as an epoch in the process of Enlightenment when at least in Christianity "the seed" of this faith is growing unhindered, so that the "invisible Kingdom of God on earth" is continuously approximated, finally encompassing and uniting "all human beings" (Religion, 6: 131). The underlying premise of these thoughts is a doctrine of traditional Christian eschatology, namely that the next world is already present in this world (cf. KrV, A 811, KpV, 5: 115; see also Hare 1996: 73–4 and Beiser 2006: 599). Kant sides with the eschatological doctrine of the Gospel according to Luke, where Jesus replies to the question when the Kingdom of God would come: "The Kingdom of God cometh not in visible form […] *For behold, the Kingdom of God is within you!*" (Luke 17, 21–22). As is to be expected, Kant interprets this passage as the triumph of the true moral religion of inner moral disposition, as the calling of each human being to become a citizen of the universal ethical commonwealth (cf. Religion, 6: 135–6), and the final attainment of this ideal at the end of – or rather beyond – history (Religion, 6: 135 note; refl. 1396, 15: 608–9). The Kingdom of God from the Lord's Prayer ("Thy Kingdom come") is both "within us and outside us" (Religion, 6: 192). It is inside us as soon as we as individuals have ordained our moral disposition to this Kingdom; it is outside us as soon as we as the human species have realized it with divine assistance in the world, by giving ecclesiastical faiths a new moral content. In my account, I have tried to take these elements into account by distinguishing between the global ethical community (the highest moral good) and the kingdom of God (the highest good proper).

If we look at the eighteenth-century context, a similar picture emerges (Beutel 2009, Bohatec 1938, Sommer 2006, Winter 2000: 49–113 and 425–76). The overwhelming majority of philosophers and theologians in German-speaking territories endorsed a form of theism and rational theology. Neologians like Johann Joachim Spalding (1714–1804), Wilhelm Abraham Teller (1734–1804) or Johann Salomo Semler (1725–1791) developed a dynamic theology that focused on individual morality and an authentic religious life. The neologian Johann Friedrich Wilhelm Jerusalem (1709–1789) perceived history as a process of divine education (and anticipated Lessing's theory). Representatives of the emerging philosophy of history developed the ideas of perfectibility, of moral and religious progress and of the "advancement" of the invisible church of God. In particular, the tradition of eschatological Christianity, of chiliasm or millenarianism can be found in Johann Albrecht Bengel (1687–1752) and Christian August Crusius (1715–1775), who both influenced Kant. There are similarities between Kant's religious cosmopolitanism and the "prophetic theology" of Bengel and Crusius: the Kingdom of God is an "embryo" or "germ" that will eventually develop in the course of history; this end is marked by the triumph of the good principle; the progress is "guaranteed" by providence and a theistic concept of "moral" nature. There are two major differences: Kant's critical approach denies that we can have theoretical knowledge in the sphere of metaphysics; and his criticism of the Jewish faith and its exclusion from church history proper (see Bohatec 1938: 489–93). In short, the majority of philosophers and theologians in German-speaking territories took it for granted that the kingdom of God could and should be promoted in this world, following traditional Christian eschatology (see also chapter 5 on Basedow and Rousseau and Cavallar 2015).

Kant never held that a concern for this world was incompatible with a moral belief in the afterlife; that moral faith had to neglect mundane matters; that we have to choose between either promoting the highest good on this earth or believing in divine distribution of proportionate happiness. All these juxtapositions fly in the face of Kant's holistic approach. The secularists have imposed an understanding of immanence and transcendence that is anachronistic and apparently goes back to the nineteenth century (and perhaps to the young romantics; see Beiser 2002: 361 ff. and 2003: 51 and 175).

Some secularists claim that Kant reworked his doctrine of the highest good in the 1790ies, arriving at a secularized, merely immanent concept of the highest political good. Francis Cheneval, for instance, has claimed that Kant abandoned his original dualism in favour of his philosophical chiliasm, dropping the cosmic-theological chiliasm (referring to Idea, 8: 27). According to Cheneval, Kant endorsed this version because philosophical chiliasm respected the limits of theoretical reason and was thus more moderate by focussing on external freedom and right independent of moral progress (Cheneval 2002: 404–79). A cosmopolitan legal society as the highest good is, Cheneval asserts, the final result of

2.2 The concept of the highest good: immanent or transcendent?

Kant's constantly revised intellectual development in the late 1790s, culminating in the clear statement in the *Conflict of Faculties* that progress would only yield "an increase of the products of *legality* in dutiful actions" (Conflict, 7: 91; Cheneval 2002: 440 f., 450 f. and 478 f.). Cheneval is right when he keeps Kant's philosophy of history separate from that of religion (for some secularists, they usually merge). However, Cheneval's thesis that Kant abandoned his so-called dualism is not convincing. If Kant focused on legal cosmopolitanism in the late 1790ies, then this does not necessarily prioritize this form, or imply that Kant deliberately dropped the religious dimension. In the philosophy of history Kant does not refer to the highest good proper, only to the highest political good for methodological reasons. This means that a particular entity is bracketed because it does not belong to a particular field under inquiry. For instance, the issue of the freedom of will is bracketed in the philosophy of history of the 1780ies, because that philosophy is concerned with empirical actions determined by natural causes rather than moral dispositions (cf. Idea, 8: 17). In a similar vein, the doctrine of right focuses on legal duties of humans towards each other, and therefore religious issues and theology are bracketed (exceptions are MM, 6: 280 note, 303 and 319, which relate to legal issues). It would be absurd to conclude that Kant has abandoned the postulates here, moral faith in freedom of the will and God's existence. – A line of thought similar to that of Cheneval can be found in Eckart Förster, who has claimed that over the years, Kant reworked his moral theology, to arrive in the *opus postumum* at a completely subjective and immanent version of religion which dropped the postulates of the second *Critique*. According to Förster, Kant held already around 1786 that "the highest good [...] must be located not in an afterlife but in this life, in this world" (Förster 2000: 127; see also ibid., 147 and Förster 1998: 343, 346 and 362; see also Michalson 1999: 112–22 and the criticism in Gawlina 2004).

The transformation thesis is refuted by textual evidence. In "The end of all things" (1794), published one year after the *Religion*, but quoted neither by Cheneval nor Michalson, Kant again combines his theological chiliasm of a Kingdom of God on earth and the hope of moral progress with an individualist as well as transcendent version of the highest good (see End, 8: 328, 330, 334–5 and also Conflict, 7: 54–59). Right at the beginning of the essay, Kant distinguishes between humans as "temporal beings" on the one hand and as "supersensible" beings on the other and discusses the possibility (from a theoretical perspective) as well as the religious hope (from a moral perspective, from "a practical point of view" or "in a moral regard"; End, 8: 330 and 327) that as supersensible beings, humans live on after death. Therefore, "it is wise to act as if *another life* – and the moral state in which we end this one, along with its consequences in entering on that other life – is unalterable" (ibid., 330; emphasis deleted, my own emphasis added; see also

28: 298–301, 25: 696–7). Kant's main concern in these paragraphs is not even a discussion whether "the future eternity" (End, 8: 328) should be doubted or not – he investigates what kind of moral belief concerning it should be held. Finally, it is worth noting that Kant develops the idea of the immanent ethical commonwealth, stressed by most secularists, only once in his writings, namely in the *Religion*, though it can be argued that it is anticipated in the Groundwork (see Groundwork, 4: 438–9 and Flikschuh 2010: 134–6). At the same time, Kant continues writing about the individualist and transcendent version of the highest good well into the *opus postumum*. In addition, the introduction of the idea of the ethical commonwealth in the *Religion* clearly has one central function, namely to account for the fact of religious communities (which are then interpreted as visible representations, symbols or archetypes of the idea).

Kant does indeed ponder the possibility that humans themselves could be the authors of their own happiness and that of others, provided that they fulfil their moral duty. Kant calls this a "system of self-rewarding morality", which would not require the idea of God (KrV A 809; 19: 202; Förster 1998, 342–3). Whereas Kant does not develop this possible "system" any further in the first *Critique* (cf. KrV A 811), it does live on in the philosophy of history, and especially in the *Religion*, where Kant asserts that promoting the highest moral good *in this world* is the task of the ethical commonwealth (cf. Religion, 6: 94–5 and 97–99). However, even here Kant clearly distinguishes between promoting and realizing the highest good, and between the highest political good, the highest moral good and the transcendent highest good proper.

The historical development of the human species in the juridical sphere towards more external freedom and legality on the one hand and the moral hope of the individual concerning the afterlife can be seen as two legitimate aspects which complement each other. This co-existence is suggested in various passages. In the *Critique of Practical Reason*, happiness in this *and* in a future life are two sides of one and the same coin and *both* are legitimate interests of reason (cf. KpV, 5: 61). As mentioned above, in "The end of all things" (1794), Kant distinguishes between humans as "temporal beings" and as "supersensible" beings and claims that from a moral perspective, it makes sense to believe in life after death. Therefore, "it is wise to act as if *another life* – and the moral state in which we end this one, along with its consequences in entering on that other life – is unalterable" (End, 8: 330; emphasis deleted, my own emphasis added; see also 28: 298–301, 25: 696–70, Brandt 2009: 17–8 and 179). Kant's main concern in these paragraphs is not at all whether "the future eternity" (End, 8: 328) should be doubted or not, but he investigates what kind of moral belief concerning it should be held, and discusses the systems of the unitists and the dualists, ultimately siding with the latter (cf. ibid., 8: 328–30). Apparently the main thrust of

Kant's reasoning is to show that both legal progress in history, promoting the highest moral good and belief in the afterlife are not impossible objects of volition, since impossibility would imply not being obliged to follow the moral law, and this in turn would undermine its unconditional command (Silber 1959: 477, Forschner 2010: 117 f., Geismann 2009: 44 f.).

Kant's own philosophy is different from the secularist interpretation. Both legal and moral commonwealths (the visible churches) are just preliminary steps in the true goal of world history, which lies beyond history and is "a visible Kingdom of God on earth" (Religion, 6: 134; cf. 15: 608–9). Kant hopes that gradually the true religious faith, natural religion or the pure faith of moral reason will spread across the globe; he sees his own century as an epoch in the process of Enlightenment when at least in Christianity "the seed" of this faith is growing unhindered, so that the "invisible Kingdom of God on earth" is continuously approximated, finally encompassing and uniting "all human beings" (Religion, 6: 131; see also Enlightenment, 8: 37–42). Jesus Christ is credited for introducing this "pure religious faith" which has the potential to become "a universal world-religion" (Religion, 6: 131). The "world religion" which Kant favours and which is universal since it is valid for every human being (Religion, 6: 157) is identical with the authentic Christian religion – a stance that contemporary commentators usually eye with suspicion since it seems so un-cosmopolitan and Eurocentric (examples abound: Dierksmeier 1998: 175 f., Louden 2002: 130–2, McCarthy 1986: 89–91 and 101, Sala 2004: 230). I make no attempt to discuss this complex issue here. Suffice it to say that Kant tries to mediate the a priori idea of an ethical community with the human condition and historical developments (cf. Louden 2002: 125–30, Bielefeldt 2001: 186–9), and consequently interprets the visible churches as symbols or archetypes of the idea of an invisible church (cf. Religion, 6: 101). The winners, at any rate, are the Christian churches (cf. Religion, 6: 52, 157–167), though Kant harshly criticizes the history of Christianity and some of its deformed practices (cf. Religion, 6: 130–1 and 167–71; see Cavallar 2015 for more).

Religious belief aims at fighting off moral despair, once the moral agent has become aware of the split between the world as it ought to be and world as it is, and her realization that fulfilling the moral command may result in undermining one's own pursuit of happiness in the world. In itself, this does not undermine the possibility of moral endeavours, but it undermines its *likelihood*. Kant claims that in order for the moral law to be binding on us, we have to be sure that the highest good and the moral world are at least possible (from the point of view of theoretical reason). I am only obliged to obey the categorical imperative if its aim (the moral world or the kingdom of ends) is not beyond reach. Thus, according to Kant, the decision to choose moral good rather than evil leads to another decision with the form of an either/or: either rational faith in God or the moral despair of the atheist faced with the possible futility of her endeavour (cf. KdU, 5: 452, Groundwork, 4: 438–9, Beiser 2006: 616–7, Caswell 2006: 208, Flikschuh 2010: 136, Munzel 1999: 212, Wood 1970: 160). Kant does not deny that atheists can acquire good moral dispositions, but he sees a problem in their steadfastness and unwavering commitment to morality. The righteous atheist Spinoza might strive unselfishly for a morally better world here on earth, and this is just what his own practical reason demands him to do. However, he will be faced with his limited powers to change the world for the better, he will have to acknowledge that nature is indifferent to morality, he will meet other humans who are evil and undermine his well-intentioned efforts, he might lead a life that is nasty, miserable and short, and has to face the prospect of an absurd end, namely being thrown back "into the abyss of the purposeless chaos of matter" (cf. KdU, 5: 452).

According to Kant, this attitude or belief-system of the righteous atheist is not in the "interest of reason" and the "interest of humanity" (KrV, A 462–76, A 798; cf. KdU, 5: 455). It might undermine our willingness to steadfastly pursue the highest good as the goal of our moral volition as well as our virtue, "the moral strength of a human being's will in fulfilling his duty" (MM, 6: 405, emphasis deleted). The idea of God as the omnipotent being which combines the two distinct elements of the highest good, namely virtue and proportionate happiness, "meets our natural need, which would otherwise be a hindrance to moral resolve" (Religion, 6: 5). Our resolve would be hindered if we assumed that, though we knew how a moral world should look like, we still held that it was impossible. In all likelihood, our resolve would melt away (see also KpV, 5: 126; Collins, 27: 317–20).

2.3 Kant's philosophy of history: The manipulation, education or self-education of humankind?

The question I raise in this section is the following: How does the highest political good in this world (a cosmopolitan legal society of peaceful states and individuals) come about? There is a tension in Kant's writings between the human species propelled or instigated by Nature towards moral ends on the one hand and an understanding of human history as a collective learning process, whereby humans are seen as autonomous agents not manipulated by Nature. Thus Kant's philosophy of history seems to offer two divergent interpretations. In the first case, Nature or providence educates the human race towards a cosmopolitan condition, and history is the education of the human species on a grand scale. In the second case, the human race educates itself. Perhaps Kant even had a more elaborate combination of the two possibilities in mind, where Nature helps humans to help themselves actualize their potentials (on Kant's philosophy of history see Brandt, 2009: 179–222, Cavallar, 1992: 253–96, Kater, 1999: 135–75, Kleingeld, 1995 and 2008, Pauen, 1999, Pollmann, 2011). The secularists usually rely on Kant's philosophy of history to support their approach. Understanding world history as the self-education of the human species on a grand scale seems to offer the intended secularized reinterpretation of Kant's philosophy, devoid of any references to divine interference.

I will start with the first, more widespread interpretation, where Nature educates the human race. In his *Lectures on pedagogy*, Kant distinguishes among three kinds of formation or *Bildung*. The education of skilfulness and of prudence cultivates acting on hypothetical imperatives, which have the form "If you want x, then you should do y". The action is good "merely as a means *to something else*" (Groundwork, 4: 414). The child cultivates imperatives of skilfulness (*Geschicklichkeit*) to attain certain ends and prudence (*Klugheit*), learning how to use other people for her own ends and thus also learning how to fit into civil society (LP, 9: 455, Moran 2009: 475–9). The result is legality, not morality of disposition. The third form of practical education is moral education based on the categorical imperative, "by which the human being is to be formed so that he can live as a freely acting being". It coincides with cosmopolitan education, since "through *moral* formation" the human being "receives value in view of the entire human race" (LP, 9: 455).

Kant transposes this tripartite structure to the philosophy of history, where the human species is supposed to face the task of cultivating the imperatives of skilfulness, prudence and morality. This train of thought is especially developed in "Idea toward a Universal History with a Cosmopolitan Aim" (1784) and "Conjectural beginning of human history" (1786). Kant deplores the fact that in the course of history, the third and most important kind of formation or *Bildung* has remained underdeveloped: "very much is still lacking before we can be held to be already *moralized*" (Idea, 8: 26). According to Kant's philosophy of history, Nature educates humankind to reach this final goal, and this is a critical, reflective and teleological interpretation, systematically developed in §§ 82 to 84 of the *Critique of Judgement*. The main theses of Kant's complex train of thought are the following (for more extensive analyses, see Ameriks 2006, Bielefeldt 2001: 132–68, Cheneval 2002: 494–562, Honneth 2004, and the contributions in Rorty and Schmidt, 2009 and in Höffe 2008): The purposiveness (*Zweckmässigkeit*) of nature is a reasonable assumption, based on the reflective power of judgement. An ultimate end (*letzter Zweck*) of nature presupposes a final end (*Endzweck*) of creation (KdU, 5: 429–36, Rorty 2009: 35,

Cheneval 2002: 545, Geismann 2009: 88–9). Since only the human species can possibly be related to an unconditional, moral end, this species is the ultimate end of nature. The final end for humankind is moral, and morality is the result of the freedom of the will. Therefore, nature cannot produce a final end, but nature can reflectively be interpreted as a "moral facilitator" (Allison 2009: 40, cf. Cheneval 2002: 534). Nature promotes its ultimate end with the help of culture, which comes in two forms, namely as the culture of skill (*Geschicklichkeit*) and as the culture of discipline (*Zucht*), which liberates us from sensuous desires. The culture of skill is the more important one for the philosophy of history, since the "cunning of nature" uses this form to promote its ultimate end (KdU, 5: 432, Allison 2009: 41, Geismann 2009: 90–1). Thus nature prepares the ground for genuine morality, which can only be the work of humans themselves. One method is the manipulation of human "unsocial sociability" by nature to trigger the establishment of republican constitutions, which in turn facilitate the growth of moral dispositions, since "the good moral education of a people is to be expected from a good state constitution" only (Peace, 8: 366; see also chapter 7 below).

Yet culture itself is still part of nature; the moral vocation of humans lies beyond nature and thus also beyond history. Possible morality (based on the freedom of the will) is not an object of the philosophy of history (cf. Idea, 8: 17 and above). The philosophy of history belongs to the "teleological doctrine of nature" (Idea, 8: 18), thus focuses on culture as the ultimate end of nature, on phenomenal virtue defined "as a facility in *actions* conforming to duty (according to their legality)" (Religion, 6: 14, cf. 47), *not* on inner morality, the final end of creation or on the highest good (cf. Geismann 2009: 90–7). Attempts of the secularists to relocate the cultivation of morality in the realm of history are therefore fraught with paradox: they would have to abandon one cornerstone of Kant's critical philosophy, the distinction between the phenomenal and the noumenal (see above).

I will now turn to the second way of interpreting Kant's philosophy of history, where the human race educates itself and legal progress is the result of a learning process (again, this would be a reflective, critical judgement; this interpretation is offered by Honneth 2004; see also Bielefeldt 2004 and 2008, Kleingeld 2008: 524 and 526, Pollmann 2011: 78–82 and Cheneval 2002: 501–60). The interpretation of history as a collective learning process is suggested by the second part of *The Conflict of Faculties* (1798), and seems to do without the hypothesis of a natural teleology. Given "immeasurable time" (Conflict, 7: 89), the principle of plenitude states that any possibility will sooner or later be realized (Cheneval 2002: 526–7). For Kant, the French Revolution is a case in point. He interprets the constitutional phase of the French Revolution (1789–91) as a symptom of the "moral tendency of the human race" (Conflict, 7: 84) since the civil constitution designed by the revolutionaries corresponded with the idea of right. In addition, Kant explains the universal sympathy of the onlookers as the outcome of a "purely moral" disposition in humanity (ibid. 86). Even if the revolution should fail, Kant muses, a cumulative learning process for the whole human race might be the overall result. "For that occurrence is too important, too much interwoven with the interest of humanity, and its influence too widely propagated in all areas of the world to not be recalled on any favourable occasion by the nations which would then be roused to a repetition of new efforts of this kind" (Conflict, 7: 88). According to this interpretation, history is an intercultural learning process, and the education of humankind is partly self-education. This is a perspective reserved for the cognitive, moral and legal cosmopolitan, "who does not consider what happens in just some one nation but also has regard to the whole scope of all the peoples on earth" (ibid.).

The second interpretation, the self-education of humankind, is the more secularized one, as the concept of God or providence (which looms behind the more modest notion of Nature, cf. Peace, 8: 361 note) is not essential there. It is obvious that the philosophical reflections developed in 1798 (in the *Conflict of Faculties*) are distinct from those of the 1780ies (in the "Idea" and "Beginning"). Whereas the early essays work with a strict separation of the phenomenal from the noumenal, Kant's last statement on the philosophy of history does not abandon this cornerstone of the critical philosophy, but permanently moves back and forth between these spheres and infers from phenomenal change that noumenal change has taken place: moral improvement is said to be the cause of observable human behaviour. In favour of the secularist interpretation, it can be argued that Kant does expand the scope of the philosophy of history in 1798 to include the sphere of inner morality. In addition, the secularist might counter the following possible criticism of the secularist interpretation: even if history is understood as a collective learning process, Nature or divine supervision is still required to make sure that the learning process advances properly and eventually reaches the desired goal. The secularists might counter with a thin version of moral teleology, stripped of all theology. On the other hand, the central arguments raised in the second section against the secularists fully apply here as well: first, the moral paradox remains unsolved since the connection between morality and happiness still cannot be conceived as either necessary or synthetic. Secondly, the secularist interpretation still remains anachronistic. By contrast, understanding history as a collective learning process is fully compatible with the approach of the system thinkers, provided that they do not drop the postulates of individual agency and autonomy (this is what some theologians of the first group do).

2.4 The ethical commonwealth: the duty of the human race towards itself

No matter which interpretation of Kant's philosophy of history we prefer, both highlight a key problem, namely the transition from culture or civilization (revolving around skilfulness and prudence) to moralization. In the Starke manuscript of 1790–91, Kant explains: "The most difficult condition of the human race is the crossing-over [*Übergang*] from civilization to moralization ... [O]ne must try to enlighten human beings and to better establish international law ... We are now, those of us who are working on the unity of religion, on the step of this crossing-over from civilization to moralization. Inner religion stands in now for the position of legal constraint. In order to reach the great end, one can either go from the parts to the whole, that is to say, through education, or from the whole to the parts" (quoted in Louden 2000: 42). According to this passage, Kant envisions several methods to promote moralization (since morality is the result of freedom, it can only be fostered, nurtured or helped indirectly): education or rather formation (*Bildung*, with Enlightenment as one element), reform of domestic as well as international politics, and the reform of ecclesiastical faiths. "Inner religion" coincides with Kant's version of moral religion with its emphasis on the moral disposition, morality and virtue rather than statutes, rituals and dogmas (Religion, 6: 168, for introductions see Fischer and Forschner 2010, Höffe 2011). Formation, going "from the parts to the whole" or following a bottom-up procedure, is one way to approximate the "great end", trying to realize one element of the highest good, namely morality, to which humans themselves can contribute (proportionate happiness would be God's task). The second way "from the whole to the parts" could either refer to providence or Nature (Conflict, 7: 93) or to political change on a grand scale, such as reforms of constitutions or governments (like under Frederick II. of Prussia), to events like the French Revolution, or reforms of international law or international organizations.

I have mentioned in the second section that Kantian ethics postulates that all rational beings, irrespective of their race, are ends in themselves and lawgiving members of "the universal kingdom of ends" (Groundwork, 4: 438 and 429), an intelligible world which humans as rational beings form by dint of being self-legislating; these beings respect each other as ends in themselves, and a moral whole of all ends is achieved (Groundwork, 4: 438, Bielefeldt 2001: 101–2 and 184–8, Cheneval 2002: 467–72, Louden 2000: 125–32, Sala 2004, Wimmer 1990: 186–206, Wood 1970: 189–200, Wood 2008: 259–69, Wood 2011b). Since only a morally good, omnipotent and omniscient being "who knows the heart" (*Herzenskündiger*, Religion, 6: 100) can guarantee the highest good, the necessary connection of morality and deserved happiness, this commonwealth has God as its founder and author of its constitution (Groundwork, 4: 434–441 and KpV, 5: 128, Religion, 6: 100). The ethical commonwealth or community encompasses "the entire human race" and is distinct from a political community, which governs the external actions of humans (Religion, 6: 95–6), is a "universal republic based on the laws of virtue" (ibid.: 98), coincides with the invisible church, and is the moral destiny of the human race (Religion, 6: 101; 15: 608–9). God and humans together try to realize it, with humans promoting (*befördern*) and "preparing" this ethical community, and God offering fulfilment (attainment, realization or *Verwirklichung*; ibid.; Geismann 2009: 49, Silber 1959: 478–9, Wimmer 1990: 11 and 74–7).

Kant calls the duty to promote the highest good as a member of this cosmopolitan moral community or "union [...] of well-disposed human beings" (Religion, 6: 97–8) a duty "*sui generis* [...] of the human race toward itself", since the highest good is a good "common to all" (ibid., 6: 97). This is an enhancement of the legal goals in the philosophy of history, but eschatology remains immanent and part of history; Kant refers here to the highest moral good in this world. The ethical commonwealth has to be global in reach since each ethical community *in concreto* – the Lutheran church, for instance – is just a "particular society" which remains in a state of nature in relation to others, thus would not overcome its imperfections or the constant threat of conflict and strife (Religion, 6: 96).

Reiner Wimmer has argued that Kant offers three distinct arguments for the duty to found the ethical commonwealth, which make use of the doctrine of radical evil, the ethical state of nature, and the highest good (cf. Wimmer 1990: 187–97; see also Sala 2004: 236–43). In the *Religion*, Kant adds a third level of human "propensity to evil" which is absent in the philosophy of history: apart from frailty and impurity of the heart, there is depravity or corruption (Religion, 6: 30). Radical evil is not in our biological nature (Kant does not offer a restatement of the doctrine of original sin), but our *Willkür* has a tendency towards the reversal of our moral maxims, subordinating "the incentives of the moral law to others (not moral ones)" (ibid.). Radical evil has a social dimension. As Kant puts it, as soon as humans have contact with each other, "they will mutually corrupt each other's moral disposition and make one another evil" (Religion, 6: 94). The task of the ethical community is to overcome this very situation of mutual moral corruption, and since it affects all humans, "the entire human race" has a duty to establish this society "in its full scope" (ibid.: 130). Promoting the highest moral good is a collective or communitarian, not an individual task. Radical evil can be held at bay – if not completely overcome -, as freedom also includes the freedom to choose morality (Guyer 2009: 148–9; for a full argument see Anderson-Gold 2001b: 25–52 and Wood 2011: 131–5).

There is a difference between the "people of God" on earth (Religion, 6: 100) or the ethical community on the one hand and the transcendent kingdom of God where "nature and morals come into a harmony" (KpV, 5: 129) on the other, a harmony which is impossible on this earth. In contrast to the secularist interpreters, Kant never abandons this distinction. The two cannot merge; they are only related to each other, since the ethical community is above all supposed to promote or preserve morality and virtue "by counteracting evil with united forces" (Religion, 6: 94), and *not* to make proportionate happiness possible. Happiness might be an unintended by-product and will in all likelihood not always be proportionate to morality.

Why not an ethical commonwealth without God? In the relevant passage itself, Kant resorts to a familiar claim, namely human finiteness, incompetence and wickedness. "But how could one expect to construct something completely straight from such crooked wood? To found a moral people of God is, therefore, a work whose execution cannot be hoped for from human beings but only from God himself" (Religion, 6: 100). Earlier in the text, Kant made a weaker claim, suggesting that "single individuals [...] on their own" are in no position to realize this "universal republic" of virtue (Religion, 6: 98). Their organizational incompetence, limited knowledge, their finite volition and limited powers are decisive. At any rate, humans are in need of divine assistance (there is an additional argument based on God as supreme and public lawgiver of the ethical community developed by Wimmer 1990: 194–6). Kant's arguments fit into the list of reasons why the philosophy of history and that of religion cannot merge in Kant's system (see above section 2, Kant's fourth argument).

It is often assumed that God's grace or providence is incompatible with human freedom of choice, since the former would determine the latter. However, divine grace could also be understood as liberating and complementary, enabling humans to overcome their initial predisposition to evil. As Leslie Mulholland has argued, "there can be an external condition of moral improvement even though it is not determining of the action produced" (Mulholland 1991: 98; see also Nonnenmacher 2011, Wimmer 1990: 158 and Wood 1970: 238–48). Divine grace could precede free choice in so far as it provided the favourable circumstances to restore this freedom, complemented the disposition or receptivity to morality one has acquired (Religion, 6: 47–8), and helped in the realization of the highest good with God as "a moral ruler of the world". Kant refers to divine "cooperation" and "management", which clearly indicates that human endeavours are a necessary condition of God's involvement (ibid., 139). There are passages where Kant hints at this possibility, though he quickly adds two familiar critical caveats. The first one is epistemological, namely that this issue "cannot be resolved theoretically, for this question totally surpasses the speculative capacity of our reason" (Religion, 6: 118; cf. 139, 174). The second qualification is the familiar thesis that what matters in morality and religion in the first place is what we as beings with a moral disposition and capable of rational deliberation can and should do – and not what God can do (cf. Religion, 6: 139, 144, 170, 177).

Kant offered a systematic whole, and apparently took the co-existence and compatibility of various forms of cosmopolitanisms for granted. Nowadays many interpreters pick out some of its elements as if they were independent from this system, and this is problematic. For instance, the second interpretation of the philosophy of history, the self-education of the human species, looks rather secularized, as the concepts of nature, God, providence or substantive teleology seem to be unimportant (if only for methodological reasons). This makes Kant attractive for contemporary philosophies, although a Kantian from the camp of the system thinkers might argue that the result is a truncated Kant and an interpretation which follows neither the letter nor the spirit of his philosophy. It could be argued that the notions that "nature educates the human race" and that "the human race educates itself" are integral parts of the Kantian cosmopolitan system, with the first perspective emphasizing the role of nature and the second stressing what humans can and should do, but "with the assistance – and not the determining influence – of nature". The overarching idea is the vocation of the human species, the teleological unfolding of its various dispositions in an attempt to promote the highest moral good.

I suppose there are additional reasons why Kant remains attractive for contemporary cosmopolitan philosophies, including those of the secularists. For a start, the highest moral good that has to be promoted does not require belief in God. Morality and moral religion are distinct from each other, morality is independent of religious belief in Kant's philosophy, and the agent's belief in the impossibility of realising the highest moral or political good does not diminish the possible moral quality of any honest – and even unintended – attempt to promote it. Secondly, Kant's practical philosophy leads only to the threshold of moral faith. This faith is subjective insofar as it requires "moral cognition of oneself" (MM, 6: 441), self-awareness, honesty, choice and commitment, which can only be done by the individual agent (cf. KdU, 5: 451 and the discussion in Cavallar 2015).

In this chapter, I focused on the relationship among political or juridical, moral and religious cosmopolitanisms, and tried to explain why for Kant the various forms of cosmopolitanisms were fully compatible. I have argued against a secularized and purely immanent interpretation of the highest good that does not solve the problem of the discrepancy between morality and happiness. As a consequence, the philosophy of history, which focuses on external actions, cannot solve the dialectic of practical reason, and Kant never implied that it could do this. The legal and ethical communities prepare the ground for something beyond history, namely "a visible Kingdom of God on earth" in the future "which is not itself history" (Religion, 6: 135). Contemporary cosmopolitan theories tend to use Kant as a starting point or a kind of quarry, picking out elements that might be useful for one's own philosophical enterprise. This approach faces the charge of being both anachronistic and reductive, because, as I have tried to show, Kant's cosmopolitan system includes the religious and regulative idea of a transcendent "unconditioned totality" (KpV, 5: 108). As a consequence, current debates on cosmopolitanism would either have to take this metaphysical and theological system into account or should – in all honesty – accept the insurmountable distance between these contemporary approaches and Kant's own (see also chapter 8, sections 2 and 3). In contrast to the secularist interpreters, Kant never abandoned the distinction between the ethical community on the one hand and the transcendent kingdom of God on the other. The overall result is a rich account of cosmopolitanism, where the threads of theological and more secularized Enlightenment conceptions are woven into a delicate synthesis.

3 Kant's right of world citizens: a historical interpretation

When Kant is regarded as the most prominent founding father of contemporary cosmopolitan philosophies (examples are Brown 2009, Cheneval 2002 or Häntsch 2008), part of this reputation can be traced back to Kant's essays *Idea for a universal history with a cosmopolitan aim* and *Perpetual Peace* and to one element of Kant's philosophy of peace which he termed cosmopolitan right. This cosmopolitan right, a translation of *Weltbürgerrecht*, literally the right of world citizens, has acquired a kind of cult status in recent literature. Daniele Archibugi and David Held made a start in the 1990s, taking Kant's cosmopolitan right as a point of departure to propose the normative model of a cosmopolitan democracy, a global and democratic civil society where individuals have "a voice, input and political representation in international affairs, in parallel with and independently of their own government" (Archibugi and Held 1995: 13). Jacques Derrida's "unconditional hospitality" (Derrida 2000 and 2001) is frequently quoted in conjunction with Kant (see for instance Brown 2010; Morgan 2009: 105), and helped to focus attention to this part of Kant's legal philosophy which had been quite neglected up to the 1990s (cf. Cavallar 1992: 236–40).

Publications which draw attention to the historical dimension of the current cosmopolitan discourses have been rare (exceptions are, among others, Albrecht 2005, Lettevall and Linder 2008 or Cavallar 2011). In this chapter, I will try to contextualize Kant's right of the world citizens, and offer a historical interpretation while trying to avoid the pitfalls of historical relativism, presentism or anachronism. As I have argued in the previous chapter, there is a three-part division in Kant's philosophy concerning the highest good and the future of the human species: The foundation of a cosmopolitan condition of perpetual peace, a global legal society of peaceful states, a "*cosmopolitan* whole" (KdU, 5: 432), perhaps a world republic is the highest *political* good. The establishment of a global ethical community is – secondly – the highest *moral* good in this world. Finally, the highest good proper coincides with the transcendent kingdom of God, the intelligible world, the kingdom of Heaven or a moral realm. This chapter focuses on one particular aspect of the global legal society, namely Kant's cosmopolitan right (section 2). I will also try to illustrate how this right relates to other conceptions of hospitality rights developed in international legal theory from Francisco de Vitoria up to Kant's time. I will compare them and suggest where Kant's originality should be located (section 3). I have also argued in the previous chapter that Kant distinguished between the doctrine of rights and the philosophy of history, and that they should not be lumped together. The next section focuses on this very philosophy of history, and the systematic role it has in Kant's discussion of cosmopolitan right: on the role of the "spirit of commerce" to promote more peaceable relations among communities, on the so-called four-stage theory, *doux commerce*, global integration, and mutual self-interest (section 4). I will finish with some general remarks on Kant's cosmopolitan right and how it can be criticized.

The highest political good in the world is a global juridical state (*Rechtszustand*) which approximates world peace. There has been an ongoing debate on whether Kant endorsed a free federation, a world republic or some sort of intermediate "cosmopolitan condition" in his writings, what his arguments were, and if they are convincing (see among many others Brown 2009: 87–122, Cavallar 2011: 64–84, Höffe 2006, Kleingeld 2004, Lettevall 2009 or Williams 2006). I make no attempt to discuss this complex and fascinating issue here. In my view Kant's normative ideal is a "state of nations" (*Völkerstaat* or *civitas gentium*) (Peace, 8: 357), "a universal *association of states* (analogous to that by which a people becomes a state)" (MM, 6: 350) as opposed to the universal monarchy, international anarchy, or the federation of republics (see also Byrd and Hruschka 2008: 600–635, 2010: 188, 200–205, Cheneval 2002: 572–573, 592–601 and Kleingeld 2012: 40–71). The *Völkerstaat* requires states to submit themselves to "public coercive rights" (according to *Perpetual Peace*), and is a regulative idea which cannot be fully realized, but continually approximated (MM, 6: 350). The basic thing for Kant was that this ideal should not be instituted by violence or force, but humans should try to realize it step by step with peaceful and juridically acceptable means. Kant hoped that states, even though they are reluctant to abandon their external sovereignty, might be willing to further this "continual approximation". The German phrase *sich freiwillig bequemen* (to bring oneself to do something, to find oneself compelled, to accommodate oneself) is quite telling (Peace, 8: 357): It combines free choice and the force of external circumstances. States are reluctant to cooperate, but they bring themselves to do so because under the given circumstances (e.g. threat of war, trans-border ecological problems) it is the smaller of two evils. *In thesi*, that is, according to reason, the world republic is the ideal and should be the ultimate goal; *in hypothesi*, under given circumstances and conditions, the federation or league of states establishing a permanent state congress for initiating or instituting public coercive right is the second-best option and should be an intermediate goal (Peace, 8: 357, MM, 6: 350–1; see Byrd and Hruschka 2008: 637–640, 2010: 201–205; Cheneval 2002: 599–600).

3.1 Kant's commercial cosmopolitanism

As mentioned in the introduction, Kant's cosmopolitan right has attracted a lot of attention in recent years (see Kleingeld 1998 and 2012: 72–91, 134–48, Brown 2006, 2008, Keil 2009, Milstein 2013, Morgan 2009, Muthu 2006, Thompson 2008). In this section I will leave out the question of how Kant tried to justify this right (see Byrd and Hruschka 2010: 122–132; Kleingeld 2012: 72–86; Cavallar 2002: 363–66 for this aspect) and focus on one particular problem, namely its systematic status within the doctrine of right. Various interpretations have been offered.

According to what can be termed the loophole-thesis, cosmopolitan right was designed to overcome the state of nature among states, non-state communities and individuals, thus complementing (not replacing) domestic and international right. All persons "who can mutually affect one another must belong to some civil constitution" (Peace, 8: 349 note), and all spheres of external freedom have to be subject to the rule of right. According to Kurt Borries, who wrote a book on Kant's politics in the 1920ies, Kant feared that the predominance of the right of nations would leave a loophole for European powers to violate the rights of non-European communities which lacked essential features of modern states (Borries 1928: 228; see also Morgan 2009: 117). A more widespread contemporary interpretation stresses the "individualistic turn" of cosmopolitan right (Cheneval 2002: 610). The addressees of cosmopolitan right are individuals as "citizens of the earth", and the right is read as an anticipation of contemporary developments in international right, where individuals are no longer exclusively mediated by the state, but elevated to bearers of rights they can assert on an international level (Kleingeld 1998: 83–5 and 2012: 87–9). Hospitality then coincides with international human rights, and strengthens the status of individuals vis-à-vis states and global corporations (Anderson-Gold 2001: 96 and 99). Some interpreters take this a step further and claim that Kant envisioned a "cosmopolitan public space" (ibid. 100, Kemp 2006: 155, 159 and 161), that he anticipated a global and democratic civil society, where, in the words of James Bohman, "[e]ach inhabitant of the planet is elevated to the position of international 'magistrate'" (Bohman 1997: 180).

A divergent interpretation has been offered by Sharon Byrd and Joachim Hruschka. They claim that for Kant, cosmopolitan right is nothing but "the idea of a perfect World Trade Organization" (Byrd and Hruschka 2010: 7). Kant distinguished among three forms of justice in a juridical state, corresponding to the three *leges lex iusti*, the *lex iuridica*, and the *lex iustitiae* (cf. MM, 6: 306, Byrd and Hruschka 2010: 58–62). The *iustitia tutatrix* amounts to positive legislation to make rights possible. The *iustitia commutativa* refers to the public sphere of the market where people exchange external objects "in accordance with principles of justice". Exchange is identical with *commutatio* (MM, 6: 302; see also ibid., 297, 301, Byrd and Hruschka 2010: 69, 36–8 and 71–4); commutative justice makes rights a reality. Finally, the *iustitia distributiva* represents the judiciary (making rights a necessity): A judge decides with binding force in cases of dispute. According to Byrd and Hruschka, cosmopolitan right refers to commutative justice, the public order for the market beyond state borders. International trade or "possible commerce" requires a legal framework, "certain universal rights" (MM, 6: 352; cf. Byrd and Hruschka 2010: 210) to guarantee an ordered market.

Some interpreters have been surprised why Kant's cosmopolitan right is so limited. According to the Byrd-Hruschka or commercial interpretation, Kant's cosmopolitan right is distinct from a more mainstream *moral* understanding of hospitality (and therefore also different from Derrida's conception; cf. Derrida 2001). Kant calls for a very thin global and democratic civil society where citizens of republics or states governed in a republican manner are represented indirectly via their representatives on a global level. The modern system of sovereign states is not swept "into limbo" (Bull 1995: 24), but reformed. Kant's cosmopolitanism is statist, defending "the normative relevance of political communities for the pursuit of cosmopolitan justice" (Ypi 2008: 48; see also chapter 8, section 3). Following this interpretation, Kant's international right or the so-called right of nations refers to *iustitia tutatrix* and *iustitia distributiva*, to public legislation and to an international court with enforceable and binding decisions. By contrast, cosmopolitan right offers an ordered commutative justice in the absence of a not yet fully achieved inter-state juridical condition with *iustitia tutatrix* and *iustitia distributiva*. "Consequently, an ordered *iustitia commutativa* and thus 'cosmopolitan right' can exist on the international level in the absence of a *iustitia tutatrix* and a *iustitia distributiva* in a state of nation states. Cosmopolitan right is thus (logically) independent from right in a state of nation states. It requires its own *iustitia tutatrix*, meaning public right and legislation ordering the international market, the *iustitia commutativa*, and its own *iustitia distributiva*, meaning an international trade court which can reach final binding decisions under cosmopolitan right in case of trade disputes" (Byrd and Hruschka 2010: 211).

For various reasons, the alternative interpretations are not convincing. Against the loophole-thesis, one can argue that if Kant had meant to ban or outlaw colonialism, this would have been included in the preliminary articles. For instance, he could simply have expanded the fifth preliminary article to run: "No state shall forcibly interfere in the constitution, government *or civil society* of another state or *a political community not meeting European standards of state-*

hood" (Peace, 8: 346, changes in Italics). This would have taken care of the problem of colonialism. However, the three definitive articles are not meant as "laws of prohibition" (Peace, 8: 347) but as articles to establish "a condition of peace" (ibid., 348). Cosmopolitan right includes a legal duty to actively promote this establishment of peace, not (only) to abstain from an action. Against the widespread global-society or globalist interpretation, one might argue that it simply goes beyond Kant's express statements and does not even attempt to explain why Kant shrank back from a more daring and extensive conception of cosmopolitan right. It simply takes Kant as a starting point for one's own Kantian agenda. The interpretation moves from strict exegesis to creative reformulation or extrapolation in the spirit of Kantian philosophy and explicitly goes beyond Kant's texts (as Brown 2009: 20 – 2 freely admits). This approach may be legitimate in its own right, but should clearly demarcate where the textual interpretation ends and one's own extrapolation starts.

There is a lot of truth in the interpretation that Kant initiated an individualistic turn in international legal theory. After all, *Perpetual Peace* refers to the "right of a foreigner" (Peace, 8: 357), and a footnote claims that not only states but also individuals should be regarded "as citizens of a universal state of mankind" (ibid., 349 note). However, the *Doctrine of Rights* which was published two years later only refers to the rights of *peoples* or of *nations* and not of individuals (MM, 6: 352 and Byrd and Hruschka 2010: 208). Kant has apparently changed one element of his doctrine: the right of individuals to visit has become part of international right, and does no longer belong to cosmopolitan right (cf. MM, 6: 338 and 344). Only peoples and not individuals or states are entitled to engage in international exchange of goods.

Interpreters disagree about the scope of cosmopolitan right. Some argue that *Verkehr* – roughly "interaction" – has a narrow meaning in Kant's texts, and coincides with commercial trade (Byrd and Hruschka 2010: 209; Thompson 2008: 306 and 315), whereas others claim that it is "clearly not limited to trade" and also encompasses cultural and intellectual exchange (Kleingeld 2012: 75; see also Eberl and Niesen 2011: 250 – 1, Geismann 2012: 219, Mori 2013: 344, O'Neill 2013: 365 – 6). There is a broad and a narrow meaning in Kant (for a discussion, see Byrd and Hruschka 2010: 209). The distinction between the doctrines of virtue and right is crucial. We have a moral (not legal) duty to interact with each other ("*Verkehr zu treiben*"; *officium commerci, sociabilitas*; MM, 6: 473). As juridical persons, however, we "stand in a community of possible physical *interaction*" (*Wechselwirkung*; ibid., 352). In legal terms, engaging in commerce is an exchange of property through contract (cf. Peace, 8: 358, MM, 6: 352). Now it can be argued that "property" only relates to goods and commodities, so cosmopolitan right is exclusively concerned with international trade and commerce in the narrow sense (this is suggested by passages such as Peace, 8: 364 note, MM, 6: 231 and 286). On top of that, this is also the meaning predominant in the eighteenth century, for instance in Montesquieu or Vattel (cf. Cavallar 2002: 243–4, 263–4, 314–5 and Cavallar 2013). Yet there are passages in Kant's writings where *commercium* also includes the exchange of ideas. The textual evidence is the following. In the *Metaphysics of Morals*, Kant argues that the innate right to external freedom also involves the authorization "to do to others anything that does not in itself diminish what is theirs, so long as they do not want to accept it" (MM, 6: 238). Kant's example is communicating one's thoughts, with the listeners being free to accept or refuse to believe them. In another passage, Kant explicitly identifies philosophy with a "commodity or labour about which there can be commercial transactions" (Preface to Jachmann, 8: 441). If any intellectual property, as long as it is not regarded as a "doctrine of wisdom" (ibid.), is a commodity, then cosmopolitan right is not limited to commercial activities. Along these lines, Kant defines *commercium* as "a community of possible physical *interaction*" (MM, 6: 352); selling or buying books or pamphlets or talking (communicating) with each other are also forms of interaction. This interpretation is supported by a look at the *Critique of Pure Reason*, where Kant distinguishes between the concepts of *communio* and *commercium*, both of which refer to reciprocal influence, simultaneity and interaction (see Milstein 2013: 120–4).

Let me briefly summarize my position. I agree with Byrd and Hruschka in terms of the scope of cosmopolitan right. Kant does favour a global civil society (this is also a new element), but it occupies a space that is not political in the strict, Kantian sense: there is no room for co-legislation of individuals, for "democratic structures", for political representation. Yet I disagree with Byrd and Hruschka in terms of the meaning of "property" and "commodity". Cosmopolitan right is more than the idea of a well-functioning World Trade Organization, it designates a global public sphere of nations that exchange commodities as well as ideas. It is an almost classical misinterpretation to claim that Kant disregarded human needs and well-being (see the Introduction). Consequently, trade and commerce do have a legitimate place in Kant's cosmopolitan legal theory. Yet the scope of interaction is expanded to include the exchange of ideas, so that the global public is in a position to gradually enlighten itself, analogous to the public described in the Enlightenment essay. Kant is interested in this dynamic and world-wide process of Enlightenment, to which any mature citizen can and should contribute (by writing books like this one, for instance). The secret article of Perpetual Peace asks governments to respect and protect this sphere of dynamic interaction, especially when inter-state relations are concerned (see Peace, 8: 368–9).

Kant's shift from the rights of states to the rights of peoples in cosmopolitan right is consistent with the role he assigns to the state in domestic right. Here, the state should not interfere in the market, but should regulate it, to make a free and just public market possible. The guiding principle is the external freedom of the citizens, not their happiness as interpreted by the sovereign (TP, 8: 290–1, 298–9, MM, 6: 318, Byrd and Hruschka 2010: 41 and 209). Relevant passages are usually interpreted as an endorsement of economic libertarianism and a rejection of welfare measures for the poor. Presenting Kant as an early liberal has to be qualified, though (see also chapter 7 below). He is all in favour of freedom of choice, individual initiative, competition, and equality of opportunity, but he also argues for a right of the poor to be supported by the government, provided that poverty was not their own fault (MM, 6: 325–7; see Wood 2008: 193–205 and Kleingeld 2012: 136–45 for a discussion). By analogy, states have a duty to regulate international trade through treaties based on "certain universal rights" (MM, 6: 352) while abstaining from interference. Since the ideal of a "state of nations" (*Völkerstaat* or *civitas gentium*), "a universal association of states" cannot fully be realized, only approximated, since, in other words, the international state of nature might not be left completely, and since a free international public market is a natural right of all nations, it has to be regulated and ordered, that is brought under the rule of right. Free trade, for instance, is therefore not an unconditional right. States are entitled to restrict or even prohibit trade if its natural right of self-preservation is at stake (cf. TP, 8: 299, Peace, 8: 359). As Pauline Kleingeld put it: "The positive role Kant attributes to international trade does not imply an unconditional endorsement of *"free"* trade, although a considerable liberalization of trade is compatible with Kant's views, provided that the conditions of international justice are in place" (Kleingeld 2012: 147; see also 137–48). In this way, Kant qualifies the free-trade doctrine, developed in the eighteenth century by authors such as Dietrich Hermann Hegewisch (1746–1812), who endorsed a version of free-market cosmopolitanism and whose relevant essays were probably know to Kant (see Kleingeld 2012: 124–34). I assume that Adam Smith, who is usually (mis)interpreted as a champion of free trade, should be positioned between Kant and Hegewisch (see below).

3.2 The historical context I: international legal theory

In this section and the next one, I want to contextualize Kant's cosmopolitan right. Here, I argue that its topic, the right to visit and to seek commercial contact, has been controversially discussed in international legal theory since Francisco de Vitoria in the 1530ies. I think we can press the positions which evolved in these debates rather brutally into three "schools" or camps in terms of hospitality rights: the imperialist school, the society of states school and the cosmopolitan school (for the following see Cavallar 2013; a different contextualization is offered by Milstein 2013: 128–37).

Representatives of the imperialist school assumed a thick conception of the good, and posited a material end of human volition, which trumped the rights of a community or state in case of conflict. Hospitality was conceived as an extensive natural right and could be enforced. The term "imperialist school" is misleading with respect to Francisco de Vitoria (1486–1546) and the Second Scholastic, because the theological dimension was dominant in their writings, and the consequences of the close cooperation with the Spanish crown (which resulted in Spanish colonialism and imperialism) were apparently unintended. Vitoria's thick conception of the good coincided with the Gospel and the teachings of Catholic Christianity. The goal of his famous lecture *De Indis* (1539) was to justify preaching the Gospel unhindered and bringing salvation to the Native Americans. The Spaniards were the ambassadors of Christ, who were therefore protected by the right of nations (*ius gentium*, roughly the basic norms of conduct shared by [almost] all [civilized] nations or *gentes*). The right to travel, to contact others, to trade and to settle, based on natural right and the right of nations in this sense, was merely a means to an end, namely the spreading of the Gospel, not an end in itself. Similar to Kant, Vitoria's concept of property also includes ideas, yet reciprocity is absent: only the Catholics are entitled to communicate their religious ideas which are held to be the only true ones. In addition, Vitoria conceptualized extensive hospitality as a perfect, enforceable right of the visitors, who have – in a famous passage – the consent and the sanction of "the whole world" on their side (Vitoria 1528/1991: 40). Hugo Grotius, a more straightforward representative of the imperialist school than Vitoria, carefully hid a material end in his writings, especially in *De Jure Praede* (written in 1604–1608). This end was Dutch colonialism, in particular the interests of the United Dutch East India Company (VOC or *Vereenighde Oostindische Compagnie*). Aiming at vindicating the VOC's privateering campaign in the East Indies, Grotius employed the language of natural right and rights and various philosophical and classical sources to offer arguments for this political goal. For instance, Grotius used and abused Stoic "cosmopolitan" philosophy to defend Dutch interests in free trade and navigation (see especially Ittersum 2006 and 2010). In Grotius' account, commercial goals replaced theological ones. In all fairness, it should be added that Grotius has presented a more impartial and less imperialist account of the law of nations in his major work of 1625, *De Jure Belli ac Pacis* (see Cavallar 2002: 121–51).

In the course of the eighteenth century, the second "camp", the society-of-states school, gradually gained the upper hand. It endorsed an international legal theory which is closest to so-called "classical" international right. It was state-centred, emphasised the sovereign right of each community to restrict or prohibit trade, and turned hospitality into an imperfect moral duty. The two crucial authors establishing this tradition were Thomas Hobbes and Samuel Pufendorf (cf. Armitage 2006, Hüning 2009, Hunter 2001 and Schröder 2001 and 2010). The key and long-term changes were the following. First, a dualistic concept of right developed after 1750, where jurists now distinguished between natural right and positive right (*lex*). The latter was more and more identified with the will of the legislator and seen as quite independent of the idea of natural justice and natural right. Secondly, jurisprudence became an independent and autonomous science. A third change was the secularization of politics, or its "deconfessionalising" or "desacralizing" (Ian Hunter); the weakening of moral theology was part of this process. The consequences of this new legal philosophy were far-reaching. It meant the end of traditional *jus gentium* as a source of right (almost) all *gentes* (peoples) had in common. This was a result of the dualistic concept of right (natural or rational versus positive), which left no room for the older version of *jus gentium* (cf. Schröder 2010: 259–282 and Simons 2003). Secondly, the right of nations was assigned to the sphere of natural right and seen as a distinct field of right applying to a unique set of legal subjects, that is, to sovereign rulers or states (*civitates*) only. Pufendorf, for instance, conceptualized the sovereign state as a composite moral person (*persona moralis composita*), constituted by the union of individuals under a government. The third consequence was a state-centred political philosophy, the result of the developments just mentioned. The impact on hospitality rights was tremendous, because the perfect right of ownership became trumps. Pufendorf not only dismissed Vitoria's first just title of "natural partnership and communication" and the right to preach the Gospel, but also Grotius' arguments on behalf of Dutch commercial interests. Instead of a natural, enforceable right to trade, Pufendorf posited that hospitality was an imperfect moral duty and any trans-border contact dependent on the native communities' express permission, which could be revoked if this contact conflicted with the duty of self-preservation, defined and interpreted as the communities or the sovereign saw fit.

The rather marginal cosmopolitan school posited a formal end of international society, namely peaceful interaction and exchange, based on reciprocity and equal spheres of external freedom, and sometimes focused on individuals and their rights rather than states. Representatives went beyond the state-centred approach of the second school and emphasised natural rights of global reach, but tried to avoid the imperialist and hegemonic implications of the first school. Hospitality, Vitoria's right to travel and to communicate was now an end in itself or the means to peaceful interaction, trade or exchange. I consider Christian Wolff the first important representative of this school (see Cavallar 2004 and Cheneval 2002: 132–213). He developed a new concept of right (*lex*) as a binding body of rules no longer connected with the feature of the legislator. The decisive criterion was the obligatory force of the right, with the right of nature based on the essence of man and of things (and not on God's will; see Schröder 2008: 66–67). The idea of *civitas maxima*, a hypothetical international legal commonwealth based on tacit consent, underlined the primacy of natural right, and was logically prior to the society of sovereign states. Yet Wolff's regulative idea of *civitas maxima* did not have any bearing on the right of hospitality: Wolff refused to qualify or soften the principle of state sovereignty here, was thus actually close to both Pufendorf and Vattel.

Most international lawyers after Wolff belonged to the mainstream society-of-states school, for instance Achenwall and Pütter, Vattel and Martini, whereas the cosmopolitan school remained marginal. The imperialist school receded for some time into the background, to become dominant in the second half of the nineteenth century. Gottfried Achenwall (1719–1772) and Johann Stephan Pütter (1720–1807) wrote a widely used textbook on natural right, *Elementa iuris naturae* (1750), which incorporated elements of Grotius, Wolff, Thomasius, and Gundling (Achenwall and Pütter 1750/1995; Schröder 1995). Achenwall later published his own treatises, namely *Ius Naturae, Iuris Naturalis pars posterior* and finally *Prolegomena Iuris Naturalis*. These subsequent books profoundly influenced Kant, who held lectures on them for more than twenty years (Byrd and Hruschka 2010: 16–8). In the *Elementa*, Pütter and Achenwall endorsed the primacy of positive legislation and of the *salus publica*, defined as the common welfare of the community as interpreted by the sovereign. The category of imperfect duties towards strangers disappeared. The Swiss lawyer and diplomat Emer de Vattel (1714–67) replaced Wolff's *civitas maxima* with the moral concept of the *société humaine,* which implied that humans were only bound by conscience to assist each other, provided that this imperfect duty of mutual assistance was compatible with the perfect duties towards oneself (Vattel 2008, "Introduction", §§ 10–13 and 3.12.189). The Austrian Karl Anton Freiherr von Martini (1726–1800) belonged to the younger generation of natural lawyers after 1780, with a new focus on the individuals and their rights, and a new function for natural/rational right. Gradually, natural law was merely supposed to replenish or complete positive legislation. Disciplinary demarcations were set up, for instance, between political science, moral philosophy, philosophical legal theory and natural right (cf. Brockmöller 1997: 36–42 and Hebeis 1996). Influenced by Wolff, but close to the society of states school, Martini claimed that there was no general (*allgemeines*) positive right of nations, only a particular, namely European, right of nations, which included the American free states, presumably because they were of European descent (Martini 1791: II § 22). Martini did not even endorse the minimalist notion of a European political community of states as Vattel had done. States had no legal authority over other states, which were "by nature" independent (Martini 1791: II, §§ 19–20 and II § 29). Martini also closely followed the society of states school in terms of hospitality rights. Each nation had a right to refuse entry to foreigners. Martini criticized Grotius, whose opinion on duties towards strangers was, according to Martini, too "vague" (Martini 1791: II §57).

In the following paragraphs, I am going to compare Kant's cosmopolitan right with these three schools. Kant attacked the society of states school and its emphasis on state sovereignty and incipient legal positivism with his famous description of Grotius, Pufendorf and Vattel as "sorry comforters" (Peace, 8: 355; cf. Cavallar 2011: 64–84), although he endorsed some of its key tenets, especially the secularization of politics. His legal theory focused on external actions, jurisprudence was an autonomous discipline separate from theology, right was divided into positive and rational right, and *ius gentium*, the right of nations, was the right of sovereign states. Kant did not dismiss state sovereignty out of hand; rather, it enjoyed legitimacy and had to be qualified. However, he differed from the society of states school with his thesis of the *provisional* quality of sovereignty and its dismissal of hospitality as an imperfect *moral* duty – or its complete eclipse. Kant was close to the cosmopolitan school of authors such as Wolff, who had posited the *civitas maxima*, akin to Kant's own long-term goal or regulative idea of a limited republican world government. Yet there are again Kantian modifications: a clear-cut distinction between norms and facts, between the rational idea and the will of the majority, between pure practical reason and the practice of "more civilized nations". These distinctions illustrate Kant's new methodological approach, the programme of a pure practical philosophy, or "completely isolated metaphysics of morals, mixed with no anthropology, theology, physics, or hyperphysics and still less with occult qualities" (Groundwork, 4: 410 and chapter 8, section 2). In *Perpetual Peace* as well as in the "Doctrine of Rights", Kant criticized European colonialism, which suggests that he rejected the imperialist school and the religious titles of theologians such as Vitoria. Scattered passages in other writings of the 1790ies attacked central tenets of this school, such as the agricultural argument or titles based on the superiority of European civilization, although at times it seems that Kant believed in this very superiority. Perhaps Kant believed in it, while at the same time denying that any rightful claims could be derived from it (this would also be a consistent position). Giving a fully adequate account of this complex issue here is beyond the scope of this inquiry (see Introduction, section 3).

Pufendorf had conceptualized hospitality as an imperfect moral duty. Achenwall, Pütter, Vattel and others stand for the eclipse of imperfect moral duties towards strangers, and the rise of "international morality". Kant, by contrast, claimed that we are talking about a right, not morality or philanthropy (Peace, 8: 357, MM, 6: 352), since right delineated external spheres of freedom and was connected with coercion. Any form of rightful (*rechtmässig*) contact was based on the mutual prohibition of injury: *neminem laedere*. Kant, for instance, asserted that European colonial endeavours were so unjust and violent that Chinese and Japanese inhospitality was justified (Peace, 8: 359). For methodological reasons, Kant keeps legal and moral duties apart; the doctrine of right should not be confused with the doctrine of virtue. Kant's main target of criticism was probably Vattel, whose book *Droit des Gens* was available in Kant's library in a German translation (Warda 1922: 8 and 16). There is another small detail which underlines Kant's clear-cut distinction between spheres of right on the one hand and morality or virtue on the other: legal relations among communities and nations can be "peaceful" and "peaceably", but must not necessarily be "friendly" (MM, 6: 352; see also Peace, 8: 358), which would be the term reserved for moral relations, as in personal friendship (cf. MM, 6: 470–3).

In terms of content, Kant's cosmopolitan right did not differ profoundly from what authors before him had written about the subject. Others had also criticized colonialism, defended Chinese or Japanese isolationism, or attempted to balance the rights of visitors with those of the natives (Cavallar 2002 and 2011: 17–38). The novel element in terms of content is Kant's emphasis on the mutual exchange of ideas, that is, a wide understanding of *commercium* (see above). Kant's justification of cosmopolitan right is revolutionary, stressing mutual spheres of freedom and original community. What I find surprising is that Denis Diderot is especially close to Kant, though his publications were not part of his library (cf. Warda 1922) and it is unclear whether he influenced him. As a philosopher, Diderot did not explicitly contribute to international legal discourses of his time, and apparently had little impact on them. He can be interpreted as a creative representative of the cosmopolitan school. Though partly following familiar distinctions, Diderot added new arguments to the debate. In his contributions to the *Histoire philosophique et politique des établissements et du commerce des Européens dans les deux Indes* (edited by Abbé Guillaume-Thomas Raynal; revised and enlarged edition 1780), he offered an explicit attack on European colonialism. Diderot supported familiar hospitality rights, and distinguished between a right of necessity, a right to visit, a right to be a guest and the right of settlement. If travellers wanted to settle in a foreign country, it was up to the natives to grant permission (Diderot 1780: 175). The right to visit was only a perfect one if the traveller's life was at stake. The right to be a guest, by contrast, was imperfect, and contingent upon the consent of the parties involved. Like Kant, Diderot considered the actual history of European commercial expansion as one of unmitigated moral disaster (cf. Diderot 1780: 178–179, 197 and 173 and the discussion in Muthu 2003: 87–104).

The main differences between Diderot and Kant are the following: Diderot's normative ideal and goal was more extensive than Kant's, including not only trade and the peaceful and mutual exchange of ideas but also possible intermarriages which might lead to the creation of a new people. As in Adam Smith and others (and later Ward), hospitality was historicized. Diderot tended to idealize ancient hospitality, claiming that it was universally practiced in the ancient world and lead to innumerable friendships – so again, hospitality is located in the sphere or morality and philanthropy. Finally, and again unlike Kant, Diderot perceived the history of hospitality as a history of decline, and the key factors were modern technology as well as a form of moral disorientation. The latter was a result of European travellers finding themselves so far away from home that they felt "outside the network of reciprocal relationships and expectations that had once given them the cultural contexts for their actions, beliefs, and values – for their *moeurs*" (Muthu 2003: 86). In addition, Diderot denied that European incursions and atrocities could be stopped.

The originality of Kant's contribution lies in his revision of the traditional argument from original ownership, his methodological distinctions (between right and virtue and between the philosophies of right and of history, for instance), his new justification of hospitality rights, and the thinness of his account. In addition, his philosophy of history embedded cosmopolitan right in a teleological and tentative reconstruction of political history as continuous progress towards more peaceful trans-border interactions. Though Kant found clear words denouncing European, especially British and Dutch colonialism, Diderot's pessimism and cynicism were absent in his account, and an optimistic tone prevailed. Two elements of Kant's originality deserve special attention: the goal of cosmopolitan right and the just mentioned thinness of his account.

I have argued that in Vitoria or Grotius, a material end, or a thick conception of the good prevailed in their accounts of hospitality rights. Kant has become famous for his criticism of teleological ethics or consequentialism where the purpose is crucial, and his own theory is usually labelled "deontological" (cf. Groundwork, 4: 393–400). Along these lines, Kant attacked – in the context of cosmopolitan right – authors who had argued that "the good end justifies immoral means": Non-European peoples could be subjugated, expelled or exploited because it was "to the world's advantage", because those savages would "become civilized" or the home country could be "cleaned of corrupt men" (MM, 6: 353; cf. Cavallar 1992: 232–4). Kant held that an obvious injustice remains just that irrespective of consequences, that is, even if morally acceptable (and usually unintended) consequences should follow. This criticism of consequentialism has sometimes been misunderstood as implying that any end of volition is incompatible with Kant's ethics. In fact, material ends are acceptable, provided that they do not conflict with the formal principle of morality or right. Ends and states of affairs do matter, but actors have to avoid the pitfalls of consequentialism, for instance by violating a moral principle "by the lure of some great good to be gained in the relatively near future" (Wood 2008, 260). Proper moral reasoning combines the conformity with the categorical imperative or the principle of right with aiming at a common, rationally defensible set of moral or legal aims that are compatible with this imperative or the respective legal principle. Kant conceptualizes these ultimate aims or goals as the highest moral and political goods (see Introduction, section 2 and chapter 2, sections 2 and 4). It is therefore not contradictory when Kant claims that cosmopolitan right *does* have a formal end, namely "the possible union of all nations" (MM, 6: 352) under the rule of right, or the approximation of a "cosmopolitan constitution" (Peace, 8: 358), where the reciprocal spheres of freedom of all humans are respected.

The second element of Kant's originality is the thinness of his account. I have tried to show that natural hospitality rights have been interpreted in divergent ways from Vitoria to Kant. Vitoria himself argued for a very extensive right which was, in addition, enforceable and included the right to dwell in the countries or territories visited for an unspecified amount of time, the freedom to use common property, the freedom of residence, nationalization and citizenship and finally the negation of a right of expulsion without just cause (cf. Cavallar 2002: 108–11). Kant rejected all these extensive rights. Achenwall, Pütter, Martini and Martens belong to a second group where hospitality rights have virtually vanished, usually in the name of state or community sovereignty. Kant himself was closest to a third group, which limited or qualified hospitality rights and included Pufendorf, Wolff and Diderot: hospitality is not a right to settle (cf. MM, 6: 352), it is not a "*right to be a guest*", but only a right "to *seek* commerce" and "to present oneself for society" (Peace, 8: 358). Only this thinness guarantees due respect for the equal spheres of external freedom of all parties involved.

It has been argued that around 1794, Kant's theoretical philosophy "was falling out of fashion" in Germany, with a younger generation moving into very different directions (Kuehn 2001: 378). This also seems to have been the case with Kant's legal philosophy. The three main trends in the late 1790ies, when Kant elaborated cosmopolitan right, were legal positivism, incipient historicism, and the turn to Europe. I do not find any traces of these developments in Kant's texts. I start with legal positivism. A member of the younger generation was the international lawyer Georg Friedrich von Martens (1756–1821), who became well-known for his collection of treaties, the *Recueil des principaux traités* (1791). His main work, *Précis du droit des gens moderne de l'Europe fondé sur les traités et l'usage* (1789), was edited in German under the title *Einleitung in das positive Europäische Völkerrecht* one year after Kant's essay *Zum ewigen Frieden*, namely in 1796. Martens' work is nowadays considered the final breakthrough of legal positivism (cf. Ziegler 1994: 201–202). Martens moved from generic *ius inter gentes* to state-centered European right of nations and from natural and volitional right to positive right (Martens 1796: §§ 2–3; for a brief introduction see Cavallar 2011: 96–8). While he did not deny that there was a "pure natural right of nations" (*reines natürliches Völkerrecht)*, natural and volitional rights of nations coincided with international morality or *Völkermoral* (Martens 1796: §§ 1, 5, 117, 122 and 136). Martens' paragraph on the right of immigration (now the traditional concept of hospitality was really dead) reads like a succinct summary of previous authors' key statements as well as legal practice (the only *explicit* sources here). His starting point was the perfect right of the sovereign territorial state or nation to prohibit entry, passage or permanent residence of foreigners, for whatever reasons. The only exceptions were cases of necessity such as distress at sea. These were obvious remnants of natural-right doctrine, now justified by state practice. In Marten's legal system, there is not even room for Kant's very thin natural right to offer to engage in commerce.

I continue with incipient historicism. *An Enquiry into the Foundation and History of the Right of Nations in Europe* by the thirty-year-old Robert Plumer Ward (1765–1846), published in the same year as Kant's *Perpetual Peace* in 1795, is usually considered the first historical study of the right of nations. Ward doubted that the right of nations was universally valid, as European codes were not. This European right became a historical phenomenon, subject to change depending on geography and historical periods (Ward 1995: vol. 1, XV, XX, XIII-XIV, 60, 130–131; for an introduction see Cavallar 2011: 98–101). Ward was obviously influenced by the "philosophical historians" of the Enlightenment such as Montesquieu, Adam Smith, David Hume, Lord Kames, Adam Ferguson, Edward Gibbon and John Millar. In Ward's book, their delicate balance between philosophical principles and historical embeddedness tilted towards the latter. Like Diderot, Ward historicized hospitality, noting its many examples among Germanic tribes during the migration of peoples in the fifth century A. D., when hospitality was a virtue, a personal quality of individuals and perhaps an established custom (cf. Ward 1795: vol. 1, 232–233). While Ward was not a full-blown cultural or moral relativist, his balance between moral universalism and culturally sensitive relativism or particularism was a very precarious one. At any rate, Kant's claim that there were universally binding rights a priori was seriously challenged (cf. Ward 1795: vol. 1, 58), together with traditional forms of moral or legal cosmopolitanisms.

This has to do with Ward's turn to Europe, European culture and Christianity, the third and final trend I want to mention. The right of nations became a European phenomenon in his account, historically and culturally embedded as well as rooted in Christianity. In spite of elements of cultural relativism in his account, Ward tended to see non-European cultures as inferior, and claimed that Chinese isolationist policies demonstrated their "barbarity" and the "inferiority" of their concept of the right of nations (Ward 1795: vol. 2, 4). Forgotten were those European lawyers like Gentili, Leibniz, Wolff or Vattel who had defended Chinese isolationism as legitimate since it was interpreted as a clear case of self-defence in the face of European aggression or threats. Authors like Martini or Martens had anticipated this turn to Europe in their respective writings. This was a general trend after 1750, when cosmopolitan elements were gradually and partly replaced by the ideas of "Europe" and "civilization" (see Cavallar 2011: 85–108, especially 107–108). I cannot detect traces of this trend in Kant's published writings of the 1790ies.

3.3 The historical context II: the spirit of commerce, the four-stage theory, *doux commerce*, global integration, and mutual self-interest

In this section, I continue with my contextualization of Kant's cosmopolitan right, turning to the writers of what came to be called political economy, and especially to David Hume and Adam Smith. A lot of what I write about possible influences is mere conjecture. Sometimes influence is evident, for example in the case of Smith (see Fleischacker 1996). The books of Kant's personal library which were sold after his death offer another clue, though the book list might be incomplete (see Warda 1922). I suppose that another possible source were Kant's famous dinner talks, which started at 1:00 P. M. and often lasted until the evening. Kant "liked to disregard learned matters. At times he even cut off such associations. He most loved to talk about political things. Indeed, he almost luxuriated in them" (quoted in Kuehn 2001: 325). So Kant might have learned about the investigation against Warren Hastings in the House of Commons in the late 1780ies and early 1790ies (see below). Another source might have been Kant's friend Christian Jacob Kraus, who was also a professor at Königsberg University and taught courses in economics (cf. Kuehn 2001: 324). Finally, Kant might have borrowed books from friends or from his publisher Friedrich Nicolovius, or just have read available newspapers. Thus it is possible that Kant was, for instance, familiar with some of the ideas of Johann Heinrich Gottlob von Justi (1717–71). Be that as it may, it is obvious that Hume and Smith had some impact on Kant, and I will therefore focus on these two philosophers. In the next paragraphs, I am going to take sentences or half-sentences from Kant's section on cosmopolitan right, and try to embed them within eighteenth-century discourses. My aim is to show that the theories about the spirit of commerce, the four-stage theory, *doux-commerce* thesis, the assumption of global integration, and conceptions of self-interest and (unsocial or commercial) sociability were recurrent themes in Kant's time, that Kant joined these debates, and that in many cases he integrated these theses and assumptions into his framework of a critical, namely reflective and tentative philosophy of history (this philosophy is not my issue here; see Rorty and Schmidt 2009 and chapter 2, sections 2 and 3 for introductions). Kant distinguished between the doctrine of right, which focuses on the original right to external freedom, and the philosophy of history. The latter investigates into the natural forces and trends in history and into possible unintended consequences and beneficial results of – possibly determined – human actions. Like the other two relations of public right, the gradual approximation of cosmopolitan right is guaranteed by "the great artist *nature*" (Peace, 8: 360) since humans know what they "*ought* to do in accordance with rights of freedom" but usually simply refuse to do it (ibid., 365).

The key factor Kant hoped might promote his cosmopolitan ideal of a legal world community was the spirit of commerce (*Handelsgeist*), "which sooner or later takes hold of every nation" (Peace, 8: 368). Here, Kant briefly hints at the four-stage theory, widespread since the middle of the eighteenth century, and developed since the late seventeenth century by diverse thinkers such as Pufendorf, Bossuet, Locke, Montesquieu, Rousseau, John Dalrymple of Cranstoun, Lord Kames, Mirabeau, Ferguson, Millar and Turgot (cf. Cavallar 2002: 236–9; Hont 2005: 159–84; Morgan 2009: 109–110). The key tenet was that all communities and nations moved naturally through various stages until they became commercial societies. One function of the stages scheme was to explain why norms differed in various societies. Smith interpreted these differences as symptoms of divergent cultural and economic developments, offering a socialized and historicized theory of natural right and stressing natural factors as well as human efforts (Cavallar 2002: 236). Kant was definitely familiar with Smith's elaborate account. An early reference to the four-stage theory can be found in his *Conjectural beginning of human history*, published in 1786 (Kant was an early reader of the *Wealth of Nations* in Germany; see Fleischacker 1996: 379–83 and 390). The passage compared the life of the hunter and herdsman with that of the farmer, offering economic, cultural and social explanations to account for differences (Beginning, 8: 118–20; see also Peace, 8: 363–4 and 364 note and Fleischacker 1996: 389).

The four-stage theory is crucial for Kant's right of world citizens since commercial societies tend to be more peaceful than previous stages of development (cf. Peace, 8: 364). Kant claims that the "*spirit of commerce* ... cannot coexist with war" (ibid., 368). This is an obvious reference to the *doux-commerce* thesis developed since Montesquieu, who had claimed that commerce destroys prejudices, promotes gentle mores, polishes barbarous ones, unites nations, leads to peace, and "produces in men a certain feeling for exact justice" (Montesquieu 1748/1989: 20.1–2, 338–9; cf. Cavallar 2002: 243–4 with secondary literature). Softness or *douceur* is the antonym of violence, commerce also conflicts with despotism, and in a republic based on rights and equality commerce does not corrupt mores, but brings "the spirit of frugality, economy, moderation, work, wisdom, tranquillity, order, and rule" (Montesquieu 1748/1989: 22.14, 416–417; cf. 5.6, 48). While Montesquieu's analysis of commerce is ambiguous, as he only partially broke up the link between commerce and what the civic humanist tradition called corruption, many Enlightenment intellectuals were more enthusiastic. They offered a range of positive effects of commercial interaction: people had to learn to please and serve others, the arts and sciences might profit, and a focus on this-worldly welfare and wealth would replace uncompromising religious fanaticism. Finally, commerce might increase cross-cultural interaction and overcome parochial attitudes like narrow patriotism and dated and potentially violent pursuits of military glory and honour (cf. Mendham 2010: 606–607 and Hirschmann 1981: 59–62). Kant was particularly interested in the last two, the pacifying effects. For him, the high esteem attributed to military courage is typical of "savage" cultures before the dawn of commercial society, such as the European age of chivalry (Peace, 8: 365).

There is one thinker whom Kant adored and who explicitly attacked the *doux-commerce* thesis in his writings: Jean-Jacques Rousseau. "The ancient politicians forever spoke of morals and virtue; ours speak only of commerce and of money" (Rousseau 1997a: 18). Rousseau, who closely followed the civic humanist tradition in this respect, criticized the thesis from a moral perspective, and also doubted that commercial interdependence would foster peaceful relations (cf. Mendham 2010 and Cavallar 2002: 287–90). The society created by mutual needs was a Hobbesian state of anarchy and instability. There was no natural order or alliance between private interests and the general good. Proponents of the *doux-commerce* thesis, Rousseau claimed, deceived us into believing that commercial society constituted a kind of moral whole, while it was not even a society. "They live together without any real union, like men grouped on the same piece of land but separated by deep ravines" (Rousseau 1887/1991: 121).

Both Hume and Smith distanced themselves from this pessimistic assessment. Hume praised commercial society as a training ground of the arts, of improved industry, sociability, politeness and good manners (Cavallar 2002: 246–9). Smith stressed two aspects Kant was particularly interested in. First, commerce, the result of an expanding division of labour, had beneficial political effects: it undermined paternalistic and dependency-generating social institutions like slavery, feudalism or unfree labour and offered more political freedom for individuals (Hill 2010: 463–464 with references; see also Cavallar 2002: 251 and Hont 2005: 278). There was a good chance that the paternalistic and despotic governments loathed by Kant might gradually be replaced by republican governments where the original or natural "principles of external human right", namely freedom, equality and independence would be guaranteed and individuals could start to overcome their immaturity (TP, 8: 290–1, Idea, 8: 28, Anthropology, 7: 209 and Fleischacker 1996: 385, 387–8 and 401–2). Secondly, Smith assumed that unhindered commerce would expand indefinitely, eventually transgressing national borders, helping to create a global society of distant strangers, "uniting ... the most distant parts of the world, ... enabling them to relieve one another's wants", and encouraging "one another's industry" (Smith 1762–3, 1766/1978: 4.7.c.80, 626; cf. Hill 2010: 463–5). There was a good chance that destructive "national jealousies", the irrational "jealousy of strangers" (Smith 1762–3, 1766/1978: 6.164–5, 391–2, Smith 1776/1976: 1.10.c.22, 142) would eventually be replaced by "habituation to foreigners", a "general attitude of restrained amity" and "forms of amicable *strangership*" in the commercial *cosmopolis* (Hill 2010: 470–1 and 473, referring to Smith 1776/1976: 4.3.c.9, 493). Kant's formulation of cosmopolitan right as the "idea of a *peaceful*, even if not friendly, thoroughgoing community of all nations" (MM, 6: 352) suggests that he had a similar vision in mind. "*Freundschaftlich*" (translated as "friendly") belongs to the realm of virtue, not to the market, where peaceful (*friedlich*) interaction is more likely (and indispensable). Friendship, at least for Kant, is not based on mutual self-interest, but on a moral disposition, namely "equal mutual love and respect" where the friend is regarded as an end in him- or herself (MM, 6: 469 as opposed to Smith 1776/1976: 1.2.2, 27). However, friendship is not required for market relations, the exchange of goods or ideas.

To sum up, the essential advantage of commerce was global integration or economic globalization, whose beginnings Smith quite accurately dated back to the 1500s (Smith 1776/1976: 4.1.33, 448–9, 4.7.c.80, 626; Hill 2010: 450–451). Kant's philosophical reconstruction of world history stresses its paradoxical elements. For instance, the European conquerors who did not distinguish between visiting and conquering a country committed injustices and brought havoc upon the natives, while at the same time these very activities opened up the trade routes between the continents, thus contributing to a possible cosmopolitan world order which might eventually approach the ideal of just and peaceful relations among nations (cf. Peace, 8: 357–8). This is very close to Smith's assessment, who praised global integration – just like Abbé Raynal and Diderot (cf. Cavallar 2002: 257) -, but criticized the "savage injustice" of Europeans from a moral point of view. The discovery of America or the passage to the East Indies opened new markets, promoted the divisions of labour and improved the arts, but the Europeans spoiled what could have been "advantageous" and "beneficial" for all sides (Smith 1776/1976: 4.1.32., 447–448; see also 4.7.b.59, 588 and Hill 2010: 451–452). Apparently drawing on Smith, Kant claimed that modern history moved towards a global economy, where, for example gold and silver mines in Peru and New Mexico were inextricably linked with European manufacture of goods. Both productive industries stimulated each other, causing a mutually reinforcing process. "In this way industry [or industriousness, diligence; the German original uses the term *Fleiß*] always keeps pace with industry" (MM, 6: 288). Humans invented money as a means to measure this industry and to facilitate trade among individuals as well as nations (ibid., 287–8).

Kant briefly mentioned in *Perpetual Peace* that the Europeans often did not even profit from the crimes committed against the natives in the colonies, and that "trading companies" were "on the verge of collapse" (Peace, 8: 359), citing some examples. Several writers before Kant had written against conquest, colonies, imperialist adventures, or trading monopolies, among them Montesquieu, Bayle, Hume, Rousseau, Davenant, Rutherford, Blackstone, Raynal, Diderot, Marmontel and Justi (Adam 2006: 61–70, Cavallar 2002: 254–9 and Muthu 2003). Abbé de Raynal mused about the disadvantages of the immoral behaviour of the European conquerors, colonists, and slave owners: in the short run, it works and leads to prosperity, but in the long run power based on "goodness, kindness, benevolence and humanity … is more solid and long-lasting" (Raynal 1780/2006: 31). Jeremy Bentham considered colonies an economic disaster, their emancipation was thus above all in the interest of the home countries. Colonial expenses by far overbalanced profits, and trade should replace colonial exploitation (cf. Cavallar 2002: 258 and Cavallar 2011: 50–1). A few years before Bentham, Smith arrived at similar conclusions, offering moral as well as economic arguments against colonies and ensuing privileges for trading companies like the East India Company. Like others before him, Smith rejected the assertion of mercantilism, neo-Machiavellism and civic humanism that war and expansion were "the keys to national survival and *grandezza*" (Hont 2005: 75). Colonies were not only unjust but also economically self-defeating, since the mother country would eventually ruin its own finances, investments, resources and trading capacities (cf. Smith 1776/1976: 4.7.c.16–108, 594–641, 5.3.92., 946–947; Hill 2010: 452–4.). Provided that the "jealousy of trade" and the fallacies of mercantilism such as monopolies were avoided, a condition of commerce was synonymous with peaceful relations (cf. Smith 1776/1976: 4.3.c.9, 493, 4.3.c.11, 494; Hill 2010: 469). Kant seems to have subscribed to Smith's analysis. Perhaps there was some additional meta-analysis involved on Kant's side: Smith could be seen as one of the scholars who used their own reason "before the entire public of the *world of readers*" (Enlightenment, 8: 37) to promote enlightenment, the cultivation of reason, the exchange of ideas and thus a cosmopolitan condition with more political freedom and peaceful interaction. Writing books and criticizing colonialism could be a cosmopolitan enterprise.

According to Kant's philosophy of history, the driving forces of these changes were part of the phenomenal world and results of mundane factors such as "mutual self-interest" (Peace, 8: 368) and "unsocial sociability" (Idea, 8: 20). Both had been stock themes of Enlightenment moral philosophy and political economy. Theories about the sociable and unsociable character traits of the human species can be traced back to Hugo Grotius and Samuel Pufendorf in modern European history (see Schneewind 2009: 95–103; Cavallar 2002: 237–9), and Kant transformed this concept in new and interesting ways (cf. Hedrick 2008: 253–5, Schneewind 2009: 104–9 and Wood 2009). As for self-interest, this was a recurrent theme in nascent psychological theories of Enlightenment moral philosophies, which Kant could easily find in authors he read and liked, such as Hume, Vattel, Rousseau or Smith (Cavallar 2002: 245, 251, Cavallar 2012b; Stapelbroek 2008: 75–76; Schneewind 2009: 102–103). Smith in particular held that self-interest or self-love – and not benevolence – had led to more individual liberty and justice in the legal systems in the past, and that it was natural that humans put themselves, their families and friends first (Cavallar 2002: 251, Hill 2010: 455 and Hont 2005: 397 with references). In a manner reminiscent of Rousseau, Smith attacked the Stoic notion of universal benevolence as psychologically implausible and counter-productive (Hill 2010: 456–8). Self-love and self-interest were more reliable motive-forces than benevolence (Smith 1776/1976: 1.2., 26–27), and this also applied to the international realm. Self-interest had the potential to weaken nationalist feelings, the irrational "jealousy of strangers" mentioned above, and foster a "general attitude of restrained amity" and amicable, commercial strangership among communities (Hill 2010: 470–471, 460–461).

Kant's advocacy of a cosmopolitan society based on the natural right of hospitality should not be identified with the idea of an "ethical commonwealth" (Religion, 6: 86–102 and chapter 2 above). Kant keeps both types of commonwealths apart, though they are related to each other. The right to visit regions and to engage in commerce, though justified deontologically as being based on innate freedom and original collective possession, has the function to promote a possible "community of all nations" (MM, 6: 352). Kant apparently expected that complex interdependence and globalization – empirical phenomena which per se do not qualify as sources of normativity – would drive humans towards, and urge them to establish, a global commonwealth under the rule of right. However, this union aims at the compatibility of external actions (and is based on mutual self-interest), not at morally good dispositions. Moral progress in this respect seems to have been Kant's additional hope based on his moral teleology as well as his hope and moral faith (see chapter 2 above).

I conclude with the somewhat unclear and frequently cited claim that the "community of the nations of the earth has now gone so far that a violation of right on *one* place of the earth is felt in *all*" (Peace, 8: 360). Modern economic globalization also leads to increased interaction and migration, creates new "lines of communication". It urges people to widen their circles beyond families, friends, and immediate civil society. This is the objective side, already outlined by Smith. There is another, moral or juridical dimension. As Diane Morgan puts it: "Kant suggests that injustices in one part of the globe (such as slavery in the West Indies) send out shock waves which reverberate along these ever developing lines of communication, thereby gradually consolidating a public sphere which is, which should be the concern of all rational beings" (Morgan 2009: 115). This is perhaps too dramatic a language, yet Kant indeed seems to believe that historical developments, triggered by the aforementioned economic globalization, will eventually change people's attitudes towards distant strangers, so that an at least thin "community of the nations of the earth" (Peace, 8: 360) based on mutual self-interest is established.

For me this passage is unclear since I am not sure how Kant arrived at this assessment. Which evidence did he have in mind? Perhaps it was the recurrent criticism of European theologians, natural lawyers, philosophers and intellectuals of European overseas crimes since Francisco de Vitoria, culminating in the eighteenth century (Cavallar 2002, Muthu 2003 and Cavallar 2011: 17–38 and above). It might have been Smith's criticism of European, especially English colonialism on moral as well as economic grounds (Hill 2010: 450–5). My guess is that for Kant, additional evidence might have come from another eighteenth-century bestseller, from events in Haiti, and from Great Britain.

The book I am referring to is Abbé de Raynal's monumental *A History of the Two Indies* (1770, revised and enlarged edition 1780), which became an international blockbuster with more than thirty editions (for the following see Richter 2006: 165–7 and Courtney 2006). Raynal and his co-authors, among them Diderot, fiercely attacked European colonialism, the slave trade and the violation of the rights of natives in their extensive and meticulous study, with the third edition encompassing ten volumes. For instance, one passage commented on the belated English attempt to found trading posts and colonies: "They believed that it was difficult to acquire great wealth without great injustice, and that in order to surpass or even match the nations they had criticized they had to act in the same manner" (Raynal 1780/2006: 31). The text usually – but not always – denounced slavery as immoral. Especially Diderot contrasted "savage" peoples – which were in his opinion morally superior – with the corrupt and unjust European civilized man. As Melvin Richter put it: "More than any other major work of the century the book systematically reversed prior judgements about the old world's political and moral superiority" (Richter 2006: 166).

Raynal's *Deux Indes* is said to have influenced the former Black slave and Haitian revolutionary leader François-Dominique Toussaint Louverture (1743–1803). Some passages of the book indeed invited native populations to revolt (cf. Richter 2006: 167). The revolutionary events in Paris triggered social instability on Saint Domingue, which had been the most profitable French colony due to coffee and sugar exports (for the following see Bell 2008, Blackburn 2006, Césaire 2008, Dubois 2005). Initially the rebel slaves, who outnumbered the whites by a ratio of ten to one, were willing to bargain for better conditions. In the wake of the *Declaration of the Rights of Man*, Julien Raimond and other free people of color demanded civil equality with whites. After 1791, the abolition of slavery became the goal. Though Toussaint fought the French with the help of the Spanish, he switched allegiance as soon as the French National Convention proclaimed the abolition of slavery and granted civil and political rights to black men in February 1794. In 1796, the government even held elections to choose colonial representatives for the national assembly. However, tensions between Toussaint and the French government grew when the *Directoire* was suspected of planning to reintroduce slavery on the island. Kant may have been familiar with some of these developments. Perhaps his remark that the consequences of the French Revolution would be "infinitely great and beneficial" also referred to the Haitian events (Kuehn 2001: 392).

Another political event Kant might have heard or read about could have been Edmund Burke's famous attack on Warren Hastings (1732–1818), who was the first Governor-General of India from 1773 to 1785 and was charged in the House of Commons with high crimes, corruption and misdemeanors by MPs, among them Burke, two years later. Some of Burke's arguments during the long investigation are worth mentioning. Against Hastings, Burke asserted that the English were not entitled to suspend their moral and legal standards when dealing with non-Europeans. Instead, as Jennifer Pitts summarizes, "the British had an obligation to extend universally the fundamental standards of respect, rightfulness, and humanity that applied at home" (Pitts 2005: 78). A way to overcome "geographical morality" limited to a certain region was to boost the moral imagination, and increase sympathy for strangers. In a manner reminiscent of Francisco de Vitoria, Burke compared India with Germany, "not for an exact resemblance, but as a sort of middle term, by which India might be approximated to our understandings, and if possible to our feelings; in order to awaken something of sympathy for the unfortunate natives" ("Speech on Fox's India Bill, December 1, 1783", Burke 1981–2000: vol. 5, 390). This comparison only worked – and this is the third element – if Indians and their culture and institutions were not seen as inferior. Thus Burke was at pains to show that Indian alleged inferiority and so-called oriental despotism were psychological or cognitive problems of *Europeans* in the first place: a convenient myth of Hastings and other British administrators to justify their own oppression, injustices and arbitrary rule. Burke identified with considerable historical accuracy Montesquieu as the main culprit of this distorted picture of India (see Burke, "Speech in Reply, May 28, 1794", in ibid., vol. 7, 264–265; Pitts 2005: 74–80). Hastings was acquitted in 1795, but the trial probably had a moral significance for Kant. A European criticizing the "violation of right on *one* place of the earth" – far away from Europe – by another fellow-European, so that this violation might be felt by some among his European audience: episodes like this one were perhaps what Kant had in mind when he wrote the passage quoted above. Note that Burke, in his attack on Hastings, implicitly relies on the key tenets of Kantian formal moral principles, namely impartiality and the universalization of maxims, on normative individualism (humans as ends in themselves), and the enlarged way of thinking. Kant did not refer to principles or concepts but to *feelings* in the quoted passage, so it can be claimed that he saw these and similar historical episodes as proof of his claim that every rational person has moral feelings, which are defined as one of the four "predispositions" or "*subjective* conditions of receptiveness to the concept of duty" (MM, 6: 399).

These three examples with their possible impact on Kant are in need of qualification: the text of Raynal's monumental work was ambiguous on the issue of slavery, for instance. On the one hand, this institution was condemned as immoral, on the other hand, the authors approved of the plantation systems even if they were based on slavery, provided that the slaves were treated in a humane way (Raynal 1780/2006: xxvi). Against my interpretation, one might argue that Burke was not a moral cosmopolitan or anti-imperialist thinker, that he did not really care about the Indians, did not respect cultural pluralism, and that his attack on Hastings was motivated by deeply conservative and patriotic concerns, and this criticism could find support in a recent article, which claims that Burke "remained firmly committed to the continuation of a providential imperial project in India throughout the course of his long political career" (O'Neill 2009: 497). This interpretation of Burke's thought sounds plausible, but might also be open to criticism. Be that as it may, the claim does not invalidate Kant's passage about the violation of rights in one part of the globe. What matters for Kant is the fact that colonial practices were criticized, *for whatever reasons* (the worry about proper moral motivation in politics is widespread, but can be duly ignored by the philosopher of history or the legal historian). Kant's philosophy of history does not presuppose universal benevolence or a respect for Europe's external "other", it presupposes pragmatic considerations revolving around self-interest. Finally, there are the sobering results of the Haitian revolution, which did indeed transform a society of slaves into a self-governing nation. However, after the defeat of the French forces in 1803 the mulatto descendants became the new Haitian elite which ruled the country, thus creating another two-caste society. Still, the Haitian revolution tested the ideals of the French revolutionaries and their declaration that all men are born equal and free; they were forced to investigate the meaning of their revolution. It was an opportunity – and nothing more than that – to expand one's way of thinking, or *Denkungsart*.

I want to finish with a few remarks on possible criticism of Kant. His hope that the spirit of commerce would guarantee cosmopolitan right was perhaps too optimistic: commercial interaction normally leads to exclusive hospitality rights, without extending to *all* humans. Implementation of cosmopolitan right currently depends on states, their interests, and their power, thus is often arbitrary and selective (cf. Kleingeld 1998: 82–83; Habermas 1997: 121–122). Kant could be defended with the argument that he saw commercial interactions based on mutual self-interests as deficient but with *possible* beneficial results, admittedly incomplete, but still a step in the right direction. Second, Kant's (and Smith's) enthusiastic praise of world trade seems to be outdated in our contemporary world troubled by environmental crises which are partly rooted in an excessive use of mass transportation of goods. Kant lived in an age of a relatively environmentally friendly world trade (at least if one restricts the comparison to the transportation systems), in a world of sailing ships, horses and camels (cf. Peace, 8: 358). Third, since the eighteenth century there has been an ongoing debate about restrictions on free trade and the legitimate amount of state intervention. Kant himself held that the supreme power of the state was entitled to pass rights meant as "means for *securing* a *rightful condition*", not in order to make the state's citizens happy or prosperous but in order to secure its very existence as a commonwealth, also against foreign enemies. In a footnote, Kant included "certain restrictions on imports … among these rights" (TP, 8: 298 note) – a provision that clearly qualified the free-trade doctrine.

This chapter has argued that Kant's cosmopolitan right is not the blueprint of a cosmopolitan democracy or a global and democratic civil society where individuals are co-legislators building "democratic structures". This is an anachronistic interpretation I have tried to counter with my historical analysis. Since *commercium* also includes the exchange of ideas, cosmopolitan right indeed "opens up a space" – to use a phrase dear to contemporary cosmopolitans – for a thin version of global civil society. Cosmopolitan right thus has two functions: first, it is the third segment of the juridical framework, of what Kant terms "a universal *cosmopolitan condition*" (Idea 8: 28; see also Anthropology, 7: 333) as the basis or "womb" of proper formation or *Bildung* (the other two segments are the republican constitution and the reformed right of nations). Politicians cannot and should not manipulate their respective citizenry, but they can influence the conditions that facilitate the development of their moral characters. The cultivation of our germs and predispositions requires "an immense series of generations, each of which transmits its enlightenment to the next" (Idea 8: 19), and this difficult and slow process is only possible in a condition that can be characterized with the phrases "rule of law", "republicanism", "global peace" and cosmopolitan right. Secondly, Kant holds that establishing and refining cosmopolitan right in itself has a moral significance, because it is an educational process that prepares the ground for moral formation via juridical reform (see chapter 2, section 3 and chapter 7).

Let me flesh out my interpretation with a brief comparison. In her book entitled *Toward an Imperfect Education. Facing Humanity, Rethinking Cosmopolitanism*, Sharon Todd aims at what I am trying to do in this study, offering a modern theory of cosmopolitan education. She sees Kant's cosmopolitan right as the centre of his "cosmopolitan project": "it is here, in establishing cosmopolitan right as a right of hospitality, where the kernel of cosmopolitanism is to be found" (Todd 2009: 33–4). This is a widespread assessment, but I believe it is mistaken. Todd abandons Kant's crucial distinction between the doctrines of right and virtue, calling hospitality a "moral duty" and blurring the difference between external freedom of choice and moral freedom, and between humanity and the human race (Todd 2009: 34). Her sole focus is the essay on perpetual peace; the *Metaphysics of Morals*, the writings on history or the lecture on pedagogy are left out. This results in a mistaken assessment of the systematic place of cosmopolitan right. It is not the centrepiece of Kant's cosmopolitan theory, it is only the third segment of the juridical framework that prepares the ground for possible cosmopolitan formation. Towards the end of her book, Todd stresses the importance of reflective judgements in her theory of a cosmopolitan ethic that avoids turning cosmopolitanism into yet another "ism", an ideology or a "prosthesis for thinking" (Todd 2009: 140; see 138–51). This is a very Kantian move, yet Todd does not see this. Her own theory of judgement, inspired by Hannah Arendt and aiming at justice, wants to do without "a faith in principles" (ibid., 140), and I doubt that this can be done (see chapter 8, sections 2 and 3). Todd misses the opportunity to find in Kant's philosophy what she is looking for: an elaborate theory of judgement contained in the third critique (which deeply influenced Arendt), a theory of justice in the *Metaphysics of Morals*, and the outlines of a conception of cosmopolitan education in the lectures on pedagogy. I will try to reconstruct this conception in the subsequent chapters. First, however, conscious of the fact that an investigation into embedded cosmopolitanism should itself pay attention to contexts, I will turn to Kant's crucial authors in terms of education, namely Rousseau and Basedow.

4 Educating Émile: Rousseau on embedded cosmopolitanism

Whereas the second and third chapters offered a systematic interpretation of Kant's cosmopolitanism, the next two look into the eighteenth-century context, in particular relevant educational theories. This chapter focuses on Rousseau, whose philosophy exerted a strong influence on Kant, yet whose ideas on cosmopolitanism, patriotism and nationalism flatly seem to contradict Kant's. Traditionally, the eighteenth century has been seen as a cosmopolitan age before the rise of nationalism. Though this assessment is in need of qualification, many Enlightenment philosophers were in fact more cosmopolitan than representatives of previous or later eras: there was a certain amount of openness towards and fascination with other cultures, and many intellectuals perceived themselves as members of a transnational "republic of letters". The diversity of attitudes, opinions and theories concerning cosmopolitanism was impressive, yet a common feature of Enlightenment cosmopolitanism was that it tried to strike a tenable balance between patriotism and cosmopolitan obligations. Samuel Taylor Coleridge (1772–1834), for instance, asserted: "This is indeed Cosmopolitism, at once the Nursling and the Nurse of patriotic affection! This, and this alone, is genuine Philanthropy, which like the Olive Tree, sacred to concord and to wisdom, fattens not exhausts the soil, from which it sprang, and in which it remains rooted, it is rooted in the soil of the nation: nourished and nourishing the national soil" (Samuel Taylor Coleridge, "On the Law of Nations", quoted in Wohlgemut 2009: 2–3). According to Coleridge, genuine moral cosmopolitanism was identical with philanthropy, was embedded in the culture of the country and stimulated as well as was stimulated by patriotism: they mutually reinforced each other. Cosmopolitanism was not abstract, but "rooted in the soil of the nation". Rousseau was the thinker who tried to go beyond these often easy compromises. In the first place, he emphatically rejected various types of cosmopolitanism as degenerate, deformed and immoral, such as cultural or economic cosmopolitanism. However, this did not turn him into the founding father of modern nationalism, as generations of interpreters up to the present have misleadingly asserted.

In this chapter, I argue that Rousseau offers a version of embedded cosmopolitanism. Though frequently overlooked, *Émile* includes a plan for the cosmopolitan education of the pupil. My argument develops the following way: Building on the concept of cosmopolitanism and its various types developed in chapter 2, I show how Rousseau criticizes widespread forms of cosmopolitanism in his writings. In the next section, I outline Rousseau's theory of authentic moral cosmopolitanism. One of the by-products of living in a true republic is the moral education of citizens. They learn to renounce destructive *amour-propre* or personal interests if they conflict with the general will or the greatest good. These moral citizens make moral cosmopolitanism as well as genuine legal cosmopolitanism possible, though this is a conclusion Rousseau does not draw. The next section focuses on Rousseau's vision of cosmopolitan education as developed in *Émile*. I attempt to show that Rousseau is a systematic thinker, linking cosmopolitanism with his generic moral and political philosophy, and their educational dimension. The concluding section points at various tensions and problems inherent in Rousseau's theory.

4.1 Rousseau's attack on forms of cosmopolitanism

For a long time, Rousseau has been seen as one of the "classics" of pedagogical thought (Baker 2001, Todorov 2001, Hentig 2003, Schneider 2005, Streck 2006, Oelkers 2008, Wain 2011). In addition, he is usually depicted as an anti-cosmopolitan founder of modern nationalism (Cheneval 2003: 55 and 60) or an advocate of strong patriotism, with the community more or less absorbing the individual (Yonah 1999: 366–7 and 385). This widespread interpretation is mostly based on a reading of "Considerations on the Government of Poland" (Korsgaard 2006; see also Cohler 1970 and Barnard 1988). Francis Cheneval, for instance, writes about this text: "Dans des conditions de menace extrême et donc de fortes pathologies politiques, Rousseau ouvre, dans ce texte, les portes de l'enfer d'un nationalisme aveugle et passionnel et d'une politique qui prend comme paradigme la nécessité naturelle" (Cheneval 2003: 59–60). He contrasts Rousseau's national educational programme with Kant's cosmopolitan project. It is indeed not difficult to find passages in some of Rousseau's writings which support this nationalist reading. For example, he claims about the national education of the "true republican" that the "love of fatherland ... makes up his whole existence; he sees only his fatherland, he lives only for it; when he is alone, he is nothing: when he no longer has a fatherland, he no longer is, and if he is not dead, he is worse than dead" (Rousseau 1997d: 189).

I disagree with this interpretation of Rousseau as the founder of modern nationalism, and argue for a more nuanced assessment, in agreement with other recent interpreters (see Lex 2014, Neidleman 2012, and Rosenblatt 2008). While Rousseau doubtlessly defends a strong form of republican or civic patriotism, he can be interpreted as working out an early compromise with thin moral cosmopolitanism and legal cosmopolitanism. Although he was an eccentric intellectual, his version of rooted cosmopolitanism seems rather main stream and common sense, offering a sort of "commentary" on the traditional concentric circles imagery. I start with a systematic description of forms of cosmopolitanism endorsed in the eighteenth century, and summarize Rousseau's criticism. This is the first step in my attempt to reconstruct his theory of cosmopolitan education.

Rousseau attacks what could be labelled thick cultural cosmopolitanism – or, rather, Europeanism – , that is, the belief that a single thick conception of the good life should spread all over the globe, swallowing existing cultures and traditions. Rousseau deplores the fact that Europeans of his age endorse a way of life that successively becomes more monotonous and more uniform. Linking the trend towards cultural, European-wide homogeneity with decadence, Rousseau claims that "there are no more Frenchmen, Germans, Spaniards, even Englishmen nowadays, regardless of what people may say; there are only Europeans. All have the same tastes, the same passions, the same morals, because none has been given a national form by a distinctive institution" (Rousseau 1997d: 184; see also Rosenblatt 2008: 60–1).

Rousseau also dismissed economic or commercial cosmopolitanism, doubting that commerce is primarily beneficial, as Montesquieu, Adam Smith and others had claimed (Rousseau 1997a: 18, Rousseau 1997d: 226, Rosenblatt 2008: 62, Cavallar 2002: 287 and chapter 3 section 4 above). Finally, Rousseau criticized the natural law cosmopolitanism of Samuel Pufendorf and Denise Diderot (natural law cosmopolitanism understood as an early form of cosmopolitanism that blended moral and juridical elements). Pufendorf's key concept, that of sociability or *socialitas*, Rousseau claimed, did not establish a true community. Against Diderot's article on "Natural Right" written for the *Encyclopédie* in 1755, Rousseau suggested that the "fraternité commune de tous les hommes" might be an empty idea (Rousseau 1997c: 155, Fetscher 1980: 122–3 and 185).

4.2 Rousseau's tentative republican cosmopolitanism

Rousseau's attack on the "supposed cosmopolites" (whom he denounced as mere hypocrites) aimed at making room for genuine moral and political cosmopolitanisms. One element of this theory is what can be labelled republican cosmopolitanism, which includes republican patriotism. The latter saw human fulfilment culminating in the citizenship in a free republic. Rousseau did not endorse nationalism, where coherence is based on ethnicity, language, or common heritage. For him, the true *patrie* was a republic, characterized by freedom, equality, and the rule of law (Rousseau 1997d: 179, 196–7, 224–5, Cheneval 2003: 56–7, Viroli 1995: 93–4). Like Montesquieu and other early modern European civic humanists, Rousseau adored the ancient republics as shining examples of civic virtue and material equality (Rousseau 1997d: 192 and 219, Dent 2005: 9 and 84 and chapter 7 below; on Rousseau's political philosophy see the recent publications of Gessmann 2013, Herb and Scherl 2012, Wain 2011). Emotional identification with the political community enabled citizens to overcome one's selfish tendencies, to respect the laws, to lead a life that sustained political liberty, and to develop civic virtue. This in turn would solve the problem of realizing the general will, which is accomplished if civic virtue dominates, "the conformity of the individual will with the general will". This way, all the vices associated with *amour propre* could be avoided (Rousseau 1997d: 179, 183, 221, 238–9, Fidler 1996: 130, Scott 2006). The goal of republican education is to transform a mere aggregate of selfish individuals (as in commercial society) into a "moral and collective body" (Rousseau 1997b: 11, Roosevelt 1990, chapter 5, Oelkers 2008: 161–7, Spaemann 2008: 122–3). Patriotism and civic virtue coincide, and integrate *amour de soi* and *amour propre* (on these two concepts see Fetscher 1980: 65–75, Dent 2005: 39–40 and 68–72 and Lex 125–30).

The psychological assumption behind this reasoning is that the intensity of pity (*pitié*; sometimes also translated as compassion or commiseration) diminishes the more people are involved, and the more distant they are. Rousseau saw this as a historical development, which coincided with the transformation of (desirable) *amour de soi-meme* into (a deformed version of) *amour-propre* (Fetscher 1980: 75–8 and White 2008). "It would seem that the sentiment of humanity dissipates and weakens as it spreads to the whole earth, and that we cannot be as touched by the calamities of Tartary or Japan as we are by those of a European people. Interest and commiseration must in some way be constricted [*comprimer*] in order to be activated" (Rousseau 1997b: 15). Rousseau's answer to this problem is civic patriotism. It has been argued that *amour-propre* is simply turned into a kind of collective egoism (cf. Fetscher 1980: 78). However, this interpretation probably misses the complexity of Rousseau's account of *amour-propre*. Nicholas Dent has persuasively argued that the contrast between *amour de soi-meme* and *amour-propre* should not be cast in simple black-and-white terms. According to Rousseau, patterns of competition, domination and submission are historically contingent. *Amour-propre* is not necessarily aggressive and competitive. In Rousseau's ideal political community, the requirements of *amour-propre* are met as members enjoy equality of status, due recognition, and mutual respect. It is the task of legislation and of education to promote and cultivate the development and flourishing of this benign and socially acceptable form of *amour-propre* (Dent 2005: 71–2 and 104–6; see also Yonah 1999: 370 and Lex 2014: 130–1). This is the dynamic and educational interpretation of *amour-propre:* it is contained and tamed but at the same time also nourished in certain directions to become morally acceptable. The underlying psychological assumption implied in the passage quoted above about the intensity of pity is plausible, but can be challenged. Let me just add that the theory has found its followers; it can be found in authors such as Kant or Martha Nussbaum.

Republican cosmopolitanism is a form of legal cosmopolitanism (see chapter 1, section 1 and chapter 2, section 1 for definitions). There are two versions: Like John Oswald or Friedrich Schlegel, Rousseau advocated an alliance of republics, whereas Anacharsis Cloots was in favour of a world republic with *departments*, but without states (Cheneval 2004 and Poulsen 2014). Rousseau's ideas are notoriously difficult to interpret. He praised the plan of a European federation developed by Saint-Pierre, but also mocked his naivety and the plan's focus on princely sovereignty (Rousseau 2008: 95 and 123–5). Rousseau developed different concepts in other writings. His scattered comments do not allow for a comprehensive reconstruction, but occasionally he suggests that small republics could peacefully co-exist with each other, or form loose defensive alliances, even confederations, to deter aggression (Asbach 2000, Hoffmann 2006: 42–3, and Cavallar 2012a).

Rousseau's theory can be understood as an attempt to show that genuine moral cosmopolitanism is compatible with republican patriotism (this is the compatibility thesis). For Rousseau, cosmopolitanism was acceptable if squarely rooted in and evolving from adherence to one's particular community. It could be argued that Rousseau went a step further and implied that republican patriotism, properly understood, might lead to thin moral cosmopolitanism. According to this interpretation, Rousseau endorsed an evolutionary approach, and a bottom-up procedure. Civic patriotism was the first and indispensable step in the evolution of a genuine "love of humanity". Civic patriotism and cosmopolitanism, if both are properly understood and cultivated, do not exclude each other, but can form a synthesis with the help of education. Both form concentric circles. "Willing generally" can only be properly learned in a specific community. A global general will might be created by continuous republican practice (Rosenblatt 2008: 67). Participation in a community governed by just laws and the general will helps people to form ideas of justice with a more extensive application. Human history would be a learning process, and the crucial lesson is parallel to Emile's, who, as a first step, has to cultivate his moral sensibility to those he knows and has relations with. After all, "the word *mankind* will signify anything to him. … It is only after long training, after much consideration on his own sentiments and on those he observes in others, that he will be able to get to the point of generalizing his individual notions under the abstract idea of humanity, and add to his individual affections those which may identify him with his species" (Rousseau 2007: 184). Abstract moral reasoning has to be practised, learned and perfected in order to achieve a true cosmopolitan attitude. A more limited sensibility is a necessary if not sufficient condition of emotionally identifying with the whole species. According to this interpretation, Rousseau is a peculiar kind of cosmopolitan, who believes in the human capacity to learn, form syntheses, and develop one's moral potential.

4.3 Rousseau's vision of cosmopolitan education

According to Rousseau, one of the by-products of living in a true republic is the moral education of citizens. They learn to renounce destructive *amour-propre* or personal interests if they conflict with the general will or the greatest good. These moral citizens make moral cosmopolitanism as well as genuine legal cosmopolitanism possible (in the form of the law of nations based on reason). A succinct passage in the "Geneva Manuscript" drives this point home: "Extend this maxim to the general society of which the State gives us the idea, protected by the society of which we are members, or by that in which we live, the natural revulsion to do evil no longer being offset by the fear of having evil done to us, we are inclined at once by nature, by habit, by reason, to deal with other men more or less as [we do] with our fellow-citizens, and this disposition reduced to actions gives rise to the rules of reasoned natural law" (Rousseau 1997c: 160; see also Fetscher 1980: 138–9). Republican citizens have learned to respect universal laws by habit. They are no longer exclusively controlled by passions, have developed their rational capacities (*droite raison*) and have become part of a wider moral whole. Now – and not sooner! – they are in a position to meet foreigners "more or less" like their fellow-citizens, on a footing of equality and mutual respect. A benign and socially acceptable form of *amour-propre* has widened its circles. A moral cosmopolitan disposition has become possible.

Given Rousseau's psychology, which cognitive or emotional faculty carries this moral cosmopolitanism? Is it pity, the most likely candidate? Is it going to yield active world citizens, or rather "reluctant spectators" who are trying to avoid engagement, as one commentator has claimed? (Boyd 2004: 540). Passages in *Émile* would suggest that the relevant faculty is indeed pity or compassion, the capacity to identify with others and their suffering. "A union of mutual regard and esteem is established, created by these interconnections of feeling and concern" (Dent 2005: 103; cf. Rousseau 2007: 174–6). This moral union is gradually extended beyond state borders. The passage quoted above suggests that Rousseau has an education in mind that combines emotional and cognitive faculties, and is additionally based on habit, evoking associations with the ancient concept of virtue. This could point at a possible synthesis between cognitive and sentimental moral cosmopolitan theories, which goes beyond the binary opposition sketched in some accounts (see for instance the distinctions in Jollimore and Barrios 2006). In *Émile*, Rousseau holds that compassion should be global in scope, but limited by the demands of reason and justice. "To prevent pity from degenerating into weakness we must generalise it and extend it to mankind. Then we only yield to it when it is in accordance with justice, since justice is of all the virtues that which contributes most to the common good" (Rousseau 2007: 203). In this way, Emile learns to identify with the rest of humankind, to put himself in the place of others, to cultivate his imagination. The overall result is a combination of cognitive and emotional learning processes: compassion, for instance, is something emotional; setting limits is a cognitive feat. It may of course be disputed whether Rousseau's educational strategy or theory concerning compassion is successful (see the critical discussions in Jonas 2010, White 2008: 36–47 and Yonah 1999: 385–6).

Rousseau offered a version of embedded cosmopolitanism. He conceded key arguments of the critics of cosmopolitanisms and seems to have combined republicanism with elements of legal cosmopolitanism and a thin version of moral cosmopolitanism. Rousseau tried to strike a balance between genuine moral cosmopolitanism and defensive republican patriotism, while perceiving the dangers of chauvinism that becomes "exclusive and tyrannical and makes a people bloodthirsty and intolerant … It is not permissible to strengthen the bond of a particular society at the expense of the rest of the human race" (Rousseau 1991c: 131; see also Hoffmann 2006: 40 and 44).

I continue with a reading of *Émile*, since, as Helena Rosenblatt suggests, this book on the education of a boy "can even be read as a book about the formation of a true cosmopolitan" (Rosenblatt 2008: 65). Whereas Rosenblatt has offered only a brief sketch, I will try to support her thesis – that Rousseau was in search of true, authentic cosmopolitanism – with a more extensive discussion. Let me emphasise first that Rousseau's approach in *Émile* is different from his political writings such as the notorious essay on the government of Poland or the *Contrat Social*. In the book on education, the focus is on one individual, not on the collective entity of republican citizens.

Three elements of Rousseau's philosophy – integrated into Émile's upbringing – prepare the ground for the cosmopolitan education of the pupil: Rousseau's criticism of Eurocentrism, his moral universalism, and his pacifism. Already in the *Discourse on the Origin of Inequality*, Rousseau criticized Eurocentric assumptions in travel accounts, claiming that they were inspired by "ridiculous" "national prejudices" (Rousseau 1997e: 220). This disapproval is repeated in *Émile*, where Rousseau deplores European ignorance of other cultures and the arrogant attitude of censuring them after having read some travel books. "In no country of Europe are so many histories and books of travel printed as in France, and nowhere is there less knowledge of the mind and manners of other nations" (Rousseau 2007: 388). Travellers in turn tend to see what they want to see; and merchants are interested in profit, not in studying others (ibid. 391). It may be argued that Rousseau himself is not free from prejudice either; for instance, there are sweeping generalizations about the French and the English, such as that the "Englishman's prejudices are the result of pride, the Frenchman's are due to vanity" (ibid. 389). However, if Rousseau's statements are compared with those of, say, David Hume on the inferiority of Africans or of Montesquieu on the deficiencies of the Asians (Popkin 1993, Cavallar 2002: 355–6), then one has every reason to be lenient with him. There is a passage in *Émile* where Rousseau explicitly criticizes what we would nowadays call colonial exploitation. Emile and his tutor have been invited to dine with rich people, and a feast with servants, "many dishes, dainty and elegant china" has been prepared (Rousseau 2007: 145). The tutor whispers into the boy's ear: "How many hands do you suppose the things on this table passed through before they got here?" The question is designed to arouse interest in the morally unspoilt reason of the child. Rousseau comments: "what will he think of luxury when he finds that every quarter of the globe has been ransacked, that some 2,000,000 men have laboured for years, that many lives have perhaps been sacrificed, and all to furnish him with fine clothes to be worn at midday and laid by in the wardrobe at night" (ibid.). The ensuing conversation with the pupil aims at showing him that the fine dishes and all the luxury only promote vanity and are not worth the effort. Emile should learn to feel compassion and pity for others, even if they live far away.

The episode is a fine example of Emile's moral education, and this leads us to the second element, Rousseau's moral universalism. He claims that humans all over the world have an "innate sense of justice" (Rousseau 2007: 32), and one goal of education is to awaken and cultivate this disposition. God's moral commandments are written "in the secret heart" of everybody (164). Rousseau does not ignore cultural differences across the globe, but asserts that "among this amazing variety of manners and customs, you will everywhere find the same ideas of right and justice; everywhere the same principles of morality, the same ideas of good and evil" (237). Using contemporary terminology, it might be said that Rousseau endorses a thin concept of moral universalism, a position that is hotly contested, but also endorsed by some contemporary philosophers (see Cavallar 2002, 46–59). According to Rousseau, elements of this moral minimalism is the principle or negative virtue "never hurt anybody" (Rousseau 2007: 66) and conscience, the universal ability to judge our own actions (ibid. 237; see also 185–6, 239, 409; Dent 2005: 114–5 and Cooper 1999).

Kant followed Rousseau with his own version of weak or thin moral universalism, expressed in the principle of the categorical imperative which he conceptualised as formal as well as universal (see chapter 5, section 4 and chapter 6, section 1).

The third element is Rousseau's pacifism. When Emile and his tutor talk about his future profession, the tutor mentions joining the army, an occupation he describes in the following words: "you may hire yourself out at very high wages to go and kill men who never did you any harm" (Rousseau 2007: 393; cf. Rosenblatt 2008: 64). Given the way Emile has been educated, this is no real option; Emile has developed a "peaceful spirit" (Rousseau 2007: 201; cf. 190). Finally, in the closing pages of the book, Emile receives his political education, and discusses with his tutor how war, together with tyranny "the worst scourge of humanity", can be overcome with the formation of leagues and confederations (403). This parallels Saint-Pierre's ideas, but with the difference that the latter restricted his federation to Europe, whereas Rousseau's does not seem to be limited in this way. At any rate, the passage hints at Rousseau's republican cosmopolitanism (see Rousseau 2008 and above). It is crucial to understand that these three elements, especially thin moral cosmopolitanism, are preconditions of Rousseau's moral cosmopolitanism; otherwise it would be half-hearted or self-contradictory.

In the remaining paragraphs of this section, I will outline the unfolding of Emile's cosmopolitan education. My starting point is Rousseau's distrust of "those cosmopolitans who search out remote duties in their books and neglect those that lie nearest. These philosophers will love the Tartars to avoid loving their neighbour" (Rousseau 2007: 8). Loving the Tartars, Rousseau implies, is mere hypocrisy, as this love does not have any consequences, is but a phrase. The education of Emile has to avoid this pitfall of moral degeneration, without abandoning the goal of moral cosmopolitanism. Thus the tutor must carefully choose what to teach and when to teach it. The child should not be overburdened with knowledge it cannot grasp. "We are now confined to a circle, small indeed compared with the whole of human thought, but this circle is still a vast sphere when measured by the child's mind" (ibid. 123). The remedy is again a bottom-up procedure. Teaching geography, for instance, should start with the smallest circle, the home town and its immediate surroundings (ibid. 127).

The same approach applies to moral education. Rousseau uses the familiar imagery of concentric circles – widespread in the eighteenth century – to illustrate how he conceptualizes "the expansion of [Emile's] relations" (ibid. 165). The Stoics conceived humans as surrounded by a series of concentric circles: the self, one's immediate family, one's extended family relations, neighbours, fellow citizens, and finally the whole species (Heater 2002: 44–52). Thus Rousseau starts with the self and its self-love or *amour de soi-meme* which is "always good, always in accordance with the order of nature" (Rousseau 2007: 164). The child discovers that "those about him" (usually his parents) are not only useful, they also "desire to be useful to him" and they are inclined to help him, so he learns to love them (ibid. 165). If everything goes well, "he gets the habit of a kindly feeling towards his species" (ibid.). However, there are many pitfalls which have to be avoided, especially the transformation of (desirable) *amour de soi-meme* into (a deformed version of) *amour-propre*. This possible development of course parallels that of the human species described in the *Discourse on the Origin of Inequality*. In the case of the individual, the roots of evil are (again) "a multiplicity of needs and dependence on the opinions of others" (ibid.).

How does the education of Emile counter these possible negative developments? Rousseau holds that the adolescent should form friendships first, and avoid losing his innocence by early contacts with women. Rousseau advises the tutor to "take advantage of his dawning sensibility to sow the first seeds of humanity" in the pupil's heart (ibid. 172). This is done by making the pupil realize the fact of the "common sufferings" of humankind (the cognitive aspect) and by a careful cultivation of the feeling of pity (the emotional aspect). "Our common sufferings draw our hearts to our fellow-creatures; we should have no duties to mankind if we were not men" (ibid.). Our duties towards mankind are based on human frailty and weakness, on various forms of sufferings, not on our needs, on mutual dependence, or on what others think of us. The teacher stimulates and nourishes pity by fostering the following cognitive and emotional capacities: first, the adolescent learns to change his perspective and to put himself "in the place of those who can claim our pity" (Rousseau 2007: 174). Secondly, he learns to realize that human condition and fate is alike for all, so that when we see someone suffering "we know we may suffer in like manner ourselves" (ibid. 175). Finally the pupil learns to identify with others in an emotional way, which goes beyond the mere cognitive exercise of changing one's perspective: he feels the feelings of others. Thus the third maxim: "The pity we feel for others is proportionate, not to the amount of the evil, but to the feelings we attribute to the sufferers" (ibid. 176; see also White 2008: 36–9). Again and again, Rousseau emphasizes that humans are similar in their passions and feelings all over the world (Rousseau 2007: 176).

I have described one example of how the tutor tries to cultivate Emile's pity, his sense of justice and virtue above (the dinner with rich people). Later, Emile's moral character is tested, when he has already found his love and future wife Sophie. He passes the test with flying colours. His cognitive, moral and emotional capacities have developed in a way that he is able to respect "the rights of humanity". Emile has dates with Sophie, who is eager that she is respected by him, and being late would be a violation of this right to be respected. One day Emile and his tutor do not show up. Sophie meets Emile with "scornful irony" the next day (Rousseau 2007: 378). Emile has helped an unlucky peasant the day before, who fell off his horse and broke his leg while his wife was about to give birth to another child. Emile addresses Sophie with a beautiful speech: "You may condemn me to die of grief; but do not hope to make me forget the rights of humanity; they are even more sacred in my eyes than your own rights; I will never renounce them for you" (ibid. 379). There is a clear hierarchy of moral duties. Helping those in distress is a perfect duty which trumps the minor duty to respect one's love by not being late. Sophie's answer shows that she has developed the same moral character as Emile. She accepts him as a future husband and spends the following day as an angel of charity in the home of the poor peasant. If readers manage to ignore the romantic kitsch, they can see that Emile's moral education has come to a successful conclusion. Pity and justice (in this case: knowledge of the hierarchy of duties) have formed a perfect synthesis. Emile is ready for the last stage of moral development, moral cosmopolitanism, which combines sentimental and cognitive elements. As Rousseau puts it: "Extend self-love to others and it is transformed into virtue, a virtue which has its root in the heart of every one of us. [...] the love of the human race is nothing but the love of justice within us. [...] Apart from self-interest this care for the general well-being is the first concern of the wise man, for each of us forms part of the human race and not part of any individual member of that race" (ibid. 203).

The tutor puts the finishing touches to Emile's cosmopolitan education during their Grand Tour. All Emile has to do now is overcome possible patriotic prejudices. How can he do that? Rousseau's remedy is very simple. Emile has met men "of worth" in all the countries he visited, and now they become his pen-friends. Finding them was not difficult. As Rousseau asks rhetorically in another passage, "Are there not, in every country, men of common-sense, honesty, and good faith, lovers of truth, who only seek to know what truth is that they may profess it?" (ibid. 251). Corresponding with these worthy men abroad "is also an excellent antidote against the sway of patriotic prejudices, to which we are liable all through our life, and to which sooner or later we are more or less enslaved" (Rousseau 2007: 408). A friendly and respectful interchange of opinions helps both partners to overcome their respective set of prejudices. The correspondence helps them to "set the one set of prejudices against the other and be safe from both" (ibid.). Emile finally practices what I have called epistemological or cognitive cosmopolitanism in the first section, a cognitive orientation with the key feature of impartiality, a disposition which entails openness towards others, and an appreciation of diversity.

When Emile and his tutor return from their Grand Tour, the former is ready to marry his beloved Sophie. Searching for the perfect place to live in Europe was one of the motives for the tour in the first place. The two main characters provide two slightly different answers. Emile has arrived at what Ulrich Beck and others nowadays call "global thinking", and at a genuine form of moral cosmopolitanism. He declares, "What matters my place in the world? What matters it where I am? Wherever there are men, I am among my brethren; wherever there are none, I am in my own home" (ibid. 409). The tutor does not simply dismiss Emile's opinion; he qualifies it by distinguishing between one's country or republic and the land where we live. He replies, "Do not say therefore, 'What matters where I am?' It does matter that you should be where you can best do your duty; and one of these duties is to love your native land. Your fellow-countrymen protected you in childhood; you should love them in your manhood" (ibid. 410). This is embedded moral cosmopolitanism, partly characterized by the worn-out phrase "think globally, act locally". The inner concentric circles should not be neglected, even if one's native land does not correspond with the idea of a perfect republic outlined in the *Contrat Social*. Emile should not become one of those caricatures of cosmopolitans mentioned at the beginning of the book, who neglect their duties "that lie nearest" (ibid. 8).

At the end of his formal education, Emile seems to have reached the intellectual and moral heights of those "few great Cosmopolitan Souls" Rousseau refers to in the Second Discourse: they "cross the imaginary boundaries that separate Peoples and, following the example of the sovereign being that created them, embrace the whole of Mankind in their benevolence" (Rousseau 1997e: 174). The loss of "natural commiseration" was, according to Rousseau's philosophical history of humankind, the result of the establishment of societies and states. Note how the quotation again summarizes the two key aspects of cosmopolitanism, namely its cognitive dimension (crossing imaginary boundaries that separate peoples) and the moral one (global benevolence). Emile has returned to this natural attitude.

4.4 The limitations of Rousseau's approach

Rousseau saw as negative what many of us tend to see as positive virtues: a vague indifference towards others, frequent travelling abroad, commercial interaction, and superficial socializing. Rousseau probably had authors like Fougeret de Monbron in mind when he attacked allegedly cosmopolitan frequent travellers. De Monbron, who published his travel memories under the title *Le Cosmopolite ou le Citoyen du Monde* (London 1753), displayed an aesthetic and individualistic cosmopolitan attitude. He lacked critical self-reflection and a careful analysis of his own prejudices and of the cultural and moral norms of his own society (see Lettevall 2008: 23 and Heuvel 1986: 45–6). According to Rousseau, a moral attitude or virtue, the willingness not to overlook those close to oneself, genuine cognitive as well as moral cosmopolitanism, and legal cosmopolitanism are essential. For people corrupted by commercial society, Rousseau's advice could be summarised like this: "Human beings need to turn inward, to consult their consciences, to listen to their natural sentiments, and thus find their true and shared humanity, before they could love others as they loved themselves" (Rosenblatt 2008: 66). I am going to argue later on that this is exactly Kant's understanding of moral cosmopolitanism (see chapter 6). Perhaps the common root of their conceptions is Saint Augustine's famous *in interiore homine habitat veritas*. Though I will also show that Rousseau and Kant differ in their respective cosmopolitan theories (see the next chapter), they share certain key tenets. Above all, both claim that moral cosmopolitanism is not something added to cultivated morality, but they are identical (the identity thesis). Recall that Rousseau claimed that "the love of the human race is nothing but the love of justice within us" (Rousseau 2007: 203). This is Kant's central message: the cognitive and emotional predispositions (*Anlagen*) of each individual are the only possible foundation of moral cosmopolitanism, and their cultivation by each individual herself with the help of teachers is the task of cosmopolitan formation or *Bildung* (see chapter 6). Furthermore, Rousseau argues that cognitive, moral and emotional capacities should be developed proportionally, and this is also Kant's mature position.

In this conclusion, I won't deal with aspects of Rousseau's position which relate to generic philosophical problems, such as the conception of a thin moral universalism, the differences – or tensions – among Rousseau's various writings, or the thesis of an essential similarity of humans. Instead I am going to focus on what might be called Rousseau's utopianism, the thin dividing line between nationalism, patriotism, and republican patriotism, Rousseau's pessimistic philosophy of history and the tensions in Rousseau's writings between communitarian and individualistic elements. First, Rousseau's utopianism: I suppose that Rousseau would have partly subscribed to the following statement of one of Nussbaum's critics: "Teach children instead to be 'citizens of the world', and in all likelihood they will become neither patriots nor cosmopolitans, but lovers of abstraction and ideology, intolerant of the flaw-ridden individuals and cultures that actually exist throughout the world" (McConnell 1996: 81). Rousseau suggests that we do not need a fake moral cosmopolitanism or a shallow sociability, we need true moral cosmopolitanism. However, will this distant goal ever be reached? Will not moral cosmopolitanism be too remote and too abstract to have any actual bearing on the ground? Rousseau's relevance for today's educational philosophy seems very limited for another reason: the tutor's education Émile receives cannot easily be translated into contemporary forms of state schooling. Our distance from Rousseau's age also becomes apparent if we look at his sexism and stereotypes about women and men (for a subtle analysis see Schneider 2005). Cosmopolitan education is clearly reserved for Émile; Sophie has to fulfil her duty as an "angel of charity" at home.

Secondly, the reader is left with an obviously very thin dividing line between nationalism, patriotism, and republican patriotism. However, I think one should give Rousseau credit for sincerely reflecting upon this very problem. In the *Confessions*, he admits that his love of France during the war of 1733 "became so rooted in my heart, that when I later played the anti-despot and proud republican at Paris, in spite of myself I felt a secret predilection for that same nation that I found to be servile, and for that government which I affected to criticize. What was funny was that, since I was ashamed of an inclination so contrary to my maxims, I did not dare to admit it to anyone, and I scoffed at the French for their defeats, while my heart bled more than theirs" (Rousseau 1995: 153). Patriotism is seen as a strong emotion that clouds rational considerations of impartiality, a necessary condition of cognitive as well as moral cosmopolitanism. A true cosmopolitan will judge nations and states impartially, by republican principles for instance. Rousseau admits that he himself was unable to do this, calling his partiality for France a "madness" he could not cure. Rousseau's mad inclination ultimately triumphed over his rational maxims in the reported episode. However, his intellect attempts to explain the "blind passion"; for Rousseau, it was caused by his continued and exclusive reading of French national heroic literature, an educational measure – or poison – he – somewhat ironically – advocates for Polish patriots. Rousseau's ability to abstract and reflect upon himself helps him to understand patriotism as a strong, ambivalent, often logically inconsistent, and potentially dangerous emotion.

Third, there is Rousseau's pessimistic philosophy of history. Like many other civic humanists of early modern Europe, he is deeply worried about the almost inevitable decline and fall of European or "western" civilization as a consequence of commercial activities, ensuing wealth, corruption, and loose morals. Rousseau is a cultural pessimist who believes that European civilization is in a process of irreversible decline, and in certain respects he is deeply conservative in the sense that he wants to preserve traditional institutions like marriage and the nuclear and patriarchal family (see for instance Wain 2011: 18 and 38). Incidentally, this also explains why he rejects modern commercial and cultural cosmopolitanism (see above). Examples of Rousseau's cultural pessimism abound. Right at the beginning of *Émile*, Rousseau deplores the fact that French city women of his time "refuse to nurse their own children". He continues: "Not content with having ceased to suckle their children, women no longer wish to do it; with the natural result motherhood becomes a burden; means are found to avoid it". He predicts that eventually all of Europe will be faced with declining birth-rates and depopulation (Rousseau 2007: 12; see also ibid. 14). He contrasts his own "age of degradation" and its soft education where almost no virtue can be found (ibid. 15, 17, 49 and 167) with the tough and warlike education of the Spartans, who "were not taught to stick to their books, they were set to steal their dinners" (ibid. 81). Rousseau praises the women who get married, disappear from the public and devote their lives to husband, household and children, playing their parts "in the physical and moral order" (ibid. 302; cf. ibid. 310, 167, 305, 307, 405 and Dent 2005: 117–21). Émile has to avoid decadent society at all costs, in particular a life of debauchery and early sexual experiences (cf. Rousseau 2007: 167, 172, 283, 332 and 350). In contrast to the countryside, cities and especially capitals are corrupt and uniform (ibid. 391, 404–6). Globalization erases national differences, but fails to create a moral community (ibid. 390–1 and above). Commerce leads to "the passion for money", opulence, urbanization, the decline of the family, and the end of the political community or the civilization. "Rich peoples have always been beaten and conquered by poor peoples" (Rousseau 1997d: 225 and 226; more references are in Dent 2005: 50–80). This element of Rousseau's philosophy is a serious challenge to all interpretations that present him as a founder of modern liberal or social democratic thought (see for instance Dame 1997 and Streck 2006).

Finally, there are clearly tensions in Rousseau's writings between communitarian and individualistic elements. At the beginning of *Émile*, he writes: "Forced to combat either nature or society, you must make your choice between the man and the citizen" (Rousseau 2008: 8). If education fails, the young person will be neither in the end. The tutor's advice to Emile shortly before his wedding is that he should live in the countryside, turn into another Socrates telling his fellow-creatures the truth, "cultivating their friendship" and serving as a shining example. If prince or government require his services, Emile should "fulfil the honourable duties of a citizen" in the post assigned to him (ibid. 410–1). This looks like a compromise which tries to overcome the stark opposition, the either-or at the beginning of the book. At heart, Emile has become a kind of Christian and cosmopolitan Stoic who has cultivated his conscience and his humanity (cf. Spaemann 2008: 129–35). This leaves room for the role of citizen, but Emile would avoid what Nicholas Dent calls "maximal identification" with the political community (Dent 2005: 164). Most recent interpretations try to find a compromise between or a dynamic synthesis of "citizen" and "man". Nicholas Dent, for instance, argues that Rousseau favoured the priority approach, the thesis that in case of conflict, concern for one's fellows should take priority (ibid. 164–6; see also Bolle 2012 and Neuhouser 2010). I have argued at the end of section 3 above that it might be claimed that Rousseau endorsed an evolutionary approach and a bottom-up procedure, with civic patriotism as the first and indispensable step in the evolution of a genuine "love of humanity." Civic patriotism and cosmopolitanism, if properly understood and cultivated, could then form a synthesis with the help of education. This interpretation definitely weakens the tension between "man" and "citizen", so pervasive in Rousseau's writings, yet does not solve it, and is at odds with Rousseau's texts. I am going to turn to this problem in the next chapter.

5 Sources of Kant's cosmopolitanism: Basedow, Rousseau, and cosmopolitan education

In the course of his reflections on historical greatness, Rousseau offers the following moral assessment in *Émile*: "Great men are under no illusion with respect to their superiority; they see it and know it, but they are none the less modest" (Rousseau 2007: 195). Their modesty is striking; they are full of knowledge about their own inner selves, also and in particular about their weaknesses. "[A]mong the good things they really possess, they are too wise to pride themselves on a gift which is none of their getting. The good man may be proud of his virtue for it is his own, but what cause for pride has the man of intellect?" (ibid.: 195–6). One can easily see how Kant the intellectual was struck by this passage: the arrogance of the academic is unfounded, for she is proud of something that might not be due to her own effort; perhaps her wit is a natural talent. The morally good person (virtuous in Rousseau's terminology) deserves our respect and admiration, for her moral disposition and her ensuing moral character are the result of her own efforts, of her own endeavours. The old motive of the *vanitas* reappears in a new context. In the Parable of the Pharisee and the Tax Collector, Jesus criticized those "who were confident of their own righteousness and looked down on everyone else" (Luke 18, 9) and concluded that the humble tax collector rather than the proud Pharisee "went home justified before God. For all those who exalt themselves will be humbled, and those who humble themselves will be exalted" (ibid. 18, 14). The new context is academic life. Whenever interpreters deal with the relationship between Rousseau and Kant, the following famous passage is quoted or mentioned. I suppose that the passage from *Émile* quoted above about the vanity of the intellectual and the value of autonomy as self-legislation inspired Kant to the following lines: "I am myself by inclination an investigator. I feel a complete thirst for knowledge and an eager unrest to go further in it as well as satisfaction at every acquisition. There was a time when I believed that this alone could constitute the honour of mankind, and I had contempt for the rabble who knows nothing. Rousseau brought me around. This blinding superiority disappeared, I learned to honour human beings, and I would find myself far more useless than the common labourer if I did not believe that this consideration could impart to all others a value in establishing the rights of humanity" (Notes and fragments, 20: 44). This establishes *in nuce* the primacy of practical reason over theoretical reflection. Vanity is a weakness of character; we find our true vocation (*Bestimmung*) if we develop our predisposi-

proportionately. A one-sided "thirst for knowledge" may lead us down a wrong path, towards the amassment of theoretical knowledge and a continuous strive for quantity rather than quality, that is, moral wisdom. Rousseau's philosophy – this is how Kant read him – aimed at a generic formation of the individual towards an authentic personal identity based on freedom and genuine happiness (*eudaimonia* rather than pleasure), an identity that would include a moral disposition, maturity and striving for *perfectibilité* or perfection. Kant apparently saw *Émile* as one of the key works, providing a perspective that integrated Rousseau's diverse writings (see below). According to Kant, Rousseau understood the difference between conventional education, where the educator is "creator" and "former" of the young person, and formation, where the tutor becomes a "companion" who respects each person's autonomy, identity, and individuality, knowing that morality cannot and should not be forced upon the younger generation. The goal of formation is autonomy. "The chief intention of Rousseau is that education be free and also make a free human being" (Notes and fragments, 20: 167). This highlights the dilemma of "making" a free being: this can only mean guiding, assisting and helping (for a discussion see Cavallar 2005). Kant cherished Rousseau's normative universalism: "Rousseau discovered for the first time beneath the multiplicity of forms human beings have taken on their deeply buried nature and the hidden law by the observation of which providence is justified" (Notes and fragments, 20: 59). This is an explicit rejection of any form of cultural relativism. Like Rousseau, Kant posited an a priori core of moral standards, a formal and universal normative principle; the "hidden law" is of course the categorical imperative. The wider implication of the passage is the following: moral formation (*Bildung*) is about acquiring an enlarged conduct of thought (*Denkungsart*) and a moral comportment of mind or disposition (*Gesinnung*). This moral formation coincides with cosmopolitan formation (this is the argument of chapter 6 below).

To my knowledge the possible influence of Johann Bernhard Basedow and Rousseau on Kant's cosmopolitanism and concept of cosmopolitan education has not yet been analysed. The goal of this chapter is to fill this gap. One of the reasons why I have chosen Basedow is because he is still a widely unknown figure of the Enlightenment educational reform movement, especially outside Germany. Basedow's *Philanthropinum* institute was admired and supported by Kant and who envisaged a form of non-sectarian and non-denominational education with cosmopolitan overtones. I consider Basedow one of the key authors who influenced Kant's concept of cosmopolitan education. I am going to compare Basedow's ideas with those of Kant, and will argue that Kant's encounter with Basedow and the *Philanthropinum* in Dessau helps to understand the development of Kant's concept of cosmopolitanism and educational theory "*in welt-*

bürgerlicher Absicht". Traugott Weisskopf called the 1770ies Kant's "pedagogical decade", when his interest in educational matters was most obvious (Weisskopf 1970: 350). After the publication of the first Critique in 1781, Kant's enthusiasm for the reform movement perhaps diminished, but not his attentiveness to matters of moral education, as sections on the methods of ethics in the works on moral philosophy testify (see the next chapter). Kant's encounter with the *Philanthropismus* is also a unique chapter in his biography, as it was "the only time in his life when he stuck his neck out, albeit briefly, to unequivocally champion a progressive social movement" (Louden 2012: 52).

Rousseau's role is more complex: he clearly influenced Kant; he is usually considered a precursor of modern nationalism and national education; and recent studies have stressed the cosmopolitan dimension of his philosophy (see chapter 4 above). How do nationalism – or rather, civic republicanism – and cosmopolitanism go together? My focus will be on the systematic status of cosmopolitanism within the context of Rousseau's philosophy, its relation to education and its tensions, and on Kant's attempt to make sense of Rousseau's overall philosophy and its cosmopolitan dimension. I claim that the dilemma of education according to Rousseau is that one has to choose between the cosmopolitan education of the *homme* or the patriotic education of the *citoyen*, who considers all foreigners potential enemies, and that there is no way to avoid or go beyond this stark alternative. Kant's reinterpretation of Rousseau is favourable and creative and has found many followers up to the present, but is misleading, as he ignores the dilemma and imposes his own conception of cosmopolitanism, of cosmopolitan education and of (possible) progress in history on Rousseau while claiming that this was actually Rousseau's message.

5.1 Johann Bernhard Basedow: a cosmopolitan-minded educational reformer

Born in Hamburg, Johann Bernhard Basedow (1724–90) studied theology and philosophy at the universities of Leipzig and Kiel and published his first relevant work on education in 1768, the *Vorstellung an Menschenfreunde* (Presentation to Friends of Humanity). Invited by Prince Leopold III Friedrich Franz von Anhalt-Dessau, Basedow opened the experimental school *Philanthropinum* in Dessau in 1774, where he also briefly served as director. Numerous additional publications followed, among them the major *Methodenbuch für Väter und Mütter der Familien und Völker* (1770), *Elementarwerk* (1774) and *Practische Philosophie für alle Stände* (1777; see for the following Overhoff 2004, Louden 2012: 41–3, Laursen 2010 and Munzel 1999: 266–72).

Basedow's educational methods were, by eighteenth-century standards, progressive. Partly influenced by Locke and Rousseau's *Émile*, Basedow aimed at a "profound reform" of school education (Basedow 1965: 12 and 28 f.). His methods included role-playing, teaching foreign languages based on conversations, and less emphasis on coercion and memorizing (cf. Basedow 1965: 112–38). Prospective teachers were not bombarded with lectures, but had a chance to get a taste of teaching with supervised practical training (Overhoff 2004: 212 and 217 f.). German educational scientist Otto Friedrich Bollnow has even claimed that Basedow's didactics amounted to a "Copernican Revolution" analogous to that of Kant in epistemology, as the child's subjective structure of the world, and not traditional ontology, became the starting point of educational efforts (Bollnow 1982: 29–31).

Basedow emphasised moral and religious education in his published writings (cf. Basedow 1965: 86–111 and Meiers 1969). One of the aims of religious instruction was to move beyond denominational boundaries. This was practiced in the *Philanthropinum*, which was open for Protestant, Roman Catholic, Greek Orthodox, Jewish, Mennonite and Muslim children, and the school's curriculum emphasized those elements in their respective monotheistic faiths which united or at least connected them (cf. Laursen 2010: 59–60). Basedow and other representatives of the Philanthropic movement like Christian Fürchtegott Gellert (1715–1769), Joachim Heinrich Campe (1746–1818), Christian Heinrich Wolke (1741–1825) and Johann Andreas Cramer (1723–1788) believed that humans were children of God who should interact with each other in brotherly love. Their pedagogy entailed education for tolerance towards diverse religious sects, denominations, and beliefs. It was in turn rooted in theological convictions (Basedow 1965: 8, 22–4, 41, 139–63, 166, Overhoff 2004: 9, 216 and 219–20 and Meiers 1969: 89). As a consequence, teaching pupils to become tolerant in religious matters became a core element of the Dessau Institute's curriculum, and of Basedow's educational programme (see Overhoff 2004: 219–20 and 2000: 138–41). In the work *Für Cosmopoliten. Etwas zu lesen, zu denken und zu thun* (1775), which Kant quoted and was apparently familiar with, Basedow wanted to limit religious instruction to the core tenets of "natural religion" (Basedow 1775: 22 and 37–40; see also Basedow 1777 vol. 2: 348–53). Cosmopolitan education coincided with education for religious tolerance and natural religion based on moral convictions. During courses on religious instruction, teachers would refrain from judging alleged advantages or disadvantages of religious denominations (ibid.: 38).

Kant was in full agreement with this approach (see 27: 78, Enlightenment, 8: 40, Religion, 6: 115–24, 179–80, Conflict, 7: 52, Overhoff 2000: 133–4). In addition, he liked the fact that these principles were put into practice: "Such an educational institute is now no longer simply a beautiful idea, but appears with visible proofs of the feasibility of that which has long been wished for, with active and visible proofs" (Philanthropinum, 2: 450). Basedow did not plan to work against religious communities at the Dessau Institute. Rather, he wanted to cooperate with priests and religious leaders how to "accustom" the pupils to their respective churches until they were old enough to "judge for themselves" (Basedow 1775: 38). This coincided with Kant's now famous definition of Enlightenment, the capacity and courage to think for oneself (Enlightenment, 8: 35). The goal was having mature citizens capable of "using their own understanding confidently and well *in religious matters*, without another's guidance" (ibid., 8: 40, my emphasis; cf. KdU, 5: 294–5 and Munzel 1999: 223–36).

Cosmopolitans are enlightened private citizens (usually men) who are moderate patriots with an interest in the well-being of all of humanity. Children should be educated to become "true citizens of our world" (Basedow 1776: 15, quoted in Overhoff 2000: 138). According to Basedow, the well-being of the human race was "surely more important" than the thriving of "one's own religious sect" (translated in Laursen 2010: 61). Even in the titles of his books, Basedow used terms like "cosmopolitans" or "friends of humanity (*Menschenfreunde*)" to invoke his philanthropic and non-denominational philosophy. Religious tolerance in Pennsylvania served as a shining example (cf. Overhoff 2004: 117, 120 and 124). Basedow invoked the familiar image of concentric circles: "The human species is [...] more important for me than the fatherland; this is more important for me than my neighbourhood and my family; these are more important for me than I am for myself" (Basedow 1777 vol. 1: 106). The priority of the idea of the human race over fatherland as well as sects implied not only toleration but also ideally impartiality, religious freedom and legal equality in any state (see Overhoff 2004: 116 with references). Co-reformer Cramer propagated religious instruction based on dialogues between teachers and children, relying on the light of reason and avoiding threats, coercion, repetitions, and religious dogma incomprehensible for small children (cf. Overhoff 2004: 132).

Intellectuals of the eighteenth century usually believed that adherence to a weak or thin form of moral or legal cosmopolitanism was compatible with (civic) patriotism or love of one's country (cf. Busch and Horstmann 1976, Busch and Dierse 1985, Cavallar 2011: 11–3, 60–3, 137–8). Basedow was no exception to this rule. He appealed to the "reasonable patriots of the human race and of states" (Basedow 1965: 6; cf. 13), to "private friends of the human race" (ibid.: 7). Love of one's country coincided with moving beyond self-interest and immediate concern with one's family and a willingness to help to reform institutions of the country such as schools (ibid.: 12–3). One of the goals of education was to prepare children to lead "charitable, patriotic and happy lives" (ibid.: 81). As the context suggests, this kind of patriotism had nothing to do with nineteenth-century nationalism or chauvinism.

5.2 Kant's assessment of Basedow's educational theory

The texts where Kant referred to or dealt with the *Philanthropinum* can be divided into four groups, all of which date back to the 1770ies (see Louden 2012: 39–40): the last section of an anthropology transcription (25: 722–28); the two short *Essays regarding the Philanthropin* (2: 445–52); the correspondence with persons associated with the school, such as Basedow and Campe (10: 178–81 or 190–2); and finally the *Lectures on Pedagogy*, published in 1803 but in all likelihood based on a lecture held in the winter semester of 1776–1777, which in turn used Basedow's *Methodenbuch* as coursebook. The source and authenticity of these lectures have been questioned, especially by Weisskopf; however, it does make sense to see them as a reliable source (cf. Weisskopf 1970: 239–350 and Louden 2000: 33–61).

Reactions to the *Philanthropismus*, the reform movement with Basedow as its most prominent representative, were diverse. Conservative authors were inclined to reject it, among them Georg Schlosser or Justus Möser, whereas early liberals, neologians or Enlightenment intellectuals usually endorsed its educational principles. Kant himself joined the camp of the supporters (cf. Louden 2012: 51–2, Weisskopf 1970: 60–2, Overhoff 2004: 212f. and 218; on Basedow's influence on Kant see Weisskopf 1970, Overhoff 2000, Munzel 1999: 266–74 and Louden 2012).

Kant appreciated Basedow's emphasis on moral education and his developmental approach, namely the conviction that one has to be attentive to age-appropriate methods, especially in religious instruction (cf. 25: 723 and 728). Kant also shared Basedow's – and Rousseau's – belief that education should not work against, but "wisely" follow "nature" (Philanthropinum, 2: 449). It was essential that a "plan of an education" was designed (LP, 9: 445) instead of implementing small changes. Schools are "defective in their original organization, and even the teachers must acquire a new formation (*Bildung*). Not a slow *reform*, but a swift *revolution* can bring this about" (Philanthropinum, 2: 449). Education has to become a science (LP, 9: 447), which for Kant implies a systematic plan including the concept of our vocation (*Bestimmung*; 9: 445–6). This scientific approach has a moral/philosophical, but also an empirical side. Experiments are needed to find out which educational methods really work, and here the Dessau Institute is the shining example (LP, 9: 451 and Louden 2012: 49).

Other points of convergence have already been mentioned: the emphasis on a non-denominational religious ethos, on morality rather than theological dogma, on moral formation rather than *Schulwissenschaft* or theoretical learning (cf. 10: 125 and 221, Weisskopf 1970: 67, 121, 128–30, Overhoff 2004: 219 and Munzel 1999: 267, 271 and 273). Kant's interest in a proper religious instruction, and his conviction that the *Philanthropin* met his expectations, are evident in the letters on behalf of his friend Robert Motherby, whose six-year-old son George became a pupil at the school (cf. 10: 179, 191f., LP, 9: 450, Weisskopf 1970: 64–8, Overhoff 2000: 142 and Louden 2012: 46–7).

I suppose a final reason why Kant appreciated Basedow's reform were the implied political implications. The *Philanthropismus* can be interpreted as a fine example of the process of Enlightenment, the work of a community of like-minded private persons who shared a set of common goals. They were the kind of public or "world of readers" trying to enlighten each other and promoting "the welfare of humanity" (Philanthropinum, 2: 450) under conditions of tolerance and relative political freedom, especially the freedom of expression described in Kant's political essays (see especially Enlightenment, 8: 36–40). As Robert Louden put it, "what existed for a brief period during the Enlightenment was an enviable level of international consensus on, and commitment to, making a moral world – a new force in history that has yet to be matched" (Louden 2007: 223). Educational reforms were part and parcel of this overall effort of intellectuals to contribute to a world that, from a moral perspective, was supposed to be markedly different from previous centuries. Another interesting aspect is that these reformers were not simply tolerated by the authorities; sometimes they were actively encouraged in their work, for instance, by the Danish government (cf. Overhoff 2004: 10–3, 16, 133, 140 and 222). It is understandable that Kant displayed an initial enthusiasm in a lecture in the 1770ies about the "present Basedowian institutes" as "the greatest phenomenon which has appeared in this century for the improvement of the perfection of humanity" (25: 722). Cooperation between authorities and enlightened reformers seemed to run smoothly in many cases.

"Cosmopolitan" was the umbrella term for these innovative practices. For Kant, the Institute was "dedicated to humanity and therefore to the participation of every cosmopolitan", since it promoted and cultivated "the greatest possible, most permanent and universal good" (Philanthropinum, 2: 451). This is a rather vague reference to what Kant elaborated as the concept of the highest good, the coincidence of virtue and happiness, with the latter "distributed in exact proportion to morality", and an idea of pure practical reason aiming at "unconditioned totality" (KpV, 5: 107–113). The concept encompasses three levels: The foundation of a cosmopolitan condition of perpetual peace, a global legal society of peaceful states, perhaps a world republic is the highest *political* good and coincides with political cosmopolitanism. The establishment of a global ethical community is – secondly – the highest *moral* good in this world (the dimension of moral cosmopolitanism). Finally, the highest good proper coincides with the transcendent kingdom of God, the intelligible world, the kingdom of Heaven or a moral realm (see chapter 2). A cosmopolitan theory revolving around the concept of the highest good cannot be found in Basedow; Kant apparently read his own moral teleology (dedication to humanity, promoting the highest good) into the *Philanthropin* movement.

Moral cosmopolitanism is stressed in moral education or formation, for instance in the *Lectures on pedagogy*, where Kant claims that the young student should be helped to cultivate "philanthropy towards others and then also cosmopolitan dispositions", which entails "an interest in the best for the world" (LP, 9: 499). I read this as a shorthand of the concept of the highest political and moral good. The individual has social duties: "While making oneself a fixed center of one's principles, one ought to regard this circle drawn around one as also forming part of an all-inclusive circle of those who, in their disposition, are citizens of the world" (MS, 6: 473). In this quotation, Kant picks up the ancient Stoic notion of concentric circles, with the most encompassing of all circles being that of the human race (cf. LP, 9: 499). I did not find any passages in Basedow where he would spell out this Stoic notion. It seems that Kant wanted to see in Basedow's innovative practices a background philosophy that he himself also shared.

In a manner that is more radical than Basedow's, Kant rejected moral formation exclusively based on theology. Kant endorsed a non-denominational moral religion, and his moral cosmopolitanism culminates in the Christian idea of "a visible Kingdom of God on earth" (Religion, 6: 134). However, Kant rejected what he considered the traditional hierarchical relationship between morality and religion. Religious education has to start with the moral law within humans, that is, the categorical imperative: "one must not begin with theology. A religion which is founded merely on theology can never contain anything moral", as it would lead to instrumental conditioning on the side of the educators, with threats of punishments and rewards, "resulting merely in a superstitious cult" (LP, 9: 494). Kant hoped that ecclesiastical faiths all over the world would gradually reform themselves towards the ideal of a pure rational faith revolving around a good will, good dispositions, virtue, and promoting the highest good (Religion, 6: 105f. and 178–85 and Wood 1970: 195–6). Kant disliked "sectarian squabbles" (Wood 1970: 197–8), and as a protestant, he deliberately provoked his predominantly protestant readership with the remark that there were "protestant catholics" in Europe, that is, people "whose frame of mind [...] is given to *self-expansion*" and even more "offensive examples of arch-catholic protestants", namely those which were narrow-minded (Religion, 6: 109). The hallmark of a cosmopolitan frame of mind is the extended or enlarged way of thinking beyond the narrow confines of one's own religious denomination (see chapters 6 and 7 below).

As I have tried to show, Basedow also attempted to move beyond denominational boundaries. The outlines of Kant's religious "project" just mentioned can thus be found in Basedow's writings. However, Basedow was clearly less radical than Kant in terms of the relationship between religion and morality. He believed that virtue was in need of religion and theology, claimed that humans could only be motivated by external incentives, and that "reverence for the Lord" should therefore be part and parcel of moral education (Basedow 1965: 119; "reverence" is a translation of *Furcht* (fear), which is close to *Ehrfurcht* in religious matters; cf. Overhoff 2004: 112–4 and 219). In this crucial respect and unlike Rousseau, Basedow remained rooted in a traditional (pre-Kantian) understanding of the relationship between religion and morality. For Basedow, morality could not be independent from religion, free-standing or autonomous in a Kantian sense. As a consequence, moral – and by implication, cosmopolitan – education had to be rooted in religious instruction, and required the support of various religious communities.

Finally and most importantly, Kant accused Basedow of "syncretism", the attempt "to develop contradictory doctrines as if they were in agreement" (27: 78), and his own systematic philosophy is very different from the sometimes repetitious work of Basedow (see for instance Basedow 1965: 253–4 and Louden 2012: 43). The main differences can be summarized as follows.

First of all, unlike Basedow's theory, Kant's cosmopolitan education is embedded in a comprehensive political theory, a philosophy of history and a philosophy of religion. Basedow's reform had political implications and repercussions, but he himself did not have a political agenda. Kant's educational theory, by contrast, was part and parcel of a system of cosmopolitan ideas with anthropological, political, moral and religious dimensions. From his own cosmopolitan perspective, Kant could interpret the *Philanthropismus* as a reform movement corresponding with the normative tenets of moral and political cosmopolitanism. This was a conscious reconstruction of a historical phenomenon *in weltbürgerlicher Absicht:* a reform movement was perceived as an important step in the endeavour of the human species to reach its own vocation.

Secondly, pinpointing the species' vocation required a practical anthropology, a moral teleology, a philosophy of history and a philosophy of religion. The details of these doctrines are beyond the scope of this essay. However, let me emphasize that Kant strongly believed in a "cosmopolitan predisposition (*cosmopo-*

litische Anlage) in the human species" (Anthropology, marginal note 7: 412) destined to develop in the course of history (for a full analysis see Louden 2013). There are many "germs (*Keime*)" and "predispositions (*Anlagen*)" in the human species, and our task is threefold: we have to understand what exactly they are (only animals "fulfill their vocation automatically and unknowingly"; LP, 9: 445). Secondly, we have to act, that is, "develop the natural dispositions proportionally and to unfold humanity from its germs" (ibid.). Finally – and this is another aspect that cannot be found in Basedow -, humans have to be attentive to methods and favourable environmental factors. They have to create appropriate and suitable external, especially political conditions to achieve their moral goal. The most important one is a rightful civil constitution, which is supposed to reform itself towards the republican form of government (cf. Idea 8: 22, MM 6: 321–2, Conflict 7: 89–90 and 93). A rightful civil constitution is essential since it makes possible civil freedom, including freedom of religion, triggers the process of Enlightenment (cf. Idea, 8: 27–8, 27: 234) and prepares the ground for proper moral and cosmopolitan education. This is the case because in a republic, citizens learn how to use their external freedom in a way consistent with that of all the others, and this in turn is a precondition for learning how to apply the categorical imperative and develop one's moral potential (see chapter 7 for a comprehensive analysis). Kant goes a step further and claims that "a universal *cosmopolitan condition*", that is, a global juridical condition approaching the ideal of a world federation is "the womb in which all original predispositions of the human species will be developed" (Idea 8: 28). This claim is rooted in Kant's conviction that wars and the condition of international anarchy (equivalent to Hobbes' state of nature among states) are the main obstacle that prevent the ordered, peaceful and systematic development of societies and thus of their members' moral *Anlagen*.

Finally, there is what Robert Louden calls Kant's postulate of "species perfectionism" (Louden 2000: 37), the conviction that the proper objective of formation is not only cultivating the individual's skilfulness, prudence and morality. Rather, it is the perfection, that is, the complete and proportionate development of all predispositions, of the whole human race. The explanation is a very simple one: as reason is not an instinct, but a capacity that "needs attempts, practice and instruction in order to gradually progress from one stage of insight to another" (Idea, 8: 19), and since the lifespan of each individual is limited, each generation depends on the work already done by previous ones (see also Idea, 8: 23 note; Beginning, 8: 115, LP 9: 445). Along these lines, for instance, Kant might have shared the belief that each culture (like Medieval or Renaissance European culture) depends on previous ones (like Ancient Greek and Roman cultures).

These are the main differences between Basedow and Kant. The latter's comprehensive and systematic philosophy as the background of his educational theory is no doubt open to various criticisms, but it would make no sense to accuse Kant of syncretism. Kant's philosophy may fail as a systematic whole, but there is no denying that he was aiming at just that. A similar attempt cannot be found in Basedow's writings, and this is the point where Kant clearly departed from Basedow.

5.3 Rousseau: The split between cosmopolitan *homme* and patriotic *citoyen*

The relationship of Kant and Rousseau has been the topic of scholarly debate for a long time, and agreement has been rare (see Cassirer 1939, Dieterich 2009, Gebhardt 2012, Knippenberg 1989, Peltre 1999, Quadrio 2009, Reich 1936, Schalowski 2010, Williams 2009, Zöller 2011). An analysis of this relationship requires a systematic approach, a comprehensive interpretation of both philosophies, as cosmopolitanism is an embedded issue within broader philosophical topics such as the tensions between natural morality and civilization, the individual and society, and the vocation of the human species. In this section, I focus on one key aspect of Rousseau's cosmopolitan education, namely the tension in his writings between patriotic *citoyen* and cosmopolitan-minded *homme*.

There are divergent interpretations of Rousseau's philosophy, but most commentators agree that there are tensions between communitarian and individualistic, patriotic and cosmopolitan, political and moral elements (for an introduction see Forschner 2010). At the beginning of *Émile*, Rousseau put these tensions into the following words: "Forced to combat either nature or society, you must make your choice between the man and the citizen" (Rousseau 2007: 8). If education fails, the young person will be neither in the end. When Emile's education is finished, he has turned into a moral cosmopolitan, into a stoic Christian who lives the universal religion of the heart, who is free and will "be free in any part of the world" (ibid. 409). He has opted for the cosmopolitan-minded *homme* at the expense of the patriotic *citoyen*. This is the dilemma of education according to Rousseau: there is no alternative to this stark either-or.

Interpretations of Rousseau's philosophy can roughly be divided into two camps. The first and larger group claims that Rousseau actually attempted to solve the dilemma mentioned above and offered a synthesis. Some, more cautious representatives of this group assert that Rousseau himself did not offer this solution, but that his writings can be reconstructed in such a way. According to some of these interpreters, Rousseau tried to show that civic patriotism was compatible with genuine moral cosmopolitanism as well as republican cosmopolitanism (the compatibility thesis). Recent representatives of this first group are Rainer Bolle, Mark S. Cladis, Nicholas Dent, Nils Ehlers, Frederick Neuhouser, Michaela Rehm, and Kenneth Wain. This leaves room for the role of citizen, but Emile would avoid what Nicholas Dent calls "maximal identification" with the political community. According to this approach, Rousseau favoured the priority approach, the thesis that in case of conflict, concern for one's fellows should take priority. The interpretation definitely weakens the tension between "man" and "citizen", so pervasive in Rousseau's writings (Dent 2005: 164–6). Along these lines, Nils Ehlers sees the solution in the concept of the "new bourgeois", who manages to combine the desire to individual self-fulfilment with the duties of the citizen towards society (Ehlers 2004: 105). According to Michaela Rehm, Rousseau's notion of civil religion is an attempt to unite the religion of the citizen with that of the human being (Rehm 2006: 145–7). Other authors have tried to offer related solutions (cf. Bolle 2012, Cladis 2007 and Neuhouser 2008). For various reasons, interpretations of this sort are not completely convincing (see below). At any rate, the first group has a famous founding father: Kant. In two key passages, Kant claims that Rousseau's writings should be divided into two groups, those which offer a diagnosis of human and social ills and those which present a remedy (see below). The link connecting both is moral and political education (I label this the synthesis-through-education approach). In a chapter on the relationship between Rousseau and Kant, it is tempting to follow this tradition and claim that Kant understood Rousseau's philosophy better than Rousseau himself, that Rousseau offered the sketch of a philosophical system that was complemented by Kant, in a word, that Kant was the *Vollender* of Rousseau (see for instance Cassirer 1939: 34 and 59–60, Dent 2005: 218–222, and Gebhardt 2012: 19 and 29–30).

However, I believe that this interpretation (which is both Kant's and fairly common among Kantians) is mistaken, simply because it lacks textual evidence. I side with the second group of interpreters, notably with Robert Spaemann: the moral cosmopolitanism of Rousseau, rooted in Christianity, is different from, and incompatible with, the republican patriotism of Rousseau's political writings, inspired by classical antiquity. This implies that there is no "solution" or "synthesis", and that Rousseau was fully aware of it. The "solution" is resignation, the isolated life of a morally free Emile who is nowhere at home and winds up as a slave, as described in the fragment "Les Solitaires". At heart, Emile has become a kind of Christian and cosmopolitan Stoic who has cultivated his conscience and his humanity and has abandoned the collective egoism of and identification with the ancient city-state. If at all, he has a country (*pay*), but definitely not a fatherland (*patrie*). The solitaire is an outsider, but he is in agreement with his own (moral) self, thus finding his identity (Spaemann 2008: 19–46, 129–35; see also Wain 2011: 31 and 44–8).

A careful reading of *Émile* shows that this is a book about the formation of a moral and cognitive cosmopolitan, who avoids the deformations of a commercial society influenced by processes of globalisation. This form of rooted moral cosmopolitanism is logically consistent with republican patriotism and republican cosmopolitanism as envisioned by Rousseau (it is of course incompatible with modern nationalism and chauvinism). This logical consistency should not lead to the interpretation that Rousseau actually saw them as compatible, or even proposed a bottom-up procedure where one (moderate republican patriotism) leads to the other (moral cosmopolitanism), made possible by educational means (see the previous chapter for an extended version of this argument).

Even if embedded moral cosmopolitanism is logically consistent with republican patriotism and republican cosmopolitanism as defined by Rousseau, he never argued in favour of their compatibility in his published writings. He also never proposed a coherent educational programme with republican patriotism as a means to further the ends of moral cosmopolitanism. Rather, Rousseau apparently never went beyond the central dilemma – either education of the stoic, Christian individualist or education of the republican patriot -, nowhere offered a solution, and in all likelihood believed that a solution was impossible, given the paradigms of the modern world. Rousseau has repeatedly argued that once *amour de soi* has perverted into selfish *amour propre*, the education of humans to become either republican citizens or moral cosmopolitans has become impossible. This is the gist of the three discourses (see Dent 2005: 49–80 for references).

Rousseau also offers an explanation of this inevitable dilemma: the rise of Christianity in history as an inner, moral and cosmopolitan religion of individual identity and of the heart, which is incompatible with the collectivism of the true republic that requires a substantial community of life with no clear distinction between private and public, intimacy and transparency (Herb 2012: 97–100). In the *Social Contract*, he juxtaposes Christianity, "this saintly, sublime, genuine Religion" (Rousseau 1997f: 147) with the political religion of the Greeks and Romans. As a politician, Rousseau deplores the fact that Christians cannot create the social unity and cohesion that is required of a republic, since Christianity, "far from attaching the Citizens' hearts to the State, [...] detaches them from it as from all earthly things. I know of nothing more contrary to the social spirit" (ibid. 147). Christians make bad soldiers and they are the born slaves since they do not care about earthly matters (see ibid. 148–9). As a moral philosopher, Rousseau appreciates Christianity as true and authentic, as "the Religion of man" (ibid. 147) which spread "the healthy ideas of natural right and of the common brotherhood [*fraternité*] of all men" (Rousseau 1997c: 158). Again, this moral cosmopolitanism of Christianity is incompatible with the city-state centered patriotism of the ancients. In a letter to Usteri (18 July 1763), Rousseau therefore concludes that a vigorous civil society peopled by true Christians is a contradictory idea; but Christianity is "favourable" to the traditional idea of the *societas humani generis*, the "great Society" based on "humanity, on universal beneficience" (Rousseau 1997: 266). Poland is an exception simply because the country is still close enough to the spirit of the ancients, their "vigour of soul", their "patriotic zeal" and the "esteem for the truly personal qualities" (Rousseau 1997d: 192; cf. ibid. 182, 185, 218, 233 and 242). Rousseau's pessimism was rooted in his all-or-nothing understanding of Christianity, individualism, republicanism, and patriotism, and his conviction that there was no way out of the impasse presented above. It was a pessimism that Kant clearly did not share.

5.4 Reinterpreting Rousseau: dynamic moral cosmopolitanism

There are several positive statements by Kant on Rousseau, and Kant explicitly asserted that Rousseau's influence had been profound. The most famous statement comes from a marginal note, written in the 1760ies which was quoted at the beginning of this chapter. The passage highlights the influence of Rousseau's writings on Kant's own moral disposition (*Gesinnung*), and is a rare example where Kant expressed his inner thoughts. The key terms are "the honour of mankind" and "the rights of humanity", which will be discussed below. Thirst for knowledge belongs to culture, not to the stage of moralization which is the final end of our existence and our moral vocation.

In his "Essay on the maladies of the head" (1767), after having defined enthusiasm as a disposition without which "nothing great has ever been accomplished in the world" (2: 267), Kant praised Rousseau as one of those enthusiasts who are ridiculed by many, but have to be distinguished from fanatics. The idealists are moral enthusiasts who promote the highest good. Together with the Abbé de Saint-Pierre, Rousseau is mentioned as propagating the juridical and indispensable idea of a peaceful "federation of nations" to overcome interstate anarchy (Idea, 8: 24), thus advancing the highest political good. Kant also often agreed with Rousseau in terms of education, and he also acknowledged that (see for instance LP, 9: 456, 461 and 469). Weisskopf has documented the direct influence of Rousseau on Kant's lecture on education (Weisskopf 1970: 168–9, 287–313 and 349; see also Louden 2011: 140, 144–5 and Moran 2012: 138–42).

Many Enlightenment intellectuals believed that the improvement or reform of external institutions would eventually lead to internal moral development (cf. Louden 2007: 128, 150 and 208). Kant also cherished this hope, but was more sober in his assessment of chances of success, perhaps under the influence of Rousseau, who famously claimed that cultural progress might even *undermine* morality. Kant partly agreed with Rousseau in this respect, emphasising the ills and self-imposed miseries humans who live in commercial societies are confronted with (cf. Idea, 8: 26, Beginning, 8: 120–3). However, occasionally Kant also explicitly criticized Rousseau, for instance, when he denied that "savage nations" love freedom "as Rousseau and others believe", but rather have not yet begun to develop "humanity' (*die Menschheit*)" as the intelligible, moral element in humans or rational beings (LP, 9: 442).

I have argued above that the tensions between cosmopolitan *homme* and patriotic *citoyen* are "not convincingly solved" by Rousseau himself, or rather more aptly, that Rousseau probably *never intended* to solve them, because he believed that they could not be solved in principle. Kant did offer a solution, and he claimed that it could be found in Rousseau's writings. In an attempt to smooth Rousseau's tensions, Kant presented a favourable reinterpretation and a cosmopolitan history of progress instead of a history of decline. The two key passages are in the "Idea toward a Universal History with a Cosmopolitan Aim" and in the Anthropology lectures, which are coextensive and which I will therefore analyse together (cf. Beginning, 8: 116–8 and Anthropology, 7: 326–7; see also 15: 890).

Kant's first hermeneutical move was to distinguish between Rousseau's diagnosis and the remedy he had offered. Along these lines, Kant divided Rousseau's writings into two groups: the first one, including especially the first two discourses, described "the unavoidable conflict of culture with the nature of the human species" which hampers our duty to reach our vocation (Beginning, 8: 116). Historical developments caused three deformations: culture "weakened our strength", civilization led to "inequality and mutual oppression", and "presumed moralization" did not lead to moral progress but to "unnatural education and the deformation of our way of thinking" (Anthropology, 7: 326). For Kant, Rousseau's diagnosis is a correct analysis of our situation and thus justified, even though the portrayal might be somewhat "hypochondriac (ill-humored)" (ibid.).

The second group of writings are those where, according to Kant, Rousseau offered a solution, especially in the *Social Contract* and *Émile*. It is important to note that Kant glossed over the tensions between these two books outlined above; they are seen as part of one coherent theory. In one passage, Kant referred to the "true principles *of education* of human being and citizen" (Beginning, 8: 116), suggesting that these two goals are complementary rather than incompatible. The first task of the human species is to look back at the state of nature with the help of Rousseau (and not to "return to nature", a phrase that can actually not be found in Rousseau's writings). The second task is to spot the key problem, namely the gulf that existed between cultivation, civilization and moralization. This also includes a sober assessment of our nature, which is "good in a negative way" (Anthropology, 7: 327), that is, only includes morally good predispositions (*Anlagen*), but which also includes a radical propensity of our will to evil (the claim defended extensively in the first part of *Religion Within the Boundaries of Mere Reason*), or, the words of the *Anthropology*, entails "(innate or acquired) corruption" (ibid.; see also Beginning, 8: 115 and Idea, 8: 26). Third, humans should become aware of their vocation, namely "to develop the predispositions of humanity" (Beginning, 8: 116), which again should be understood as the intelligible, moral element in humans or rational beings. Finally, humans should realize that this goal can only be accomplished with the help of moral education – an almost impossible task, since the educators themselves are prone to the same moral corruption as all other members of the human species (Anthropology, 7: 327). Kant's optimism concerning this Herculean task is expressed in a footnote: "That there is a cosmopolitan predisposition in the human species, even with all the wars, which gradually in the course of political matters wins the upper hand over the selfish predispositions of peoples" (ibid.: 326 note). It is an optimism that can rarely be found in Rousseau's writings.

In the next paragraphs, I am going to comment on the central concepts prevalent in Kant's interpretation of Rousseau's philosophy: culture, civilization (and the corresponding terms skilfulness and prudence) and moralization; the transition from the former two to the latter; education or formation; the vocation (*Bestimmung*) of the human species and its main obstacle, radical evil. Kant abandoned Rousseau's philosophy of history revolving around decline and decadence and replaced it with a philosophy of history *in weltbürgerlicher Absicht*. Kant's cosmopolitanism is dynamic, with the notion of the final vocation (*Bestimmung*) of the human species as its cornerstone. The human species has the moral task to realize its vocation, the establishment of a cosmopolitan society.

In his *Lectures on pedagogy*, Kant distinguished among three kinds of formation or *Bildung*. The education of skilfulness and of prudence cultivates acting on hypothetical imperatives, which have the form "If you want x, then you should do y". The action is good "merely as a means *to something else*" (Groundwork, 4: 414). The child cultivates imperatives of skilfulness (*Geschicklichkeit*) to attain certain ends and prudence (*Klugheit*), learning how to use other people for her own ends and thus also learning how to fit into civil society (LP, 9: 455; Koch 2003: 17, Moran 2009: 475–9). The result is legality, not morality of disposition. The third form of practical education is moral education based on the categorical imperative, "by which the human being is to be formed so that he can live as a freely acting being". It coincides with cosmopolitan education, since "through *moral* formation" the human being "receives value in view of the entire human race" (LP, 9: 455). Eckart Förster has pointed out that *Bildung* – together with history and *Entwicklung* – was one of the new concepts of Enlightenment philosophy. According to the new, no longer purely theological concept of formation, humans manage to reach a stage in their development when "they form *themselves* a picture of what they want to achieve" (Förster 2009: 189), thus becoming both objects and subjects of formation.

Especially the *Critique of the Power of Judgement* (1790) highlights a key problem of Kant's philosophies of history and religion, namely the transition from culture or civilization (revolving around skilfulness and prudence) to moralization (cf. 5: 425–45; see Höffe 2008, Rorty and Schmidt 2009). In the Starke manuscript of 1790–91, Kant explains: "The most difficult condition of the human race is the crossing-over [*Übergang*] from civilization to moralization ... [O]ne must try to enlighten human beings and to better establish international law ... We are now, those of us who are working on the unity of religion, on the step of this crossing-over from civilization to moralization. Inner religion stands in now for the position of legal constraint. In order to reach the great end, one can either go from the parts to the whole, that is to say, through education, or from the whole to the parts" (translated in Louden 2000: 42). According to this passage, Kant envisions several methods to promote moralization (since morality is the result of freedom, it can only be fostered, nurtured or helped indirectly): education (with Enlightenment as one element), politics based on the idea of right, and religion. "Inner religion" coincides with Kant's version of moral religion with its emphasis on morality, pure rational faith, and duties towards others rather than statutes, dogmas, statutory laws and observances, and it is very close to Basedow's and Rousseau's understanding (Religion, 6: 167; on Kant's philosophy of religion see Firestone and Palmquist 2006, Fischer and Forschner 2010, Höffe 2011; see Cassirer 1939: 44–55 on the relationship to Rousseau's religious faith; and Louden 2007: 16–25 on the Enlightenment context).

The *Bestimmung* (destiny, vocation) of each individual as well as of the whole human race is, together with the doctrine of the highest good, the core of Kant's critical practical philosophy (cf. Brandt 2009, Geismann 2009, Kater 1999: 166–70, Louden 2000: 37, 53–4 and 101). The *Bestimmung* of humans is *Selbstbestimmung* or autonomy, moral freedom (cf. KrV, A 464, Groundwork, 4: 396, KdU, 5: 434–6, Anthropology, 7: 325; Brandt 2009: 15–7, 19). Our "moral vocation" is "the ultimate end (*letzter Zweck*) of our existence" (KdU 5: 431 and 435). Picking up elements of Stoic and Christian metaphysics, Enlightenment theologians and philosophers such as Johann Joachim Spalding revived the debate about human vocation after 1750. Like some authors before him, Kant moved from the focus on individuals to the species as a whole and its history and future; this is one key aspect of his dynamic cosmopolitanism (see Cavallar 2016 for more).

The *Religion* explicitly states that the main obstacle of virtue and moral progress is an internal opponent, namely the will's tendency to subordinate the incentives stimulating morality or the rational commands of duty to the incentives of self-love (cf. Religion, 6: 32–9). Radical evil is not simply the corollary of our freedom and capacity for choice. It is the conscious and deliberate subordination of the moral law under a disposition (*Gesinnung*) that gives the "subjective principle of self-love" priority (Religion, 6: 36). This way, the human being "reverses the moral order of his incentives in incorporating them into his maxims" (Religion, 6: 36): the maxim of self-love comes first, and moral maxims have to take a back seat. Evil is thus an act of freedom based on an evil disposition and therefore radical, rooted in the very structure of our volition (for an introduction see Louden 2011: 107–20). As evil cannot be eradicated, the problem of moral education remains the most difficult task the human race has to face. The problem of evil exacerbates the problem of education, and thus also the social task of promoting an ethical commonwealth, an ideal community promoted by humans who are in the process of cultivating their moral predispositions to promote the highest moral good. Moral formation is supposed to contribute to the promotion of this ethical commonwealth (In Kant's theory of the division of labour between God and humans, it is God's task to guarantee the *realization* of the highest good as happiness *proportioned to* virtue). Kant appreciated Rousseau's acute awareness of the moral deficiencies of the cultivated and civilized Europeans of their times: "everything good that is not grafted onto a morally good disposition is nothing but mere semblance and glittering misery". In a way, Kant mused, Rousseau was right when he preferred the lives of savages over the "glittering misery" of civilized nations (Idea, 8: 26).

The differences between Rousseau and Kant are considerable, and can be summarized as follows. In contrast to most philosophies developed before him, Rousseau's concept of nature and human nature is non-teleological (cf. Spaemann 2008: 17, 119–21, 138–9). Human development is no longer seen as a necessary progress from imperfect to perfect. Kant, by contrast, returns to a teleological interpretation of nature and history, especially in the third *Critique*. He distinguishes among three types of teleology (see Principles, 8: 179–83): natural teleology, the teleology of freedom, and finally a teleology of nature with respect to the final purpose of freedom, "a doctrine of pure ends" (ibid., 8: 182). It purports to be a critical teleology: the idea of purposiveness is not a constitutive principle, only a "heuristic" and regulative principle that does not establish knowledge of objects (KdU, 5:

379, 404, 411, 457–8, cf. Höffe 2008: 211–222, 259–74 and 289–308). Kant's philosophy of history, developed since the "Idea for a universal history with a cosmopolitan aim" (1784), looks at historical and political phenomena from a "*cosmopolitan* perspective", which means "a view to the well-being of the *human race* as a whole and insofar as it is conceived as progressing toward its well-being in the series of generations of all future times" (Theory and Practice, 8: 277; cf. 8: 307, 15: 517 and Geismann 2009: 94). Kant praised Basedow and Rousseau, who presumably had been concerned about the well-being of the entire human race, from this cosmopolitan perspective.

A second difference is Rousseau's ensuing pessimistic philosophy of history, which was deeply entrenched and culminated in a theory of decadence, formulated especially in the three *Discourses* (see the end of the previous chapter). Kant, by contrast, offered a critical philosophy of moral hope: hope that our moral predispositions would eventually unfold (Anthropology, 7: 333), hope that humans would learn from past mistakes (Beginning, 8: 123, TP, 8: 313), hope that Enlightened reformers like Basedow and Rousseau would make a difference, hope in "education from above" (Anthropology, 7: 328), that is, hope in a benign divine providence (Idea, 8: 30, Beginning, 8: 121), hope in "discipline by religion" (7: 333 note). Kantian hope encompasses various dimensions, according to Robert Louden (cf. Louden 2007: 216–23). One element are signs like the French Revolution or the founding of schools like the Philanthropinum, another one is moral hope in improvable human capacities as well as in divine assistance, that combined human efforts will not be in vain, but complemented and assisted by a benign nature and divine providence. All these strategies are also employed to fight off resignation and despair, so dominant in many of Rousseau's writings. These attitudes must be avoided at all cost, because a pessimistic outlook on the future of the human race may lead to "moral corruption" and inactivity (Beginning, 8: 120–1).

The methods or means of improvement are threefold: political or legal/juridical education, moral education, and religious instruction. The education of citizens (the legal sphere) and of human beings (the moral sphere) are not mutually exclusive. In fact, Kant claims that the first is a precondition of the second. Kant hints at this theory when he remarks that "the good moral education of a people is to be expected from a good state constitution" (Peace, 8: 366). This constitution is indentical with the republican one. One of its benefits is that, since it is based on juridical freedom, equality, the rule of law, the separation of political powers, and legitimate coercion, it constrains each member "to become a good citizen even if not a morally good human being" (ibid.). However, Kant hopes that eventually morality might follow from juridical legality, the willingness to obey laws without genuine moral disposition. In a republic, citizens may become capable of self-legislation, may cultivate their power of reflective judgement, and train their enlarged mode of thinking or *Denkungsart* – capacities indispensable for both moral and political lives in a Kantian sense (for a full analysis see chapter 7). This is an aspect of the synthesis-through-education approach: political and moral education form a coherent whole, the first type being the precondition of the second. As I have argued, this approach is often ascribed to Rousseau in the secondary literature, but was in all likelihood not adopted by Rousseau himself.

Perhaps Kant *wanted* to find this developmental, dynamic or evolutionary bottom-up approach in Rousseau. This is at least suggested by his phrasing, when he refers to education "of human being *and* citizen" (Beginning, 8: 116, my emphasis), implying that both forms of education cannot be separated from each other, let alone stand in contradiction. Like Basedow and many other Enlightenment intellectuals, but in contrast to Rousseau, Kant believed that moral as well as legal cosmopolitanism and moderate forms of patriotism – especially republican patriotism revolving around political self-legislation – were compatible with each other (Kleingeld 2006 and 2012: 19–34, Knippenberg 1989: 820–1; see also Koch 2003: 357–74). At any rate, many Rousseau interpreters claim that Rousseau followed this developmental approach, going from the inner circle of the self to more inclusive circles, from civic virtue to morality (see for instance Dent 2005: 161–6). However, as pointed out above, this interpretation may be nothing more than wishful thinking.

Rousseau and Kant do not only differ in their approaches to teleology and their respective philosophies of history. A third disagreement relates to the role of Christianity. Whereas Rousseau characterized the Christian religion as unearthly, sublime and "contrary to the social spirit", Kant depicted it as prone to becoming too earthly, too involved in power politics and open to abuse, deviating from the path of pure morality and moral faith (cf. Religion, 6: 130–1). What we get in Rousseau is absent in Kant: a binary juxtaposition of the Christian religion (individualist, unearthly, moral, potentially cosmopolitan) with Ancient republican state religion (collectivist, earthly, state-centered, uncosmopolitan). The consequences of these differences are far-reaching. To put it bluntly, Rousseau the politician cannot accept Christianity; as a moral cosmopolitan, he cannot accept politics (modeled around the Ancient ideal). The result is despair. Kant, by contrast, can accept both Christianity as a moral, inner and cosmopolitan religion in theory (the teachings of Christ, cf. Religion, 6: 131–2, 157–67, End, 8: 338–9, Conflict, 7: 44–5) *and* politics as primarily focused on another dimension, namely that of juridical relations, the *external* actions and behaviour of (prospective world) citizens.

Finally, there are key differences concerning moral education (for succinct discussions see Reisert 2012 and Scuderi 2012). Both Rousseau and Kant see the inner core of reason as the standard of morality and the "laws of nature", and both move beyond a mere "instrumental social morality" (Reisert 2012: 16). However, they differ in terms of public and private education, the role of society, and educational programmes in general. Rousseau juxtaposes domestic and public education (which mirrors and is rooted in the contrast between *homme* and *citoyen*). This binary thinking is absent in Kant. He held that even state education funded by the princes, but put into practice by "enlightened experts" like Basedow, could and should teach elements of (moral) cosmopolitanism (cf. LP, 9: 448–9). Rousseau was wary of society in general, since it makes people evil (cf. Rousseau 2007: 186–8). Kant, by contrast, offered a more nuanced assessment. To be sure, radical evil ("radical" since it is rooted in the will of the agent and not her inclinations or habits) has a social dimension. As Kant puts it, as soon as humans have contact with each other, "they will mutually corrupt each other's moral disposition and make one another evil" (Religion, 6: 94). However, Kant does not diminish or give up individual moral responsibility; what he emphasizes is that individual evil propensity manifests itself in social contexts. It is in the social condition of competitiveness and rivalry, where we compare our condition with that of others, that we tend to opt for the incentives of self-love (a fairly Rousseauean thought, to put it mildly). However, this condition only provides "the necessary context of our evil choices, but we make those all by ourselves" (Wood 2009: 127; cf. Guyer 2009: 148–9; for a full argument see Anderson-Gold 2001b: 25–52, and Wood 2011b: 131–5). In other words, social relations may only trigger an evil disposition, they do not cause it.

Consequences are again profound. In Rousseau's educational design, the tutor keeps Émile ignorant, so that he is not exposed to detrimental *amour-propre*. None of this can be found in Kant. The problem of evil exacerbates the problem of education, and thus also the social task of promoting an ethical commonwealth (to whose promotion moral education is supposed to contribute). "[H]ow could one expect to construct something completely straight from such crooked wood? To found a moral people of God is, therefore, a work whose execution cannot be hoped for from human beings but only from God himself" (Religion, 6: 100). However, there is also hope. Radical evil can be held at bay – if not completely overcome or extirpated -, as freedom also includes the freedom to choose the morally good. The task of the ethical community is to overcome the very situation of mutual moral corruption, and since it affects all humans, "the entire human race" has a duty to establish this society "in its full scope" (ibid.: 94). Promoting the highest moral good is a collective, social or communitarian, not only an individual task.

As mentioned above, the civil society of a republic can prepare this moral community with the help of political education in a broad sense. In genuine republics, citizens may become capable of self-legislation, may cultivate their power of reflective judgement, and train their enlarged mode of thinking or *Denkungsart*. In a section on "permissible moral illusion", Kant asserts that civilized humans are inclined to adopt the illusion of a moral disposition, by pretending, for instance, that they respect others. Unlike Rousseau, Kant does not see this as a major problem, but as a chance of progress. In the first place, nobody is deceived by this since everybody is familiar with the deception coming from others. In addition, moral illusion has the potential for fostering a moral disposition. "For when human beings play these roles, eventually the virtues, whose illusion they have merely affected for a considerable length of time, will gradually really be aroused and merge into the dispositions" (Anthropology, 7: 151). To sum up, both modern (republican) societies and religious communities are seen by Kant as potential sources of moral progress (on the role of the churches see Stroud 2005 und 2008). In the end, Rousseau's and Kant's educational programmes are very different. The former eventually suggests to the reader of *Émile* that his project is "impossible in principle" (Scudery 2012: 34). It is a genuine utopia, a nowhere. Kant, by contrast, anticipates a possible future that is preferable to past and present. "Kant offers hope and guidance where Rousseau expects inevitable catastrophe" (ibid. 36).

There can be no doubt that Rousseau's influence on Kant was considerable. As the unpublished note quoted above suggests – where Kant confessed that Rousseau "brought him around" -, the impact was strongest in the field of moral philosophy, revolving around the distinction between morality (*Moralität*, *Sittlichkeit*) and moral conventions, theoretical knowledge and moral wisdom, and terms such as the honour and rights of humankind, the intrinsic dignity of human beings, the ideas of moral autonomy, personal identity and political freedom, moral religion, and the vocation of the human species. Rousseau helped to sharpen Kant's awareness that, in spite of – or perhaps because of – a surfeit of cultivation and civilization, we are still very far from our proper vocation. However, not all was lost, because people like Rousseau demonstrated that we would progressively become aware of our own misery, and would look for a way out. Kant also imposed his own conception of cosmopolitanism, of cosmopolitan formation and of possible progress in history on Rousseau when interpreting his philosophy. This was perhaps a symptom of his generic (Enlightenment) belief that Rousseau participated, like all other human beings, in the same universal reason that would eventually help humans to contain radical evil and self-imposed miseries. Another possibility is that Kant wanted to defend

Rousseau's reputation and honour against what he saw as unjustified attacks and outright condemnation.

At the end of the previous chapter, I have mentioned Rousseau's pessimistic philosophy of history. Like many other civic humanists of early modern Europe, he was a cultural pessimist deeply worried about the almost inevitable decline and fall of European or "western" civilization as a consequence of commercial activities, ensuing wealth, corruption, and loose morals. Kant is usually cast as philosopher with a more optimistic and uplifting philosophy of history (see for instance the contributions in Rorty and Schmidt 2009). However, Kant's texts also contain passages that contradict this overall picture. Kant changed his mind concerning the role of education in the promotion of the highest moral good in the 1790ies, rejecting the secular claim of the 1770ies that "salvation (*Heil*)" can come from radical educational reforms (Philanthropinum, 2: 449) and expressing his religious hope in divine providence as a source of progress instead (Conflict, 7: 92–3; see Brandt 2009: 184–90 and Louden 2012: 50). A possible source of Kant's change of mind was his growing pessimism concerning human perfectibility. Improvement on the educational level is "desirable, but its success is hardly to be hoped for", since those in charge of education are just frail human beings themselves (Conflict, 7: 93), "crooked wood" which can never be transformed into "something completely straight" (Religion, 6: 100). In the rather gloomy essay "The end of all things" (1794), Kant hinted at the possibility of destroying pure morality by perhaps good-intentioned, but mistaken education (cf. 8: 338 f.). Kant did not fail to notice that Basedow himself had a rather difficult personality; in particular, he was disposed to drunkenness. In the words of Kant: "Basedow's shortcoming was that he drank too much Malaga" (25: 1538). In the *Conflict of Faculties* (1798), Kant frankly declared that an "epoch of decline" in the wake of the French Revolution was possible (ibid: 7: 83). The crucial difference to Rousseau is that this course is a mere possibility and not inevitable, as Rousseau had claimed, since due to human freedom the further course of history is open. Kant's line of defence against pessimists like Rousseau remains the same: we have a moral duty to promote progress and further the highest good, and thus to cultivate our moral faith in order not to fall victim to despair (see for instance TP, 8: 307–12)

Basedow's and Kant's conceptions of cosmopolitanism share common features. Both believed that cosmopolitanism and patriotism are compatible with each other (Busch and Horstmann 1976: 1160, Busch and Dierse 1985: 209, and Kleingeld 2006). Weisskopf's description of Basedow's programme as "national education" (Weisskopf 1970: 60) is anachronistic and misleading. It may be the case, though, that for Basedow cosmopolitanism coincided with trans-border Europeanism (cf. Munzel 1999: 272). Kant's cosmopolitan disposition or personal attitude has remained a matter of scholarly debates (see chapter 1, section 3). At any rate, for both thinkers, cosmopolitanism was closely connected with religious toleration, open-mindedness, moral education, and political reforms at the level of states. In the words of Kant, the cosmopolitans are those who do not care about the military glory or reputation of one's state, but concern themselves with the "best of the world" or the "whole of the world", at least indirectly (for instance, by promoting reforms at home; cf. LP, 9: 448, 15: 627–9; Kater 1999: 171–4). Unpublished reflections on anthropology from the 1770ies suggest that Kant worked on a refinement of conceptual categories. He distinguished the philanthropical method related to the *moral* dimension of cosmopolitanism – as in Basedow's writings – from the cosmopolitan method in a narrow sense (which might also be called cosmopolitical), which focused on the civil condition and on international law, that is, on *political* cosmopolitanism (15: 627, 628, 630; other categories mentioned in the notes are "statistical" and "biographical" approaches; see also chapter 7).

In Basedow's writings, "cosmopolitan education" is a term that has the following connotations:
1. It emphasises moral education beyond denominational boundaries.
2. It aims at fostering natural religion based on moral convictions or virtue (*Tugend*).
3. It encompasses education for religious tolerance.

Kant goes beyond Basedow's concept of cosmopolitan education in three crucial respects. First of all, unlike Basedow's theory, Kant's cosmopolitan education is embedded in a comprehensive political theory, a philosophy of history and a philosophy of religion. Secondly, pinpointing the species' vocation required a practical anthropology, a moral teleology, a philosophy of history and a philosophy of religion. Finally, Kant's educational theory explicitly encompasses the whole human race, expressed in the conviction that the proper objective of formation is the perfection, that is, the complete and proportionate development of all predispositions of the whole human race.

Rousseau's *Émile* is a book about the formation of a moral and cognitive cosmopolitan, who avoids the deformations of a commercial society influenced by processes of globalisation. This cosmopolitan formation is in conflict with the political education of the citizen of a republic and with modern society.

Kant's cosmopolitanism is a political and moral project and includes the element of formation – not only but especially of oneself: *Selbstbildung*. Moral self-legislation and self-motivation ultimately aim at a cosmopolitan conduct of thought (*Denkungsart*) and a cosmopolitan comportment of mind or disposition (*Gesinnung*). This is our supreme or highest-order maxim, the "subjective ground" as a deed of our freedom (Religion, 6: 21), the "ultimate ground and justification of our actions" relating to our character, the overall orientation concerning our lives' conduct (Caswell 2006: 195; cf. Formosa 2007 and 2012: 173). Kant takes a detour: in his moral theory, cosmopolitan values are not simply instilled in pupils. A cosmopolitan disposition is a long-term result of helping adolescents to form their own moral characters, defined as "the aptitude (*Fertigkeit*) of acting according to maxims [...] of humanity (*Menschheit*)" (LP, 9: 481; see the following chapter for more).

The core ideas for cosmopolitan education as envisioned by the three authors are the following: cosmopolitan education is a part of practical philosophy. It is in turn interwoven with philosophical anthropology and the philosophy of religion in a complex way. They share minimal assumptions of early modern liberal or republican thought, such as the focus on the individual and the value of freedom and self-determination. They perceive cosmopolitanism as the result of a *process* of individual and communal development (like formation, the reform of religious communities or the process of Enlightenment). This is the dynamic element. Cosmopolitan education emphasises moral education beyond denominational boundaries, and aims at fostering natural religion, the true religion of the heart or "inner religion" based on moral convictions or virtue rather than theological dogma. It encompasses education for religious tolerance, and tends to despise denominational or sectarian disputes. The inner core of reason is the standard of cosmopolitan morality.

Though deeply influenced by Rousseau, Kant imposed his own conception of cosmopolitanism, of cosmopolitan education and of possible progress in history on Rousseau. He seems to resemble the philosopher – in Kant's account, Christian Garve – who falls prey to "the human propensity to follow one's accustomed course of thought even in appraising the thoughts of others, and thus to carry the former over into the latter" (TP, 8: 281). Kant might even have argued that, analogous to Plato, he understood Rousseau better "than he understood himself" (KrV, A 314). Kant's reinterpretation was favourable and creative and has found many followers up to the present, but is ultimately misleading. Finally, it should be kept in mind that Rousseau's dilemma can only be overcome with the help of metaphysical assumptions concerning human nature, reason, teleology, and the vocation of the human species – assumptions of practical metaphysics Kant endorsed, but most contemporary interpreters are most likely not willing to share (see chapter 8, especially section 2).

6 Taking a detour: Kant's theory of moral cosmopolitan formation

At the beginning of his *Lectures on pedagogy* (1803), Kant claims in a key passage: "1) Parents usually care only that their children get on well in the world, and 2) princes regard their subjects merely as instruments for their own designs. Parents care for the home, princes for the state. Neither have as their final end the best for the world (*das Weltbeste*) and the perfection to which humanity is destined, and for which it also has the predisposition. However, the design for a plan of education must be made in a cosmopolitan manner" (LP, 9: 448). In this passage, key elements of Kant's practical philosophy are hinted at. It also offers a sketch of his cosmopolitan formation. Parents, when educating their children, usually aim at prudence and skilfulness (which make success in the world more likely), not at morality. Kant alludes to one of the goals of education, namely the cultivation of a moral character. Princes use subjects as mere means, thus violating the categorical imperative, which states – in one formula – that humanity in persons should always be treated as an end in itself (Groundwork, 4: 429). The highest good in the world (*das Weltbeste*) – which should be promoted by prospective "world citizens" – takes the reader right into the heart of Kant's practical philosophy and its most complex and controversial issue (see chapter 2). The passage also includes what Robert Louden calls Kant's postulate of "species perfectionism", the "claim that the ultimate objective of education is to advance not the welfare of the individual student but rather the moral perfection of the human species as a whole" (Louden 2000: 37). Finally, Kant refers to "a plan of education", which also encompasses ethical didactics, his theory of moral education.

In spite of a renewed interest in cosmopolitan educational theories in recent years, publications on Kant's theory of cosmopolitan education have been rare. Most publications still focus on Kant's political cosmopolitanism, especially his so-called cosmopolitan right (see for instance Huggler 2010 and Todd 2009: 31–5). It has been claimed that Kant's moral educational theory is actually cosmopolitan in character. At the end of his article "The education of the categorical imperative", James Scott Johnston asserts that a moral character in Kantian terms is also by definition "cosmopolitical", and that as moral beings, we have an obligation to develop "'cosmopolitical maxims' as it were; maxims that are morally worthy precisely because they seek out and maintain the conditions of cosmopolitanism" (Johnston 2006: 400–1). This interpretation is supported by Kant's texts; for instance, in one passage moral education seems to coincide with cosmopolitan education, since "through *moral* formation (*Bildung*)" the human being "receives value in view of the entire human race" (LP, 9: 455).

In the Introduction and in the second chapter, I have distinguished between various forms of cosmopolitanisms in Kant's philosophy. Kant's theory of formation especially relates to the moral, political and religious forms of cosmopolitanisms. I am going to restrict myself to the moral version in this chapter. Its key claim is that Kant's moral educational theory is cosmopolitan in character. Moral self-legislation and self-motivation ultimately aim at a cosmopolitan conduct of thought (*Denkungsart*) and a cosmopolitan comportment of mind or disposition (*Gesinnung*). This is our supreme or highest-order maxim, the "subjective ground" as a deed of our freedom (Religion, 6: 21), the "ultimate ground and justification of our actions" relating to our character, the overall orientation concerning our lives' conduct (Caswell 2006: 195; cf. Formosa 2007 and 2012: 173). Kant takes a detour: in his moral theory, cosmopolitan values are not simply instilled in pupils. A cosmopolitan disposition is a long-term result of helping adolescents to form their own moral characters, defined as 'the aptitude (*Fertigkeit*) of acting according to maxims [...] of humanity (*Menschheit*)" (LP, 9: 481), "the steadfast commitment to virtue that is realized through a resolute conduct of thought (*Denkungsart*)" (Munzel 1999: 2; cf. KpV, 5: 152 and Anthropology, 7: 294–5). The second section offers a sketch of moral formation according to Kant, outlining the unique features of this systematic educational theory. The next part claims that moral formation following Kant's principles coincides with cosmopolitan formation. A shared moral predisposition turns humans all over the world into equals. Their efforts to cultivate their respective moral potential turn them into fellow-beings of a global moral community. The conclusion briefly hints at differences between Kant's approach and contemporary cosmopolitan educational theories. In short, you cannot train autonomy like a skill; thus there is a systematic difference between formation and education. The key difference to contemporary cosmopolitan educational theories is that Kant tries to achieve his cosmopolitan goals by taking a detour: unlike contemporary approaches, Kant does not simply posit "cosmopolitan values" in an age of globalization and interconnectedness, but stresses moral formation (*Bildung*) which revolves around maxims that can be universalised, the three maxims of understanding, especially the enlarged conduct of thought, a proper comportment of mind and a moral character. In its ideal form, this moral formation coincides with a cosmopolitan formation.

I suppose that elements of this conception can be traced back to Rousseau: moral cosmopolitanism is not something added to cultivated morality, but both of them are identical (the identity thesis). As Rousseau put it, "the love of the human race is nothing but the love of justice within us. [...] Apart from self-interest this care for the general well-being is the first concern of the wise man, for each of us forms part of the human race and not part of any individual member of that race" (Rousseau 2007: 203). Morality is obedience to practical reason. Rousseau raised the genuine modern question of what our identity is (cf. Wain 2011: 44). Kant's practical philosophy is not only about maxims and their possible universality, it is also and more importantly about our life-conduct, our moral identity and our vocation (see chapter 1, section 2). A shared moral disposition turns humans all over the world into equals. This is the gist of the famous Rousseau-passage quoted at the beginning of the previous chapter, where Kant wrote that "Rousseau brought me around" (Notes and fragments, 20: 44). From a moral perspective, the brilliant "investigator", scientist or intellectual is not superior to the "common labourer"; in fact, he would miss the whole point of his existence (his vocation) if he failed to cultivate what matters most, his moral predisposition. In the words of Rousseau, cultivating "the love of justice within us" results in the kind of moral cosmopolitanism that is acceptable even for sceptics of modernity and critics of some forms of cosmopolitanisms like Rousseau (see chapter 4, section 1).

6.1 An outline of moral education according to Kant

The philosophical quality of the *Lectures on Pedagogy*, published in 1803 by Kant's former student Friedrich Theodor Rink but in all likelihood based on a lecture held in the winter semester of 1776–1777, has been a matter of debate for some time. The source and authenticity of these lectures have been questioned, especially by Weisskopf (cf. Weisskopf 1970: 239–350; see also Kauder and Fischer 1999). However, it does make sense to see them as a reliable source (cf. Beck 1979 and Louden 2000: 33–61). A viable position has been developed by Lewis White Beck, who proposed the interpretative maxim that "one should use other authentic works [by Kant] as a guide to and a commentary on the Rink compilation" (Beck 1979: 18; see also Munzel 1999: 255 and Koch 2003: 11).

The key concepts of Kant's ethics are autonomy, freedom, practical reason, maxims, duty, and the various types of imperatives (see among others Geismann 2009: 11–23, Gerlach 2010, Koch 2003: 37–105, Johnston 2007 and Wood 2008). Autonomy is "freedom in the *positive* sense" or self-legislation, "*lawgiving of its own* on the part of pure and, as such, practical reason" (KpV, 5: 33; cf. Groundwork, 4: 440). One's self-legislative activity results in the categorical imperative: our maxims should not contradict themselves; they can be universalised; they imply that we do not use others or ourselves as mere means, but as ends in themselves; they could be the basis of a "universal law of nature" (Groundwork, 4:

420–436). Finally, and perhaps most importantly, as self-legislative members who are ends in themselves, humans as rational beings form a "systematic union ... through common objective laws", a union that Kant expresses with the practical ideal of a "kingdom of ends" (Groundwork, 4: 433; cf. KrV A 808/B836 and A 812/B 840). This formula of the kingdom of ends underlines the social character of practical reason: self-legislation is inextricably tied to maxims that are universal and could be agreed to by other members of this kingdom or commonwealth. Kant's notion of autonomy is social or relational – that is, embedded in the context of the moral agent's relationship to other rational beings – rather than individualist in the sense of an unencumbered, isolated rational agent. If there is a focus on the individual's will in the *Groundwork*, then for methodological reasons (see chapter 1, section 2).

Maxims are subjective principles of actions and subsume several practical rules (KpV, 5: 19; cf. Groundwork, 4: 402–3). Rules are more context-bound, whereas maxims are abstract, so they require practical judgement to apply them in concrete situations. A typical maxim would be that of promoting one's own happiness no matter what happens. Kant's point is that moral maxims are self-legislated ("produced" by one's own practical reason) and therefore can be universalised. Previous philosophers, Kant claims, realized that "the human being is bound to laws by his duty, but it never occurred to them that he is subject *only to laws given by himself but still universal* and he is bound only to act in conformity with his own will, which [...] is a will giving universal law" (Groundwork, 4: 432). Our *Willkür* or freedom of choice is always at the crossroads, we can choose the law of practical reason or ignore it, following, for instance, our inclinations like our desire for happiness. Following our inclinations is not *per se* immoral, only if there is a conflict with "grounds of reason" (Groundwork, 4: 413). If we opt for the law of practical reason and our incentive (*Triebfeder*) of action is this very law, we do our duty: "*duty is the necessity of an action from respect for law*" (Groundwork, 4: 400).

Hypothetical imperatives have the form "If you want x, then you should do y". The action is good "merely as a means *to something else*" (Groundwork, 4: 414). In modern commercial societies, Kant claims, people above all cultivate what Kant calls imperatives of skilfulness (*Geschicklichkeit*) and prudence (*Klugheit*), learning how to use other people for their own ends (LP, 9: 455). The result is legality, not morality of disposition or comportment of mind. A moral disposition is the unconditional and unwavering commitment to the moral law, the "highest-order maxim that defines the overall practical orientation" of one's character (Formosa 2012: 173). Kant's educational theory stresses the importance of moral formation based on the categorical imperative, "by which the human being is to be formed so that he can live as a freely acting being" (LP, 9: 455), the acquisition and cultivation of a moral conduct of thought, and the cultivation of virtue, a process that culminates in the idea of a moral character. The moral ideal is the proportionate development and cultivation of the three forms of human practice, of skilfulness, prudence and morality.

According to the standard interpretation, the categorical imperative is a testing device making sure that subjective maxims meet the requirements of universalising them, of autonomy, and so on. James Scott Johnston, by contrast, claims that we apply the moral law this way only occasionally, that the context in which it is operative "is always already the existing stock of norms, rules, laws, and duties built up in interpersonal, social, and public discourse", and that the categorical imperative is not something given, but developed "*in* the process of maxim formation and *not* before this" (Johnston 2007: 243). I agree with Johnston's clarification. First, Kant's thesis about "common human reason" mentioned above implies that ordinary humans have an implicit if only vague moral knowledge, and philosophers like Socrates merely make them attentive to their own reason's principle; this is the moral predisposition in humans (Groundwork, 4: 404; cf. Munzel 1999: 66–7 and 187–8). Kant's semi-Socratic method in ethical didactics has to make this basic assumption (see below). Secondly, Kant refers in the *Kritik der praktischen Vernunft* to the fact of reason (*Faktum der Vernunft*; KpV, 5: 31–2): *Faktum* goes back to the Latin terms *facere* (to make) and *factum*, and should not be related to *Tatsache,* an empirical or transcendental fact but translated as "deed" or "act" (cf. KpV, 5: 43, MS, 6: 227, Munzel 1999: 66–7, 70–1, Dall'Agnol 2012 and Almeida 2012). Fact of reason thus indicates that moral agents create, form or make a universal principle in the process of rational deliberation and maxim formation. The context of this possible generation of a universal maxim is social, since it is rooted in the agent's interaction with other human beings.

The key issue of Kantian moral formation is motivation (see especially Koch 2003, to whom I am much indebted; Breun 2002, Cavallar 2005, Großmann 2003, Kauder and Fischer 1999, Nawrath 2010, Roth and Surprenant 2012; more secondary literature in Koch, 2003: 11 and 401–16). How can we educate pupils to become autonomous agents, to realise their self-legislating potential, to cultivate their maxims in a way that they become compatible with the maxims of others? In Kant's words, moral formation looks for the "way in which one can provide laws of pure practical reason with *access* to the human mind and *influence* on its maxims, that is, the way in which one can make objectively practical reason *subjectively* practical as well" (KpV, 5: 151). The goal of moral formation – the doctrine of the methods of ethics – is to prepare moral autonomy (cf. MS, 6: 477). Preparation has to be distinguished from manipulation, indoctrination or determination; education sometimes coincides with these. Therefore I reserve the term "formation" for activities that have moral autonomy as a goal, and are consistent with it. In Kant's terminology, *Bildung* sometimes coincides with the formation of character, so is identical with moral formation. Sometimes, he uses the term in a wider sense where it encompasses skilfulness and prudence as well (see Munzel 1999: 276 for a discussion).

Kant claimed that he was the first philosopher to have found the one and only proper method of moral formation. He criticizes teachers in the past who "have not brought their concepts to purity, but, since they want to do too well by hinting everywhere for motives to moral goodness, in trying to make their medicine really strong the spoil it" (Groundwork, 4: 412 note). Kant may have thought about his own education here, with teachers and priests warning and preaching that evil-doers will wind up in prison and later in hell, whereas good people will be rewarded by society and then in heaven. The result can only be heteronomy of the will, not autonomy. Kant calls this mixing of morals with theology and "empirical inducements" (ibid., 4: 410). Kant's own methodology is completely opposed to this approach. The moral law, he asserts, should be taught "by way of reason alone" (ibid.). This is the "autocracy of reason": reason is not only self-legislating, it can also serve as an incentive and become practical (MS, 6: 383 and 29: 626). Kant adds the psychological hypothesis that this rational and pure method is much more efficient than the mixing of rational and empirical/pragmatic elements, as its "influence on the human heart" is more powerful (Groundwork, 4: 411) and "elevates the soul" (ibid.; see Koch 2003: 11–2, 19–20 and 192–211 with more passages).

I have just outlined Kant's theses on moral motivation. This is just one part of moral formation, the other two being moral instruction and moral training (or "ethical ascetics"). Moral instruction in turn is divided into *Katechetik, Kasuistik* and *Exemplarik*. Thus we get the following distinctions (see the chart below; cf. Koch 2003: 110, 118, 189, and 383–4):

	Moral formation	
1.) moral instruction	2.) moral motivation	3.) moral training
1. Katechetik 2. Exemplarik 3. Kasuistik		
Knowledge	wanting	capacity/Vermögen

Katechetik, the moral catechism, describes the method how to teach the metaphysics of morals, the canon of virtue (MM, 6: 478–84, Koch 2003: 163–73, 384–6 and Surprenant 2010). This is no pure catechism where the teacher lectures and the pupils memorise, but a semi-Socratic dialogue which involves the pupils' reason: they have to learn to think for themselves (MM, 6: 478–9; see also LP, 9: 477). The teacher is the "midwife" who helps the pupils to become aware of their own implicit moral assumptions. "The teacher, by his questions, guides his young pupil's course of thought merely by presenting him with cases in which his predisposition for certain concepts will develop (the teacher is the midwife of the pupil's thoughts)" (MM, 6: 478). The dialogue is semi-Socratic because it combines catechism and maeutics. The teacher instructs the pupils about basic moral concepts and the system of virtue, but does so with the help of the "common human reason" of her pupils. As was to be expected, this form of moral instruction has to remain pure, that is, it must not be mixed with theology, for instance. The teacher hints at the pupils' consciousness of their own moral freedom, with Kant hoping that the instruction eventually produces "an exaltation" in the learner's soul about moral goodness and her own moral capacities (MM, 6: 483) and increases her "*interest* in morality" (ibid. 484).

Kant is convinced that "common human reason" functions the way he describes it in his writings. For instance, he asserts that we all have an implicit knowledge of the difference between prudence or cunning and morality, and that we should universalise our maxims (Groundwork, 4: 402; see also KpV, 5: 32, 105, 160–1). "The most common understanding can distinguish without instruction what form in a maxim makes it fit for a giving of universal law and what does not" (KpV, 5: 27). According to Kant, then, ordinary people in their conversations would know basic moral distinctions, know how to assess or judge human conduct, and so on (and novels, and nowadays films, would reflect these common sense moral predispositions). Kant does not hesitate to draw this conclusion. He writes about his observation that during conversations, non-philosophers usually abhor "subtle reasoning", but like to argue "about the *moral worth* of this or that action by which the character of some person is to be made out" (KpV, 5: 153). This reasoning often tells us a lot about the character of the person who makes that particular judgement. Many, Kant claims, are very strict in their attempts to find, or isolate, "genuine moral import in accordance with an uncompromising law" (ibid., 154). An example taken from politics may illustrate the point. When people judge the actions of politicians, they are often very sceptical in their assessment of the underlying motivation(s). Rarely would they claim, for instance, that a certain politician acted out of respect for the norms of international law, but they would try to find some motivation revolving around self-interest or the promotion of one's own happiness. This reasoning implicitly sets up standards of legitimate and illegitimate reasons for actions.

6.2 Education following Kantian principles as cosmopolitan formation

Kant's educational theory specifies a clear goal of education: helping to reach the *Bestimmung* (destiny, vocation, determination) of each individual as well as of the whole human species. Together with the doctrine of the highest good, this concept of vocation is the core of Kant's critical practical philosophy (cf. Rossi 2005, Brandt 2009, Geismann 2009, Kater 1999: 166–70, Louden 2000: 37, 53–4 and 101, Louden 2013). The *Bestimmung* of humans is to cultivate their capacities or predispositions (*Anlagen*), especially – but not exclusively – freedom, self-legislation as well as *Selbstbestimmung*, self-determination, morality (cf. KrV, A 464, Groundwork, 4: 396, KdU, 5: 434–6, Anthropology, 7: 325). Our "moral vocation" is "the ultimate end (*letzter Zweck*) of our existence" (KdU 5: 431 and 435). Like some other representatives of the Enlightenment, Kant expanded the focus on individuals (as in Spalding or Mendelssohn) to a perspective that included the species as a whole and its history and future. However, Kant did not abandon the individualistic perspective, but kept both (see Brandt 2009: 25–7 and 114–5 and Louden 2000: 102–6). As Robert Louden has pointed out, *Bestimmung* incorporates three meanings (Louden 2013: 6–7): first, Kant sometimes compares humans with animals or even plants, pointing out that they are equipped with certain germs (*Keime*), and they are determined to develop in a certain way. In this context, *Bestimmung* can be rendered as "determination", since it is "merely a matter of proper sowing and planting that these germs develop" (LP, 9: 445). Here humans are part of the natural world subject to its laws. The second meaning relates *Bestimmung* to the concept of indetermination, as a human being, even from the perspective of empirical anthropology, is capable of reflection, deliberation and the freedom of choice, that is, "choosing for himself a way of living and not being bound to a single one" (Anfang, 8: 112). This corresponds with the level of the cultivation of skilfulness and prudence. Finally, as beings with moral predispositions, we are *bestimmt* to cultivate or develop them. "The human being shall make himself better, cultivate himself, and, if he is evil, bring forth morality in himself" (LP, 9: 446). This is the level of moral freedom and of cosmopolitanism, and our *Bestimmung* is a vocation or a calling: humans "feel destined [or called] by nature to [develop] ... into a *cosmopolitan society* (*cosmopolitismus*) that is constantly threatened by disunion but generally progresses toward a coalition" (Anthropology, 7: 331). The regulative principle of a cosmopolitan society comes in two versions: one is a political union of the whole human species based on coercive laws that are mutual and "come from themselves" (ibid.), the other one is the moral commonwealth developed in particular in the *Religion Within the Boundaries of Mere Reason* (cf. Religion, 6: 96–102; but see also KrV A 808/B836, A 812/B 840 and Groundwork, 4: 433 and chapter 2 above).

One method or instrument of promoting these cosmopolitan societies is formation. Kant thus asserts: "[T]he design for a plan of education must be made in a cosmopolitan manner" (LP, 9: 448; see also Höffe 2008c: 148–50 and Koch 2013). Kant aims at turning pedagogy into a science, which means that it should form a coherent system based on concepts a priori (those outlined above) and not on particular interests or whims such as the needs of the labour market or the government. For Kant, an educational science that deserves this name is characterized by continuity, the intent to help promoting the vocation of the human race, and is therefore oriented towards the future. This destiny can be reached by the species as a whole – an insight of our reflective power of judgement (cf. Anthropology, 7: 324, Idea, 8: 18, LP, 9: 445), but each individual has a duty to make her or his contributions to help approach this goal. Those who are successful in this attempt are not only moral and virtuous human beings in a Kantian sense but also cosmopolitan citizens.

Kant's cosmopolitan design for a plan of education or formation can be characterized with the help of the following features (for systematic analyses see especially Koch 2002, 2003 and 2013; Johnston 2006, Munzel 1999: 254–333 and 2012). First, cosmopolitan formation is education for moral freedom: educators cannot directly influence, manipulate or effect anything in their pupils, because the ultimate goal is that *they themselves* become moral beings and adopt a moral disposition (cf. Anthropology, 7: 321). However, this does not imply that educators are helpless: they can provide a favourable environment, they can help pupils to start thinking for themselves, cultivating their faculty of judgement and stimulating in them the feeling of respect (*Achtung*) for the moral law and teaching them to feel their own dignity (cf. KpV, 5: 152). In short, educators ideally *prepare* moral autonomy or self-legislation. As Alix Cohen put it, "education can be morally relevant *despite the fact that it cannot make the child moral*" (Cohen 2012: 152; see also Großmann 2003: 186–245, Koch 2003: 64, 68, 213–7, 238, 268–9, Munzel 1999: 259–61, 330–3 and Formosa 2012: 173–4). Moral formation helps the pupil to develop her predispositions in a way that she can ultimately "live as a freely acting human being" (LP, 9: 455; cf. Anthropology, 7: 285 and 294–5). The adoption of a new disposition can only be done by the agent herself, but pedagogy can shape the conditions where this goal is achieved in a better and faster way.

Secondly, the goal of Kantian formation is *not* imparting certain values, not even cosmopolitan ones. Kant does not posit "cosmopolitan values", asserting that they should be instilled in children simply because our world has become globalized. This kind or reasoning would fall back on the type of pragmatic thinking that has its limited legitimacy, but should be kept out of moral formation proper. Instead, he stresses moral formation (*Bildung*) which is highly formal, revolving around maxims that can be universalised, the three maxims of understanding, especially the enlarged conduct of thought, a proper comportment of mind or disposition and a moral character. Cosmopolitan values would stem from outside the children; as indicated above, Kant endorses a semi-Socratic method which finds moral truth inside the subject (Koch 2003: 81, 241, 376). This is Kant's unique methodology: he criticizes previous forms of teaching particular values, sometimes supporting them with inducements based outside the student's own practical reason.

Third, Kantian moral formation turns the student to the inner core of her own reason, and this move helps to include the "generalized other" since the adopted maxims should be universalized and find the rational consent of those who are also capable of practical knowledge (for a profound analysis see Koch 2003: 59, 77, 93–4, 162–3, 265–9, 375–7). At the very beginning, the pupil has to find a proper relationship *toward herself:* this implies absolute honesty and the willingness to scrutinize oneself. "Moral cognition of oneself, which seeks to penetrate into the depths (the abyss) of one's heart which are quite difficult to fathom, is the beginning of all human wisdom" (MM, 6: 441). *In interiore homine habitat veritas.* Inside herself the agent finds the idea of freedom, the dignity of humanity, the admiration for the moral law, and the moral feeling (cf. KU, 5: 274, Ton, 8: 403, Contest, 7: 58–9; Koch 2003: 200, 208–9). Self-examination and cognition of our own selves leads to cognition of our possible freedom and ideally to the *"respect for ourselves* in the consciousness of our freedom" (KpV, 5: 161).

Finally, Kant's ethics have often been criticized for their alleged individualism. A discussion of this issue is beyond the scope of this chapter, but several interpreters have convincingly argued that the charge is ill-founded (see chapter 1, section 2). For instance, judgements – which play an essential role in politics and moral formation – are exercised in interaction with others, and the enlarged conduct of thought even *requires* others and their divergent perspectives. The individual has imperfect duties to others: "While making oneself a fixed center of one's principles, one ought to regard this circle drawn around one as also forming part of an all-inclusive circle of those who, in their disposition, are citizens of the world" (MM, 6: 473). In this quotation, Kant picks up the ancient Stoic notion of concentric circles, with the most encompassing of all circles being that of the human species (cf. LP, 9: 499). Kant grounds the duty "to be a useful member of the world" in the imperfect duties towards oneself and "the worth of humanity" in one's own person (MM, 6: 446). Humanity (*die Menschheit*) refers to the intelligible capacity for the morally good in rational beings and should not be confused with the concept of the human race or the human species (*das Menschengeschlecht*), or a biological concept of the species (see Byrd and Hruschka 2010: 286–8, Cheneval 2002: 514 and Wimmer 1990: 124–8 for a discussion). As moral agents, we should posit the same intelligible capacity for humanity in other human beings. If this predisposition has become a disposition (*Gesinnung*), then we are citizens of the world. Kant argues that we have a duty of benevolence towards all other human beings, and that it would be self-contradictory to exempt myself from this duty. Since the idea of law implies universality as well as reciprocity and equality, all humans should be included, even those one finds not worthy of love. The idea of humanity is another way to express this obligation or duty: "lawgiving reason, *which includes the whole species* (and so myself as well) in its idea of humanity as such, includes me as giving universal law along with all others in the duty of mutual benevolence" (MM, 6: 451, my emphasis). Turning to the inner core of one's reason leads to the idea of universality and thus to the idea of a global moral community of all human beings (expressed in the *Religion* as the idea of an ethical commonwealth; cf. Religion, 6: 96–102).

In the process of inner self-examination and exploration mentioned above, the educator is again not completely helpless, but functions as a tutor. She has several "tools" at her disposal: first, a moral catechism based on a semi-Socratic dialogue, where the teacher functions as a "midwife" who helps the pupils to become aware of their own implicit moral assumptions (see above). Secondly, the teacher can cultivate the pupils' power of judgement (Kant's casuistry). Third, there is Kant's *Exemplarik*, the use of examples. The cultivation of judgement, in particular adopting the extended, broad-minded or enlarged way of thinking, is of crucial importance for a cosmopolitan disposition.

Cultivating the students' faculty of judgement may promote an interest in morality, but above all it trains the capacity to apply a general rule (the moral law) in particular situations. In the process, students learn how to form, justify, and reflect upon their maxims (MM, 6: 484; see Koch 2003: 173–81 and Schüssler 2012). Kant is surprised that teachers and educators do not make use of "this propensity of reason to enter with pleasure upon even the most subtle examination of the practical questions put to them" (KpV, 5: 154). He suggests that they use biographies to present characters, situations, and moral dilemmas, helping students to develop their faculty of judgement. Kant is probably thinking of Plutarch's *Lives*, among others, just like Montaigne and Rousseau (cf. Koch 2003: 263–4). Moral casuistry as a training of our faculty of judgement implies that the pupil puts herself in the shoes of the persons involved in the case. This process of imagination or empathy with others is conducive to a cosmopolitan conduct of thought and – ultimately – to a cosmopolitan disposition.

The world citizen embodies logical or cognitive cosmopolitanism, by trying to transcend the "egoism of reason", the unwillingness to test one's judgements with the help of the reason of others. The normative ideal is one of the three maxims of common understanding – the "extended way of thinking" (*erweiterte Denkungsart*). "The opposite of egoism can only be *pluralism*, that is, the way of thinking in which one is not concerned with oneself as the whole world, but rather regards and conducts oneself as a mere citizen of the world" (Anthropology, 7: 130; cf. KdU, 5: 293–6, Anthropology, 7: 200 and 228, LP, 9: 499, MM, 6: 472–3; see Häntsch 2008, Kemp 2006, Koch 2003: 324–31, Wood 2008: 17–20 and especially Munzel 1999: 57–9 and 223–36). Someone who tries to overcome logical egoism will attempt to see things from a different perspective, consider and perhaps adopt "the standpoint of others", and weigh one's judgement against those of others. As in Adam Smith, the impartial spectator is a recurrent theme in Kantian philosophy. Ideally the result is a cosmopolitan perspective based on a "broad-minded way of thinking" where the prospective citizen of the world "reflects on his own judgment from a *universal standpoint* (which he can only determine by putting himself into the standpoint of others)" (KdU, 5: 295; 19: 184–5).

Another area where the faculty of judgement can be trained is the use of examples. Kant's position here is fairly complex (see Breun 2002, Guyer 2012, Koch 2003: 260–72, Løvlie 1997: 415–8, Louden 1992 and Munzel 1999: 288–93). On the one hand, Kant rejects them as artificial aids, as go-carts (*Gängelwagen*) or leading-strings (*Leitbänder*) of the power of judgement (cf. KrV B 173–4, LP, 9: 475). They may stifle creativity and reflection on the basis of morality, and may block people's efforts to think and judge for themselves. On the other hand, examples can cultivate the "predisposition to the good" (Religion, 6: 48; cf. MM, 6: 479); they can serve as proof that morality is not an illusion, but "really possible" (MM, 6: 480; cf. KpV, 5: 158). However, this requires that the example has to pass the test of purity first: it must be judged or "appraised in accordance with principles of morality, as to whether it is also worthy to serve as an original example, that is, as a model; it can by no means authoritatively provide the concept of morality" (Groundwork, 4: 408). Ideally, examples bridge the gap between everyday life and situations that require a moral decision on the one hand and the moral law we inherently know about and just have to become aware of on the other.

In the following paragraphs, I will try to flesh out Kant's ideas, while keeping in mind what has been written about the use of examples. Kant advised searching through "the biographies of ancient and modern times" to find persons like Henry Norris who might serve as examples of moral virtue (see KpV, 5: 156–7, Breun 2002, Guyer 2012: 136). Courtier Norris refused to calumniate innocent Anne Boleyn, though Henry VIII tried to buy him and then threatened to punish him, ultimately with death. The problem with this example is that it describes an extreme situation; however, every-day life duties are more appropriate for most of us (cf. KpV, 5: 155 and Guyer 2012: 135). My first example is fictional and taken from a book Kant himself was familiar with: Robinson Crusoe (1719), described by the author himself as an "allegorical history" about "moral and religious improvement", is the only book Rousseau's Émile was allowed to keep in his library (cf. Munzel 1999: 262). Daniel Defoe's *Bildungsroman* is a description of the three stages and dimensions of Kant's education, namely skilfulness, prudence, and finally morality (see for instance Anthropology, 7: 324 and above). The protagonist's moral development entered a crucial stage when he discovered the traces of cannibals on the island. His first reaction was very emotional: "I could think of nothing but how I might destroy some of these monsters in their cruel bloody entertainment" (Defoe 1719: 223). For weeks Crusoe pondered the ways and methods at his disposal. Eventually he reflected upon his own passions, and the moral principles behind his maxims. "I began with cooler and calmer thoughts to consider what it was I was going to engage in" (ibid.: 226). In Kant's terminology, he started thinking for himself, overcoming or rather framing his passions, though not necessarily one's moral feeling (cf. KpV, 5: 159, TP, 8: 283, MM, 6: 399–400). His doubts revolved around four questions: first, did he have the authority "to be judge and executioner upon these men as criminals" (Defoe 1719: 226)? Had they really offended or injured him to justify retaliation? Could they in any way understand that they were committing a crime? And finally, how would Crusoe know "what God Himself judges in this particular case" (ibid.: 227)? Crusoe's reflection turned into an exercise in the enlarged way of thinking, by trying to see the problem from the perspective of the "savages", by trying to overcome a Eurocentric perspective. Crusoe concluded that, though the natives' behaviour was "brutish and inhuman", they had not injured him, and that only an injury – if they attacked him – or the attempt of one victim to escape would justify action on his part (ibid.: 227–8). Assessing the Spanish *conquista* was part of his reflection. If he, Crusoe, attacked the cannibals, "this would justify the conduct of the Spaniards in all their barbarities practiced in America, where they destroyed millions of these people, who, however they were idolaters and barbarians, and had several bloody and barbarous rites in their customs, such as sacrificing human bodies to their idols, were yet, as to the Spaniards, very innocent people; and that the rooting them out of the country is spoken of with the utmost abhorrence and detestation by even the Spaniards themselves at this time, and by all other Christian nations of Europe, as a mere butchery, a bloody and unnatural piece of cruelty, unjustifiable either to God or man" (ibid.: 227–8). In this dense passage, Defoe alluded to the "cosmopolitan" criticism of Spanish writers such as Las Casas or Vitoria of their fellow countrymen's conduct in the New World (cf. Cavallar 2002: 75–119 and Cavallar 2011: 20–4). The principles Crusoe – and, by implication, Defoe – referred to were those of the natural law tradition and also Kant's: the principle of injury (*laesio*), the true *dominion* of the natives, the injustice of fighting one injustice by committing another one (cf. Cavallar 1999: 99–101, 126–31). Whatever one may think about the overall success of Crusoe's train of thought: at least he tried to transcend the "egoism of reason", and he attempted to orient himself following the normative ideal of the "extended way of thinking".

My second example relates to Kant's debate on race and culture with some of his contemporaries like Johann Gottfried Herder (1744–1803), Johann Daniel Metzger (1739–1805) and especially Georg Forster (1754–94; see Kleingeld 2012: 92–123 for a complete exposition and chapter 1, section 3). There can be no doubt that Kant was an outspoken racist at the beginning of the debate (see for instance Observations, 2: 253, Principles, 8: 174), and apparently was quite reluctant for a long time to concede any points to his opponents, in particular Forster, who became quite frustrated. One might defend Kant in that he tried to strike a proper balance between thinking for oneself (and not just submitting to the opinion of others) and considering the opinions or perspectives of others, that is, between the first and second maxims of common understanding. Ultimately, namely between 1792 and 1795, Kant seemed to have had second thoughts on non-Europeans, racism, culture, and the influence of geography. There can be no doubt that Kant's thought developed in new directions: in the second half of the 1790s, he criticized European conquests and colonialism (cf. Peace, 8: 358–9, MM, 6: 353), defended the ways of life of hunters and pastoralists like the Hottentots (cf. MM, 6: 266 and 353), and restricted the concept of race to physiology (cf. Kleingeld 2007, 2009 and 2012: 111–23). Whether all this amounts to an example of the enlarged way of thinking, with Kant ultimately arriving at a coherent conception of moral universalism and cosmopolitanism, will in all likelihood remain a topic of scholarly debate.

My third example is contemporary and has a clear cosmopolitan dimension: "The colour-blind humanity of most of my teachers, strength in the face of tyranny, taught us lessons for the rest of our lives. Britain was our home", British-born Muslim Ed Husain wrote about his school experiences in London in his autobiography (Husain 2007: 2). The tyrants were the hoodlums of the National Front in the1980ies. At the age of 16, Husain (the pen name of Mohammed Mahbub Hussain) became an Islamic fundamentalist. However, the humanity, impartiality, courage, and apparent cosmopolitan disposition of some of his former teachers stayed in his mind. They "helped me form a belief in Britain, an unspoken appreciation of its values of fairness and equality" (Husain 2007: 5). As a student, Husain could not help but admire the "neutrality" or impartiality of his history teacher Denis Judd, who did not conform to the stereotype that non-Muslims necessarily "express enmity or animosity toward Muslims and Islam at any stage" (Husain 2007: 158). These experiences were one of the reasons why Husain managed to distance himself from fundamentalist doctrines later on. In Kantian terminology, these exemplary teachers Husain encountered tried to practice the enlarged way of thinking, and perhaps had a cosmopolitan disposition. The other aspect is Husain's own development; his autobiography can be read as a kind of contemporary *Bildungsroman* where the author tries to reflect upon, assess and reassess the merits of his own religion, his tradition, of Muslim groups in England, of Western societies and of Muslim societies in the Near East. The overall result could be described as a particular form of embedded cosmopolitanism.

A presentation of possible examples has to end with the caveat that they are necessary, but not sufficient (cf. Louden 1992: 303, 306, 320–2): As mentioned above, any example must first be assessed whether it can really serve "as a model", that is, embodies the supreme principle of morality (Groundwork, 4: 408). It is therefore open to divergent assessments, reflections and discussions. If they pass the test, examples can help to become aware of one's own freedom of choice, of one's own "cosmopolitan possibilities".

When Sharon Todd, in her book on cosmopolitan education, is wary of the current academic enthusiasm about cosmopolitanism because it might turn into yet another "ism" or ideology, and – following Hannah Arendt – argues for the cultivation of judgements in education, she does something very Kantian. "Judgment is, quite simply, an engagement in a world rich with diversity; it is a cosmopolitan activity" (Todd 2009: 145; cf. 138–42 and 149–50). Kant has emphasised the key role of judgement in the context of the love for all humans, which differs in degree. I am closer to some people than to others, but this does not necessarily violate the universality of the maxim (cf. MM, 6: 451–2), and finding out whether it does or not requires deliberation and judging (see also chapter 8, section 3).

Kant's moral philosophy has had a "difficult reception" in the English-speaking world – to put it mildly (Johnston 2007: 234, with illustrative examples ibid. 235–7). Typically it has been rejected as too formal, too rigorous, too idealistic, too solipsistic, too deontological, too everything – in short, as contradicting common human reason, and therefore as indefensible. Michael Hand, for instance, concludes that Kant's theory is unsuitable for educational practice (Hand 2006). Even interpreters lenient with Kant such as John Rawls or Lawrence Kohlberg have apparently grossly distorted his educational theory, further contributing to confusion, misunderstanding, and misinterpretation (see Johnston 2012: 177–92). In this chapter, I have argued that Kant's moral educational theory is cosmopolitan in character, aiming at an enlarged, cosmopolitan way of thinking and disposition. This is a long-term process of helping children to form their own characters, and as a consequence, teachers and educators may feel they are almost powerless. No success is guaranteed, since this disposition is supposed to be the result of one's own moral freedom. No cosmopolitan "values" in an everyday sense, disconnected from the ideas of self-legislation and moral freedom: this is Kant's unique methodology. He criticized previous forms of teaching particular values devoid of any reference to the concept of moral freedom, and would also have criticized contemporary forms, for instance, today's so-called *Werteerziehung* in German-speaking countries or the emphasis on "social skills" (see also chapter 8, sections 3 and 4). Kant's reminder for our times is that taking the detour – preparing moral freedom – may be more arduous and complex, but is the only rationally defensible method, and perhaps in the long run the only successful one.

7 Res publica: Kant on cosmopolitical formation

The starting point of this chapter is Kant's surprising remark that "it is not the case that a good state constitution is to be expected from inner morality; on the contrary, the good moral formation of a people is to be expected from a good state constitution" (Peace, 8: 366). The statement is at odds with the familiar assumption that Kant's philosophy is preoccupied with inner morality rather than external circumstances; that true reform has to start with our inner lives, not with politics. In this chapter, I want to show that Kant's remark is not some odd side note, but part and parcel of a coherent pedagogical theory, whose widely ignored ramifications deserve more attention. In addition, it helps us to rethink Kant's relationship to the republican tradition.

This chapter argues that a widespread interpretation of Kant as a typical early liberal is an oversimplification. Especially because of Rousseau's influence, Kant is close to the republican tradition, even though he does not share key features. Kant's pedagogy is indeed distinct from the educational theories of the civic republicans: First of all, moral self-legislation and self-motivation ultimately aim at a cosmopolitan conduct of thought (*Denkungsart*) and a cosmopolitan comportment of mind or disposition (*Gesinnung*), thus going beyond civic humanism's focus on one's own republic. Secondly, Kant takes a detour: in his moral theory, cosmopolitan values are not simply instilled or inculcated in pupils. A cosmopolitan disposition is a long-term result of helping adolescents to form their own moral characters (see the previous chapter). Yet Kant shared with civic republicans, especially with Rousseau, the conviction that education was indispensable for morality and virtue; subscribed to their belief in law's educational function; and held that a republic – or rather the republican form of government – was the proper basis of moral formation. A final section outlines Kant's vision of progress in a genuine republic.

In the second chapter, I have argued that there is a three-part division in Kant's philosophy concerning the concept of the highest good and the future of humankind: The foundation of a cosmopolitan condition of perpetual peace, a global legal society of peaceful states, and finally a world republic is the highest *political* good (this is his *cosmopolitical* vision). The establishment of a global ethical community is – secondly – the highest *moral* good in this world (this is his *cosmopolitan* vision; on the distinction see Kleingeld 2012: 38–9 and Louden 2014). Finally, the highest good proper coincides with the transcendent kingdom of God, the intelligible world, the kingdom of Heaven or a moral realm. In Kant's account, God and humans together try to realize the ethical commonwealth, with humans promoting (*befördern*) and "preparing" it while God is believed to offer fulfilment (attainment, realization or *Verwirklichung*). Together with the process of Enlightenment, the public use of reason, the development of a "cosmopolitan perspective", for instance, in historiography, together with religious as well as domestic political reforms and reforms at the international level, moral cosmopolitan education is part of this human attempt to promote the highest moral good in this world. Moral cosmopolitanism is stressed in moral education or formation (*Bildung*), for instance in Lectures on pedagogy, where Kant claims that the young student should be helped to cultivate "philanthropy towards others and then also cosmopolitan dispositions", which entails "an interest in the best for the world" (LP, 9: 499), which I read as a shorthand of the concept of the highest political and moral good in this world.

When referring to the republican constitution or commonwealth in this chapter, I have the ideal – the *respublica noumenon* – in mind; Kant frequently states that the republic as we find it in experience can only approach this ideal. He concedes that also a monarchy can follow the "spirit of republicanism", that is, adhere to the republican form of government or "manner of governing": "The constitution may be republican either in its *political form* or only in its *manner of governing,* in having the state ruled through the unity of the sovereign (the monarch) by analogy with the laws that a nation would provide itself in accordance with the universal principles of legality" (Conflict, 7: 88). At the same time he makes it clear that even a monarchy that governs in a republican manner is only of provisional legitimacy and has a duty to reform itself towards a representative republic. This republic by definition adheres to the republican form of government, even though it can always degenerate into despotism (Peace, 8: 350–3, MM, 6: 340–1, Conflict, 7: 91).

7.1 The republican tradition and the Kantian republic

According to a widespread interpretation, Kant was a typical early liberal. Along these lines, Frederick Beiser has asserted that "the diabolic Kantian republic required no education at all" (Beiser 2003: 90, referring to Peace, 8: 366). This assessment is based on the simple juxtaposition of the liberal tradition and the republican tradition of Machiavelli, Harrington, Montesquieu, Fletcher and others. Representatives of the republican or civic humanist tradition emphasized *virtus*, *vertu politique* or civic virtue and the political participation of citizens. Civic humanists or civic republicans were extremely worried about the threat of corruption, caused by citizens who put private interests above the common good, or material concerns above civic virtue. Traditionally republicans emphasized the importance of public education to foster the desired political virtue, in particular the willingness of citizens to sacrifice their own lives for the fatherland (Pocock

1975, Skinner 1998 and Peterson 2011). Early liberals, on the other hand, emphasised enlightened self-interest and – so the story goes – saw the active cultivation of virtue by the government as an infringement of the rights of citizens, as an intrusion into the private sphere. This juxtaposition of republicans and early liberals is perhaps fraught with oversimplifications; the alleged incompatibility of the two "camps" in the eighteenth century is perhaps a myth (Goldie 2006: 50). Be that as it may, I claim that it is an oversimplification to assign Kant to the camp of the early liberals, in particular because of Rousseau's influence. Kant was a republican of sorts (see for instance Fetscher 2006: 587–92, Ripstein 2009: 42–50, 203, 229 and 292).

The distinction between and separation of the moral from the legal sphere has often been seen as "typically liberal" – and highly problematic – in secondary literature (see for instance MM, 6: 218–221 as well as Byrd and Hruschka 2010, Kersting 1984 and 2004, Moran 2012 and Ripstein 2009 for discussions). There can be no doubt that the distinction is a cornerstone of Kant's system. In the 1790ies, for instance, he distinguished philosophical chiliasm – which is political and includes the highest political good, namely perpetual peace and a world-republic – from theological chiliasm, which believes in "the completed moral improvement of the human race" (Religion, 6: 34). The clear distinction between the moral and the legal/juridical sphere seems to undermine any theory of political or cosmopolitical education. The separation of right and ethics implies the differentiation between juridical legality and morality. Things were easier for the civic republicans here: personal virtue overlapped with civic virtue, and this was identical with the activities of the citizen in the commonwealth.

I want to argue that while legal and moral spheres are distinct and Kant kept them separate, he held that they might mutually influence each other, and contribute to a dynamic process. Kant's reasoning can be reconstructed as follows (for a discussion see, among others, Willaschek 2005: 198–204):

1. All duties of right (such as keeping a promise) are also duties of virtue, even though "ethical lawgiving ... *cannot* be external" (MM, 6: 220).
2. Right is independent of the good will of citizens, since it relies on coercion of external behaviour, not on moral dispositions (cf. MM, 6: 232). Coercion guarantees that legal norms are obeyed.
3. Obedience to legal norms has to be distinguished from their possible legitimacy.
4. In order to be of lasting efficiency, legal norms are in need of the "feeling of respect for the [...] law" (KpV, 5: 75); the generic moral feeling is its basis (KpV, 5: 75, 80, GMS, 4: 460, MM, 6: 399–400).

5. A government is not entitled to enforce this inner dimension. "[W]oe to the legislator who would want to bring about through coercion a polity directed to ethical ends! For he would thereby not only achieve the very opposite of ethical ends, but also undermine his political ends and render them insecure" (Religion, 6: 96). The ethical commonwealth has its own laws and ways to promote obedience distinct from the political community.
6. Political communities have a legitimate desire to ensure compliance (cf. ibid. 6: 95), may promote formation or *Bildung*, a moral mode of thinking and so on with non-coercive means (see for instance Moran 2012: 230 – 40). The end result may be "a polity directed to ethical ends".
7. The tension between coercing external obedience to legal norms and relying on moral dispositions cannot be avoided; it can only be softened by civic education.
8. Civic education should be in agreement with humanity's vocation (*Bestimmung*) to form a "cosmopolitical unity" (Anthropology, 7: 333).
9. The republican constitution itself has a pedagogical function (see below).

The key passage is Kant's claim that "it is not the case that a good state constitution is to be expected from inner morality; on the contrary, the good moral formation of a people is to be expected from a good state constitution" (Peace, 8: 366). The good state constitution Kant refers to is the republican constitution of the first definitive article (see Peace, 8: 352–3 and Ripstein 2009: 182ff.).

7.2 Cosmopolitical education according to Kant

Traditionally, civic republicans emphasized the importance of education. Whereas despotic forms of government usually relied on fear, Montesquieu famously claimed, republics had to foster a sense of community, a willingness to sacrifice one's interests in the name of the whole, among its citizenry. He distinguished among despotism which is based on fear, monarchies relying on honour and republics aiming at virtue. As a consequence, "it is in a republican government that the full power of education is needed. [...] political virtue is a renunciation of oneself, which is always a painful thing. One can define virtue as love of the laws and the homeland. This love, requiring a continuous preference of the public interest over one's own produces all the individual virtues; they are only that preference" (Montesquieu 1989: 35–6). The key goal was inculcating pupils with this form of republican patriotism. Rousseau followed suit. He also defined political virtue as the renunciation of oneself on behalf of the community. For him, the true *patrie* was a republic, characterized by freedom, equality, and the rule of law. The goal of republican education was transforming a mere aggregate of selfish individuals – as in commercial society – into a "moral and collective body" (Rousseau 1997b: 11). Patriotism and civic virtue coincided, and integrated *amour de soi* and *amour propre* (on these two concepts see Fetscher 1980, pp. 65–75 and Dent 2005, pp. 39–40, 68–72). Rousseau's pedagogy usually relied on "inclination, passion, necessity" (Rousseau 1997d: 189) and appealed to the pupil's emotions. Yet he also offered passages that came close to a Kantian understanding of morality (see for instance Cassirer 1939 and Recki 2001). Like Rousseau, Kant subscribes to the close connection of education with politics (see Bolle 2012, Wain 2011 and Munzel 2012).

Kant's pedagogy is distinct from the educational theories of the civic republicans, and, for that matter, from standard theories of the "pedagogical age", the eighteenth century (see Munzel 1012: 5–183). First of all, he distinguished between morality and virtue or the "strength of soul" (Anthropology, 7: 293; see also Religion, 6: 57, MM, 6: 380, Munzel 2012: 234–5, 281–5). Secondly, moral self-legislation and self-motivation ultimately aim at a cosmopolitan conduct of thought (*Denkungsart*) and a cosmopolitan comportment of mind or disposition (*Gesinnung*). This is our supreme or highest-order maxim, the "subjective ground" as a deed of our freedom (Religion, 6: 21), the "ultimate ground and justification of our actions" relating to our character, the overall orientation concerning our lives' conduct (Caswell 2006: 195; cf. Formosa 2007, 2012: 173). Third, Kant takes a detour: in his moral theory, cosmopolitan values are not simply instilled or inculcated in pupils. Autonomy cannot be trained like a skill, and manipulation or indoctrination has to be avoided at all costs. Morality is not simply expanded self-love. A cosmopolitan disposition is a long-term result of helping adolescents to form their own moral characters, defined as "the aptitude (*Fertigkeit*) of acting according to maxims [...] of humanity (*Menschheit*)" (LP, 9: 481), "the steadfast commitment to virtue that is realized through a resolute conduct of thought (*Denkungsart*)" (Munzel 1999: 2; cf. KpV, 5: 152 and Anthropology, 7: 294–5). A shared moral predisposition turns humans all over the world into equals. Their possible efforts to cultivate their respective moral potential turn them into fellow-beings of a global moral community. The overall result is an educational theory that is cosmopolitan in character (see also the previous chapter).

The cornerstone of Kant's theory is the concept of vocation, taken over from Spalding and his contemporaries. In his *Lectures on pedagogy* (1803), for instance, Kant wrote: "Many germs lie within humanity, and now it is our business to develop the natural dispositions proportionally and to unfold humanity from its germs and to make it happen that the human being reaches his vocation" (LP, 9: 445; see also Collins, 27: 470–1; more passages in Brandt 2009). Humanity (*die*

Menschheit) mentioned in the quotation is the intelligible, moral element in humans or rational beings (cf. LP, 9: 442). Later in the lectures, Kant emphasised the same cluster of ideas: humans themselves have to develop their dispositions, since "Providence has not placed them already finished" in them (ibid. 446); the ultimate vocation is morality, but cultivated "proportionally" in combination with prudence and skilfulness. This is a dynamic process: Kant held that for individuals, cultivation, civilization and moralization or moral formation are part and parcel of a process. This dynamic element is also hinted at by Kant when he writes that "[f]ormerly, human beings did not even have a conception of the perfection which human nature can reach. We ourselves are not even yet clear about this concept" (ibid.: 445). There is a cognitive aspect, since humans have the task to develop a proper concept of education, which has the potential to become a science, that is, a systematic and coherent theory.

The tenets of Kant's cosmopolitical education can be summarized as follows. He developed a broad concept of education; he agreed with the civic republicans that education was indispensable for genuine morality; he subscribed to their belief in law's educational function; he held that a republic – or rather the republican constitution – was the proper basis and condition of moral formation; he believed that he followed Rousseau in constructing an embedded form of cosmopolitan formation (I am going to deal with some of these claims in the next section).

First, Kant developed a broad concept of education; places of education were not only families, schools and universities. Equally important was the education in the (republican) state, namely civic education – in particular the way the constitution "invisibly" educated its citizens. Education in a broad sense also included self-education (as depicted in the novel *Robinson Crusoe*, 1719), education in a friendship (Moran 2012: 168–203), in a society, as a member of a church community (Stroud 2005). Even dinner parties – as Kant described them – had a pedagogical function, could serve as opportunities to practice hospitality, to cultivate self-discipline, "mutual respect and benevolence" (Anthropology, 7: 281), and to promote "true humanity" (Anthropology, 7: 278; Formosa 2010). Kant explicitly claimed that social intercourse includes a cosmopolitan dimension. As Paul Formosa put it, "Friendship, enlightenment and cosmopolitanism, as well as virtue and happiness, all achieve their union only in a society that revolves around universal conversation between equals" (Formosa 2010: 21). A pleasant dinner party could be an anticipation of this universal society. Public deliberations as well as private conversations can prepare the ground for the cultivation of one's moral character and the attainment of virtue.

Secondly, education and formation are indispensable for morality. "The human being can only become human through education. He is nothing except what education makes out of him" (LP, 9: 443). This looks like an extreme formulation, and seems to conflict with the idea of autonomy. Yet if the term "education" is understood in a broad sense, and includes, for instance, self- education, then the statement makes sense. Humans can realize their vocation or calling only through education, the stepping stone of autonomy. The process of moral formation includes the following phases (see for instance Munzel 1999: 279 – 88 and Formosa 2012): there is the germ for the good at the beginning (Religion, 6: 27, 45), together with the natural propensity to evil. In society, people cultivate what Kant calls discipline, imperatives of skilfulness (*Geschicklichkeit*) and prudence (*Klugheit*), learning how to use other people for their own ends (LP, 9: 455). The ultimate goal is the acquisition and cultivation of a moral conduct of thought, and the cultivation of virtue, a process that culminates in the idea of a moral character or virtue.

Third, reason is in need of cultivation which "needs attempts, practice and instruction in order gradually to progress from one stage of insight to another" (Idea, 8: 19; cf. Beginning, 8: 115 and LP, 9: 445). This is the empirical side of the gradual progress towards perfection (the idea of progress is an assumption based on our reflective power of judgment). In educational theory, this requires, for instance, experiments (cf. LP, 9: 451) and the conscious attempt to turn education into a science (ibid. 9: 447). Since the development of all natural predispositions takes place in time, some forms of government are better suited to promote this development than others.

Finally, Kant's cosmopolitanism is embedded and dynamic. The embedded element can be traced back to Rousseau's influence, and, indirectly, to the civic humanists. Kant's juridical and moral cosmopolitanism is compatible with thin forms of patriotism (such as contemporary "constitutional patriotism"; for a discussion see Kleingeld 2006, 2010 and 2012: 13 – 39, Bohman 2010 and Tan 2004). In a manner reminiscent of Rousseau, Kant criticized the indifferent *Weltliebhaber*, "because of too much generality, he scatters his affection and entirely loses any particular personal devotion" (17: 673, translated in Kleingeld 2006: 485). Kant advocated a form of civic and moderate patriotism with citizens enjoying legal freedom and equality and regarding "the commonwealth as the maternal womb" (TP, 8: 291). The commonwealth, where citizens are "authorized to protect its rights by laws of the common will", is the opposite of despotism or a paternalistic government (ibid.). The common bond is formed by republican principles, not an ethnic or national identity, and civic republicanism is therefore compatible with forms of cosmopolitanism. This way Kant offers a form of embedded cosmopolitanism, with people identifying with the local and the embedded, while also conceiving themselves in terms of universal obligations and rights. In an unpublished note, Kant claimed that "national illusion" (*National-*

wahn) had to be eradicated and should be replaced by patriotism and cosmopolitanism (Refl. 1353, 15: 591). The principled patriot is cosmopolitan (15: 873).

Kant's pedagogics is situated between the Scylla of indoctrination and the Charybdis of utter helplessness. This becomes obvious if we compare Kant with some representatives of German romanticism. As Frederick Beiser has put it, its key paradox was "its utter commitment and devotion to the education of humanity, and yet its recognition that it cannot and ought not do anything to achieve it. We are left, then, with a striking gap between theory and practice, which it was the very purpose of romanticism to overcome" (Beiser 2003: 105). Many romantics were stuck with the dilemma that freedom cannot be taught. This is true, yet the claim has to be qualified. Education cannot guarantee the cultivation of autonomy or virtue, but can facilitate it – in spite of all coercion that is part of human society. Instructors or teachers should not manipulate their students, but they can influence the conditions that shape the development of one's moral character (Munzel 1999: 259–63, 330–3, Koch 2003, Cavallar 2005).

7.3 Kant's vision of progress in a genuine republic

I want to start with a caveat: "The philosophy of history is now widely believed to be extinct. How could anyone take seriously the idea of progress in the wake of the bloodiest century on record, in the faces of its 100 million victims?" (McCarthy 2009: 131). After the Holocaust, the philosophy of history can only be critical, tentative, and moral: wary of its tendency to wind up with dogmatic metaphysics; cautious with any predictions about the future; careful that individuals are not turned into mere means of progress, "sacrificed at the altar of world history". Kant's philosophy of history tells the story of the gradual development of human predispositions (*Anlagen*), the cultivation of our cognitive faculties, the establishment of political communities which have a duty to reform themselves to approach the spirit of a republic, and ultimately to form republics. A similar kind of reasoning is applied to religious communities, educational systems, and international relations – all of them are supposed to reform themselves to approach the ideal of reason (see Rorty 2009 and Sommer 2006 on the philosophy of history, Kleingeld 1999 and Honneth 2004 on the possibility of moral progress).

The *Endzweck* or *Bestimmung* (vocation) of the human race is of course morality. Kant claimed that he was the first philosopher to have found the one and only method of proper moral formation (see chapter 6 for more). The moral law, he asserted, should be taught "by way of reason alone" (Groundwork 4: 410). This is the "autocracy of reason": reason is not only self-legislating, it can also serve as an incentive and become practical. Kant apparently believed that the

Enlightenment was a stage in human history where people would gradually come to realize the truth behind this method, that this was the one and only method of proper moral formation. Phrases like "those of us who are working on" (Starke 1831: II, 124–5, translated in Louden 2000: 42) probably suggest that Kant saw himself as part of this Enlightenment "project" – if there ever was one – or movement.

In a first step, it is crucial to overcome the familiar cliché that Kantian ethics are individualist, solipsistic, static, and unconcerned about ends. A string of recent interpreters have challenged this cliché, and suggested that if there is a reduced account of human agency in the *Groundwork*, then only for methodological reasons. They claim that Kant's mature position is not that of solipsistic, but that of public, intersubjective and communicative reason, and that Kantian morality entails the opening up towards the world, either (only) "in thought" or also (and more importantly) in practice, by checking the validity of our judgements with the help of others (see chapter 1, section 2). Judgements are exercised in interaction with others, and the enlarged conduct of thought even *requires* others and their divergent perspectives.

The relationship between republicanism and cosmopolitical formation is of course complex (for discussions see Munzel 1996, Munzel 1999: 321–333, Munzel 2003, Meyer 2005 and Moran 2012: 204–40). I want to start with two theses:

1. Republicanism, as a system of external, enforceable and equal laws cannot have a direct influence on moral formation, internal freedom or virtue.
2. Yet republicanism can have an indirect and beneficial influence.

I divide my discussion into three possible spheres of influence: republicanism and peace; publicity and the process of Enlightenment; the pedagogical function of the republican constitution.

First, despotic states are prone to wage wars – which are the scourge of the human race – and tend to spend too much money on the military. They hinder possible legal or educational progress (see for instance Idea, 8: 26, Peace, 8: 367). Genuine republics, by contrast, are inherently peaceful – it is more likely that they contribute to the highest political good (Peace, 8: 349–353). The cultivation of our germs and predispositions requires "an immense series of generations, each of which transmits its enlightenment to the next" (Idea, 8: 19), and this difficult and slow process is only possible in a condition that can be characterized with the phrases "rule of law", "republicanism" and "global peace" – in short, in "a universal *cosmopolitan condition*" (Idea, 8: 28). In the *Conflict of the Faculties*, Kant formulated this argument in favour of the republican constitution as follows: "at least negatively, progress toward the better is assured humanity in spite of all its infirmity, for it is at least left undisturbed in its advance" (Conflict, 7: 86). True republicans are also cosmopolitans, insofar as they do not care about the military glory or reputation of one's state, but concern themselves with the "best of the world" or the "whole of the world", at least indirectly, for instance, by promoting reforms at home (see LP, 9: 448, 15: 627–9; Kater 1999: 171–4).

Secondly, the republican form of government is more likely to create a public sphere and promote the process of Enlightenment (see Blesenkemper 1987, Keienburg 2011, Ladenthin 2005). In one of his essays for the *Berlinische Monatsschrift*, Kant asked rhetorically: "Yet how much and how correctly would we *think* if we did not think as it were in community with others to whom we *communicate* our thoughts, and who communicate theirs with us! Thus one can very well say that this external power which wrenches away people's freedom publicly to *communicate* their thoughts also takes from them the freedom to *think* – that single gem remaining to us in the midst of all the burdens of civil life, through which alone we can devise means of overcoming all the evils of our condition" (Thinking, 8: 144; cf. Enlightenment, 8: 37). Kant defended the strong claim that humans all over the world share the same formal cognitive structures a priori, also in moral terms. This shared capacity can only be actualized if a public sphere is established. An individual is an animal capable of reason, an *animal rationabile* (*vernunftbegabt*), and needs others to find out whether what she or he thinks indeed reflects "common human reason", *die allgemeine Vernunft* or requires amendment, improvement or rejection. The reason of others is one indispensable touchstone of truth. This public sphere is global in principle, since bounded communities only have a provisional legitimacy. In the Enlightenment essay, for instance, Kant equals "the public" with "the world" (Enlightenment, 8: 37, 38 and 41). The public sphere is outlined by Kant as the idea of a world-wide legal community (the society or republic of states) and the more challenging idea of a world-wide moral community (the ethical commonwealth).

The public sphere encompasses three dimensions in Kant's political philosophy (for the following see Keienburg 2011: 23–42 and 167–8). First, just maxims in politics require publicity. Governments have a duty to cultivate maxims that pass the test of publicity; citizens have the corresponding right to express their own opinion. The "freedom of the pen" is "the sole palladium of the people's rights" (TP, 8: 304; see also Anthropology, 7: 128–9) and censorship contradicts the idea of the original contract. Justice can be thought of "only as *publicly known*" (Peace, 8: 381). The principle of publicity concretizes the enlarged way of thinking (see below). Publicity is not only a thought experiment, but ultimately requires discourse, debate, an actual public sphere, and the control of politics via public criticism. This in turn can only happen in a republican form of government.

Secondly, the public sphere encompasses the general public of (active) citizens who have started to enlighten themselves and to form so-called "public opinion". The proper general public is the *"world of readers"*, ultimately the community or "society of citizens of the world", where the use of reason is free, in contrast to the passive, private and heteronomous reason of subjects such as civil servants who obey orders in a "mechanical" fashion (Enlightenment, 8: 37–8). This is a sphere beyond the authority of the government. Despotism does not leave room for it, only the republican form of government does. Kant's example is the "enlightened absolutism" of Frederick II of Prussia, who, for instance, allowed intellectuals and clergymen to debate the merits and disadvantages of a new hymnbook for the Berlin parishes at the beginning of the 1780ies (see Enlightenment, 8: 40 and Spankeren 2011). The public sphere is also a vehicle of Enlightenment. Testing one's own judgement with the help of others may help us to transcend logical egoism (see below). "The opposite of egoism can only be pluralism, that is, the way of thinking in which one is not concerned with oneself as the whole world, but rather regards and conducts oneself as a mere citizen of the world" (Anthropology, 7: 130). Finally, the public sphere encompasses the activities of the general public which aims at constituting itself as the general will. Representation is the mediating principle between this public sphere and the government, which is bound to act "as if" its maxims could be willed by the citizens.

Third, the republican constitution has a pedagogical function (Munzel 1999: 321–333). The citizens' participation in a republican commonwealth guaranteeing and fostering the public use of reason will in all likelihood cultivate their predispositions (*Anlagen*) for practical reasoning. In particular, a republican form of government might help citizens to train the three maxims of the enlarged way of thinking, namely thinking for oneself, assuming the perspective of others and thinking consistently (cf. KdU, 5: 294–5, Keienburg 2011: 154–81, Munzel 1996, Munzel 1999: 175–81). There are various reasons for this: the republican citizens are helped by the form of their government to become capable of self-legislation in the sphere of politics. A republic is by definition based on *legal* equality, and this prepares the ground for the idea of *moral* equality central to the idea of the ethical commonwealth. As a consequence, Kant rejected any hereditary aristocracy and thus implicitly the *ancien régime* as incompatible with the idea of juridical equality (MM, 6: 329, TP, 8: 292, 297, Peace, 8: 351 note). Cosmopolitan formation also encompasses becoming familiar with and learning to appreciate the ideas of right and political freedom, and these ideas are – if only imperfectly – approximated in the republic. The capacity for enlarged thinking has to be linked with a moral attitude (ideally, with a version of cognitive moral cosmopolitanism). This is in turn compatible with Rousseau's concept of civic patriotism, which focuses on the rule of law, mutual respect, and the reciprocal rights and duties of citizens. Judgements are exercised in interaction with others, and the enlarged conduct of thought even *requires* others and their divergent perspectives (on the role of judgements and their presupposition of universality see Engstrom 2009: 98–126). The Kantian republic is the perfect training ground in this respect. Ideally, judgement eventually becomes "a habit" (KpV, 5: 159, cf. 5: 154–5 and Munzel 1999: 318–20). In spite of some differences, civic education and moral formation share a common basis: both demarcate spheres of freedom; both cultivate or train the power of judgement; both cultivate forms of freedom, in the case of civil education, the external freedom of choice, in the case of moral education, moral or transcendental freedom (see Cavallar 2005: 62–7 for more).

Let me stop here for a moment and point out two possible misunderstandings. The first misunderstanding assumes that the republican constitution guarantees that active citizens become "on the whole […] more virtuous" and bring "a community of agents closer to the highest good", as Kate Moran claims (Moran 2012: 240). Kant would never have asserted that there is a clear causal relationship, since this would be uncritical speculation. All we can know is that these efforts *might* promote moral legality or even morality. The second misunderstanding is the basis of the first. Again in the words of Kate Moran, it is sometimes believed that the main advantage of the republican constitution lies in the fact that "it can help provide background conditions that make virtuous action easier" since it forces criminals to comply with the law, and an "honest person" would not suffer by being virtuous (Moran 2012: 210 and 209). This is a problematic interpretation of Kant's doctrine. It blurs the distinction between right and morality and implies that moral formation is all about making it more likely in the realm of experience. In the first place, however, moral formation is about step-by-step, gradual and long-term character formation. Put bluntly, the republican constitution is not useful because it teaches citizens that "crime doesn't pay" and the moral person can expect a happy ending, it is useful because it might help citizens to understand that morality is not about usefulness, it might help them to cultivate moral judgement and the enlarged way of thinking. The republican constitution has a genuine *pedagogical* or *didactical* function.

A republican commonwealth will in all likelihood combat the tendency toward logical egoism, the *"prejudice of excessive trust placed in oneself"* (Logic, 24: 187; see also Anthropology, 7: 129–30, 219) as well as its opposite, the prejudice of passivity or imitation, where the judgements of others are simply imitated or accepted as true without further scrutiny (Logic, 24: 188; cf. Moran 2012: 230–40). We can combat the tendency to make wrong judgements only when communicating with others, which is more likely in a republican form of government. A priori elements in themselves are true, and the senses can neither be true nor false (because no judgement is involved). Yet the judgements of our understanding (*Verstand, intellectus*) may be wrong, since "error is effected ... through the unnoticed influence of sensibility on understanding, through which it happens that the subjective grounds of the judgment join with the objective ones" (KrV, B 350). When communicating with others in public we form "a common world", and can find out whether our thoughts or judgments "also agree with the understanding of others; for otherwise something merely subjective ... would easily be taken for something objective" (Anthropology, 7: 219).

In a section on "permissible moral illusion", Kant asserts that civilized humans are inclined to adopt the illusion of a moral disposition, by pretending, for instance, that they respect others. Kant does not see this as a major problem. In the first place, nobody is deceived by this since everybody is familiar with the deception coming from others. In addition, moral illusion has the potential for fostering a moral disposition. "For when human beings play these roles, eventually the virtues, whose illusion they have merely affected for a considerable length of time, will gradually really be aroused and merge into the dispositions" (Anthropology, 7: 151). A culture of respect is more likely in a republican state (on the culture of respect in modern pluralistic societies see Hill 2000).

I have argued in this chapter that according to Kant, successful moral formation is facilitated by the republican constitution. This leads to the following antinomy:

Thesis: moral formation is the product of the republican constitution (and of favourable cosmopolitical conditions).

Antithesis: moral freedom constitutes "the transcendental condition for the possibility" of political freedom (Munzel 2012: XVI).

The antithesis is developed by Felicitas Munzel in her work, especially in her recent book, *Kant's Conception of Pedagogy* (2012). She puts the emphasis on the inner self and its possible corruption by self-interest and egoism that threaten personal integrity. Political liberty presupposes moral freedom, the free capacity to contribute to the highest good. The danger is not only political despotism; it is also the despotism of self-interest and a corrupt *Denkungsart*. Munzel writes that only where honest Socratic examination "is freely exercised, where the inner freedom of integrity of the morally well-ordered conduct of thought, of the integrity of the honest and upright character, reigns, will the political, civil right of free speech be realized as a genuine freedom' (Munzel 2012: 178; cf. XVI, 83, 171–9, 233, Munzel 1999: 175–81).

I can only hint at a possible solution of this antinomy here (see also the discussion in Munzel 1999: 177–83): moral or inner freedom and formation on the one hand and political freedom and cosmopolitical conditions on the other are mutually dependent. The thesis has to be qualified along the lines of Kantian criticism: moral freedom (and thus formation) is the *possible outcome* of the republican constitution. Republics help their citizens to take "a great step ... *toward* morality", but this "is not yet a moral step" (Peace, 8: 376 note) – a step that can only be taken as an act of inner freedom. Any republic also depends on the moral characters of its citizens. The antithesis brackets Kant's insistence that the cultivation of moral freedom in part depends on certain external factors which he summarized under the term "cosmopolitan condition" (Idea, 8: 28). Yet Kant repeatedly emphasized that the stage of cultivation, civilization and quasi-republican government in the best of cases leads to an individual "of good morals", not necessarily to "a morally good human being" (Religion, 6: 30, Idea, 8: 26).

Finally, I want to point out that I do not fully share Kant's occasional optimism concerning progress in ethical didactics and republican governments. I also do not share his hope that "the times during which equal progress takes place will ... become always shorter" (Peace, 8: 386). Republican democracies at present seem to degenerate into oligarchies or democracies in the Kantian sense, that is, states with despotic forms of government (Peace, 8: 352–3). Current trends in educational sciences show a new pragmatism and utilitarianism, a focus on skills, prudence, efficiency and usefulness for the labour market, with a tendency to abandon the idea of moral formation or *Bildung* the way Kant envisioned it (for a discussion see chapter 8, section 4).

8 Conclusion: From Kant to the present

8.1 From cosmopolitanism to nation states in German philosophy: Schiller, Novalis, Fichte, Hegel, Herbart (1795–1835)

Reinhard Brandt has remarked that the moral philosophy focusing on the vocation of the human species, so prominent in the second half of the eighteenth century in German territories, is nowadays dead and buried (see Brandt 2009: 54; for an example see Anders 1980: 386–7). There have been recent attempts to recover the cosmopolitan dimension in educational science (see especially Todd 2009). It is often asserted that cosmopolitan trends or elements of Enlightenment philosophy were "lost" in the following century, with the triumph of nationalism and politics focussing on the sovereign nation state.

Many late eighteenth-century intellectuals turned towards Europe, perceived as a political or legal community, as a cultural entity, or as both. Up to the end of the eighteenth century, European thinkers had developed two distinct political roles for Europe. According to the group of political cosmopolitans such as Kant, Europe was the starting point of a global federation or world state. Authors like Saint-Pierre, on the other hand, had designed plans of an exclusively European federation. After 1789, plans and ideas of this second type, and Europeanism in general, seem to have gained the upper hand (see Bartelson 2009: 86–140, Cavallar 2011: 61–3 and 104–8). In this section, I am going to tell the fairly complex story of the transition from Kantian cosmopolitanism to the triumph of the nation state, to the "nationalization of community" (Bartelson 2009: 108) in Hegel's philosophy.

The debate on cosmopolitanism in German-speaking countries towards the end of the eighteenth century revolved around two issues. First, intellectuals discussed the significance of the French Revolution, its perceived failure, and its relationship to cosmopolitan ideas. Secondly, they continued to debate how cosmopolitan and patriotic allegiances could be combined. Many came to identify cosmopolitanism with the Revolution, and rejected both. Patriotism was subsequently replaced by forms of nationalism, and the latter sometimes declared incompatible with cosmopolitan sentiments. While some intellectuals tried to keep an uneasy balance, and still endorsed some form of patriotic cosmopolitanism, the general trend was clearly favouring nationalism (see Albrecht 2005: 319–52, Pinkard 2002: 82–5, Thielking 2000: 38–83, Viroli 2003: 95–160).

Poet, dramatist, historian and philosopher Friedrich von Schiller (1759–1805) went beyond Kant with his theory of aesthetic education, as developed in *Letters on the Aesthetic Education of Man* (1795). He freely admitted that his assertions were on the whole based on "Kantian principles"; yet he also disagreed with Kant in many respects (see Beiser 2005: 37–46, 169–190). In particular, Schiller disliked Kant's alleged dualisms and abstract philosophizing. His description of the philosopher who tries to "detain the fleeting apparition" and therefore must "preserve its living spirit in a fleshless skeleton of words" (Schiller 1795: 11) obviously has Kant in mind, whom he had studied for years. Schiller agreed with Kant that reason was capable of finding its own moral law, but held that it was not powerful enough to motivate humans to act. Art can unify the two aspects of human nature, reason and sensibility (cf. Schiller 1795: 15–6 and 103; for introductions see Beiser 2005, Bollenbeck 2007: 22–110, Matuschek 2009, Murray 1994 and Zelle 2005). Like many German intellectuals, Schiller cherished the principles of the French Revolution, but rejected the means applied, especially the use of violence and terror. Unlike Kant, Schiller held that his age was already enlightened (and not just in the process of enlightening itself). "Reason has purified itself from the illusions of the senses and from a mendacious sophistry, and philosophy herself raises her voice and exhorts us to return to the bosom of nature, to which she had first made us unfaithful. Whence then is it that we still remain barbarians?" (Schiller 1795: 33). Schiller claimed that the revolution had failed because people had not been sufficiently educated in their moral characters (cf. Schiller 1795: 32–4). Like Kant, Schiller defended a concept of the vocation that encompassed the individual and at the same time the human species. He distinguished between the enlightened, cosmopolitan and liberal *Weltbürger* with a moral disposition from the selfish *Weltmann* who had cultivated his understanding and prudence but not his practical reason (cf. ibid.: 13, 21, 139, 157). Like Kant (but perhaps more explicitly), Schiller insisted on the proportionate development of capacities as a precondition of the "aesthetic state" in the future (cf. ibid.: 29–30). Individuals as well as the species only reach their vocation if their development passes through three distinct phases: the physical condition where the human being is exposed to the power of nature, the aesthetic condition where she emancipates herself from it, and the moral condition where she controls the power of nature – but in complete harmony with nature (cf. ibid.: 97–103). The most pressing task of the present age was the cultivation of sensibility (*Empfindungsvermögen*; 34); in Schiller's account, the artist – rather than the philosopher, teacher, priest or theologian – was the proper educator of the human species. In contrast to Kant, there was no room for religious cosmopolitanism in Schiller's account of human self-perfection. The highest good was presented as an immanent and secular concept: the agreement or harmony of dignity and happiness (*Glückseligkeit*) would be achieved by culture in the course of historical progress, and not – as in

Kant – perhaps in history as well as in a moral realm beyond history (Schiller 1795: 99; cf. Beiser 2005: 2–3, 43, 127–8). There was a clear break. Schiller belonged to a younger generation where the teachings of Christianity had become marginalized.

In sum, the Schiller of the early 1790s endorsed the cosmopolitan universalism of a German *Weltbürger*. He defended a form of patriotism with people forming the aesthetic state not because of their self-interests or their (Kantian) sense of duty but because they had internalised the moral law and sufficiently cultivated their moral feelings to obey it (cf. Beiser 2005: 163–4). In Schiller's account, this patriotism was pacifist, moral, and cosmopolitan. This would soon change. The last decades of the eighteenth century had witnessed the development of a home-grown – and impressive – German culture, which led some Germans to adopt the concept of a German "cultural nation" (*Kulturnation*). Sometime after 1797, after the first humiliating defeats against Napoleon, Schiller developed the notion of "German greatness", and tried to define it as "ethical greatness". He was clearly struggling to cope with the emotional consequences of military and political defeat. Germany was supposed to be superior, and Schiller expressed his pride in *national* German culture. Jim Reed summarized his development in the following way: "his argument had shifted from national consolation to national self-assertion, from national self-assertion to claims of a unique national value, and on to the edge of nationalistic aggression. In other words, perhaps he discerned the beginnings of demagogy in what he was writing" (Reed 2006: 46).

Early German romantics, representatives of the *Frühromantik* from roughly 1797–1802, agreed with the Enlightenment and Kant on the importance of education or *Bildung* (cf. Beiser 2003: 88). Some went beyond Schiller's claim that art could unify the two aspects of human nature, reason and sensibility. They transformed their aestheticism by asserting that religion as a form of art would or could be the cornerstone of the new formation or *Bildung* (see Pinkard 2002: 136, 144–64, Beiser 2002: 454, Beiser 2003: 28, 88–105, 134, 171–86). Novalis (Georg Philipp Friedrich von Hardenberg, 1772–1801) was a case in point. He asserted in "Christianity or Europe", a fragment written at the end of 1799: "Only religion can reawaken Europe, make the people secure, and install Christianity with new magnificence in its old peace making office, visible to the whole world" (Novalis 1799: 77–8). He presented his vision of romantic Christian cosmopolitanism only six years after Kant had published his *Religion*, and only one year after the *Conflict of the Faculties*, but Kant and Novalis were worlds apart: Novalis' romantic understanding of religion contrasted with Kant's rational and moral religion; Novalis criticized Kant's cosmopolitanism as "based on an abstract and legalistic notion of human rights" (Kleingeld 2008: 270); Novalis' apparent glorification of the European Middle Ages was directly opposed to

Kant's sceptical look at Church history; Novalis' new metaphysics, his rejection of "common distinctions", his enigmatic language, his new spirituality could be seen as uncritical philosophy by Kant's standards (for a comparison see Waibel 2007 and Kleingeld 2008).

Early German romantics are often assigned to the camp of nationalists since they criticized the Enlightenment (which has traditionally been conceptualized as "cosmopolitan" in nature). This widespread cliché has to be qualified. As Frederick Beiser and Esther Wohlgemut have demonstrated, the romantics did not reject the *Aufklärung* in its entirety and continued the discourse on patriotism and cosmopolitan sentiments in a modified form (Beiser 2003: 43–87, Wohlgemut 2009; see also Earle 2005), and as Pauline Kleingeld has convincingly shown, Novalis was a cosmopolitan, if of a particular sort (Kleingeld, 2008). Although Kant and Novalis are worlds apart in terms of epistemology, metaphysics, and the proper relationship between morality and religion, both share a form of religious cosmopolitanism, insofar as they both believed in a new, ecumenical, genuine cosmopolitan Christianity. Novalis phrased the idea of an invisible church of the future in "Christianity or Europe" the following way: "The other parts of the world wait for Europe's reconciliation and resurrection to join with it and become fellow citizens of the kingdom of heaven. [...] Should not all kindred religious minds be full of yearning to see heaven on earth?" (Novalis 1799: 78–9). Christianity should form one visible church "without regard to national boundaries" (ibid.: 79), apparently an ecumenical union of Protestantism and the Catholic faith and based on "genuine freedom" (ibid.). Novalis stressed the idea of the human race united by spirituality, by "faith and love", not by "having and knowing", or by pragmatic considerations based on utility, something the romantic associated with allegedly cold Enlightenment rationality (cf. Kleingeld 2008: 270). Critics were soon upset by Novalis' explicit enthusiasm for Roman Catholicism as well as the Middle Ages.

Novalis shared with Kant a teleological and dynamic conception of history. His starting point were the dispositions and predispositions of the human species: "the capacity of the race as a whole is immeasurable" (Novalis 1799: 68), whereas the powers of the individual are limited. Here, Novalis sided with Kant, Pölitz and Hegewisch and endorsed their distinction between the vocation of the individual and that of the species, and their claim that the vocation of the species could be reached at the end of history. According to Novalis, the last step of human development was the cultivation of the "spiritual sense" (63), which went beyond mere culture, civilization and (presumably) morality. The first attempt at a lasting Christian Europe in the Middle Ages had to fail, in particular because faith was "childlike" (61) then and "mankind was not mature or educated enough" (63). Cultural progress, the cultivation of prudence and skilfulness and the rise of commercial society were "harmful [...] for the spiritual sense" (ibid.), but had helped humans to move towards maturity.

For Novalis, the human race had reached a crucial stage during his own time: now that European civilization had passed necessary stages of development, the time was ripe for spiritual progress. This progress could be slowed down, it could even be reverted, but not blocked in perpetuity. "What does not now reach perfection will do in a future attempt, or in another later one" (64) – this is the underlying teleological doctrine, in full agreement with Kant, but without his critical caveat.

Philosopher Johann Gottlieb Fichte (1762–1814) is usually considered one of the founding fathers of German idealism as well as of German nationalism. While Fichte was doubtlessly celebrated as a national hero and champion of nationalism in Germany after 1862, especially during the Weimar Republic and by the National Socialists, he himself "stood at the crossroads between cosmopolitanism and nationalism" (Albada 2012: 38; for an introduction to Fichte's legal philosophy see James 2011). Fichte's case is fascinating, not only in light of his appropriation of Kant's philosophy and the history of Germany and Europe in the last two centuries, also on its own terms. One might be tempted to construct a contrast between Fichte's *Die Bestimmung des Menschen* (1800) and his notorious *Reden an die deutsche Nation* (1808), held during the occupation of Berlin by the French after Napoleon's devastating defeat of the Prussian army. In the former book, he outlined his cosmopolitan faith in the continuous spread of formation (*Bildung*) among nations, in the vocation of the human species to unite and form a "developed body" (Fichte 1800: 111), and in the ultimate goal of global perpetual peace based on culture, freedom, and free (republican) states (cf. ibid. 115). This is one aspect of the vocation of the species, the immanent one: the philosophy of history tells us that everything that happens in this world contributes to the formation of humans and thus to the attainment of their vocation (cf. ibid. 147). Yet humans are also members of a spiritual, divine world, since they are capable of morality and have a conscience (cf. ibid. 125–9, 138–40). This philosophy has affinities with Kant's doctrine and with late eighteenth-century cosmopolitan thought, especially with Kant's legal cosmopolitanism, his cosmopolitan right and religious cosmopolitanism. While Fichte's position was similar to Kant's in many respects, he distanced himself from his former inspiration as well. For instance, he identified a problem in Kant's concept of cosmopolitan right that in his opinion Kant had overlooked, namely unequal relationships of economic dependence among states (Fichte 1797: 320–334, James 2011: 87–111 and 2013).

In the *Addresses to the German Nation*, Fichte seems to have abandoned this form of cosmopolitanism, and taken the "nationalist turn" (for a recent analysis see Abizadeh, 2005). Fichte, who gave the speeches after Prussia's momentous defeats at the battles of Jena and Auerstädt in 1806, frankly declared that he spoke "for Germans only" (Fichte 1808: 10), argued for "German uniqueness", constructed an insurmountable, essential difference between being German on the one hand and foreigners and *Ausländerei* (foreignism) on the other (see Fichte 1808: 12, 47, 72, 81, 92, 100 and passim), and proposed a "specifically German national education" (*National-Erziehung*; ibid. 19). Nothing else but "the existence of the German nation" was at stake, Fichte declared dramatically (ibid. 17), setting the tone for German nationalist rhetoric to come.

However, picking passages from Fichte's speeches does not give the whole picture. For Fichte, the nation, a community characterized by shared culture, above all language (cf. Fichte 1808: 49–51, 166–7) was only a means to promote moral, spiritual and religious progress, not an end in itself. His main thesis was that Germans should take the lead and further the cause of cosmopolitanism. In a key passage, Fichte claimed that "the true vocation of the human race on earth [...] shall be this, that it fashions itself with freedom into that which it really and originally is" (Fichte 1808: 42). This is – to use a convenient cliché – the voice of "Enlightenment cosmopolitanism", with a dose of Kantian ethics: the final end is something humans should achieve due to their freedom and moral endeavours. "Self-fashioning" has to begin in space and time, at a certain place in the world and in a certain age. According to Fichte's speculative philosophy of history, the human race has to pass through five necessary ages in history, humans having reached the third in Fichte's time (ibid. 9; see also James 2011: 168–72). Now there was the chance to enter the fourth stage entitled "Progressive Justification" which embraced truth, as Fichte had outlined in *The Characteristics of the Present Age*. Time was one aspect, space the other. "With respect to space, [...] we believe that it falls first and foremost to the Germans to inaugurate the new age, as pioneers and exemplars for the rest of humanity" (ibid. 42–3). For lack of a better term, I call this national cosmopolitanism: its core is the cosmopolitan ideal of a moral world order based on the republican spirit and of the cultivation of humanity (*Menschheit* in the sense of "human race"). According to Fichte, the vehicle of moral progress could and should be the German nation, as one particular "race that [...] will first awaken to the light" (ibid. 45), with Germans as "pioneers" and "exemplars" who "inaugurate" the new epoch of truth and freedom. This is the national element. The theory implies that other nations may follow suit; it means that the vocation thus fulfilled is universal and a goal for all the "races" of this earth. To further these goals, pupils should be educated in independent and self-sustaining communities isolated from society to provide the favourable conditions necessary for the cultivation of morality, which also includes acting for the sake of the community as a whole (James 2011: 189–91).

So far I have argued that the Fichte of the *Addresses* is not the founding father and patron saint of German nationalism, but endorsed a unique form of republican, moral and religious cosmopolitanism blended with what might be called cultural nationalism (see Abizadeh 2005 for a discussion whether Fichte should be read as a proponent of cultural or mediated ethnic nationalism; the author argues for the latter). Still, one might ask why Fichte has proven so malleable, so open to abuse, so easily misappropriated, distorted, and abused by nationalist movements, including even the so-called *Völkisch* movement, and Nazism (see Albada 2012: 39–41). A possible explanation might be the following: in the course of the speeches, Fichte moved from cosmopolitan ideals to a form of republican patriotism that became progressively more xenophobic and militant (though not aggressive). This is obvious in a passage where Fichte tried to outline "German characteristics in history" (the title of his sixth address). "True religion, in the form of Christianity", Fichte mused, has had to pass through three distinct phases in history. The first step was taken by Martin Luther, who freed religion from "external authority" (the despotism of papacy) and introduced "to it the free thinking of antiquity". The second step was taken by Kant (not mentioned in the passage), who discovered moral religion "and with it all wisdom, within ourselves". The third step that has to be taken would be "the complete education of the nation to humanity" (Fichte 1808: 81). For a professional historian of ideas, this might be nothing but pulp history and metaphysical gibberish. Yet the cosmopolitan element is still there: the progressive development of the whole human species towards fulfilling its true vocation. The national – and dubious – element is carefully interwoven into the narrative. Luther and Kant were Germans, Fichte was at pains to emphasize; "foreigners" were only credited with having "provided the stimulus" for each step (ibid. 81), and the true heroes of the mind are Germans through and through. Many intellectuals in the late eighteenth century held that Germans were cosmopolitan in character. Even Kant was a case in point. He declared that the German "has no national pride, and is also too cosmopolitan to be deeply attached to his homeland" (Anthropology, 7: 318). The twist of Fichte's argument was to add a national element to this kind of reasoning. Since Germans had not yet developed a form of national pride, they were – in preference to all other nations – entitled to be proud (and to feel superior). Germans were better cosmopolitans than others. Germany was *primus inter pares* – nowhere in his speeches did Fichte suggest that the role of Germans as "pioneers and exemplars" would amount to a profound moral, juridical or racial inequality of other nations. Yet all the nationalists in the wake of the German Wars of Liberation had to do was to remove the cosmopolitan elements, and replace them with (more and perhaps ethnic) nationalist rhetoric: Germany came first, and the other nations were not equal.

Fichte adjured "men of state" and "thinkers, scholars and writers still worthy of the name" to unite and work for the fatherland in a form outlined by him in his speeches (Fichte 1808: 190, 191). This was in line with his emphasis on the role and vocation of the scholar to promote the cause of progress (cf. James 2011: 165–8). One of the addressees might have been the Prussian philosopher and diplomat Wilhelm von Humboldt (1767–1835), a key reformer of the Prussian educational system after 1806 and the main representative of German *Neuhumanismus* (Benner 2003, Junga 2011, Lahner 2011, Tintemann 2012). He defined the "true purpose of the human being" prescribed by reason as "the highest and proportionate formation (*Bildung*) of his powers towards a whole" (Humboldt 1792: 64). This was a restatement of the doctrine of vocation, and like Kant and Schiller, he emphasized the element of proportionate and comprehensive development. In a similar vein, Humboldt asserted that the "ultimate task (*letzte Aufgabe*) of our existence" was giving "the concept of humanity in our person" as much content as possible – in this world and beyond (Humboldt 1793: 235). As in Kant, "humanity" (*die Menschheit*) was perceived as the intelligible, moral element in humans or rational beings (cf. LP, 9: 442). The goal of education was the development of our human powers to the highest degree possible, made possible through the interaction of the self with the world. Realizing the idea of one's true self also contributed to the progress of the human species (see Lahner 2011: 29–36, 39 and Benner 2003: 77–116). A full exposition of Humboldt's theory would take me far off my course, but I would like to note that it was focussed on the state, whose powers he wanted to limit in the name of personal freedom, security and property (Humboldt 1792: 69–94 and 1960: 341–2).

Traditionally, Georg Wilhelm Friedrich Hegel (1770–1831) has been interpreted as a statist hostile to any form of cosmopolitanism. His *Outlines of the Philosophy of Right* (*Grundlinien der Philosophie des Rechts*, 1821) are usually seen as an early example of political realism, with an emphasis on the state and its absolute sovereignty, on the right to go to war, and on history as the only judge among states (see for instance Cavallar 1992: 214–9 and 235–6, Brincat 2009: 50, Fine 2007: 29–30). This seems to leave little room for any theory of cosmopolitan global justice. In recent years, this traditional interpretation has been challenged. Some scholars, whom I call revisionists, have tried to unsettle and qualify the traditional approach, arguing for a Hegelian and dialectical cosmopolitan theory of mutual and expanding spheres of recognition ultimately covering the whole earth (see especially Brincat 2009, Brooks 2012, Fine 2003 and 2007, Moland 2011).

The key passage where Hegel criticized cosmopolitanism and – perhaps indirectly – Kant is the following: "It is part of education, of thinking as the consciousness of the individual in the form of universality, that the I comes to be apprehended as a universal person in which all are identical. A human being counts as a human being in virtue of his *humanity*, not because he is a Jew, Catholic, Protestant, German, Italian, etc. This consciousness, for which *thought* is what is valid, is of infinite importance. It is defective only when it becomes fixed – e.g. as cosmopolitanism – in opposition to the concrete life of the state" (Hegel 1821: § 209). Hegel criticized cosmopolitans like Kant for turning the idea into a "fixed position", thus creating an opposition to the real world; he deplored fossilizing the idea of cosmopolitanism into an "ism", a system of defined and specified concepts (Fine 2003: 616; see Fine 2003: 615–22 and Fine 2007: 29–38 for Hegel's critique of Kant's cosmopolitanism).

Hegel's attack on cosmopolitanism can be divided into two related criticisms. First, Hegel rejected Kant's juxtaposition of the deficient law of nations of the *ancien régime* on the one hand and his own idea of a cosmopolitan world order. Hegel tried to show that the former was not lawless or devoid of right, and that what scholars nowadays call the Westphalian system only *seemed* to be anarchic in a Hobbesian sense. In a second step, Hegel argued that Kant's idea was deficient (see Hegel 1821: § 331, 333, Cavallar 1992: 214–9, Fine 2003: 619–20 and 2007: 30–2). Hegel's criticism does not do full justice to Kant's account. Kant held that the "miserable comforters" Grotius, Pufendorf and Vattel played down international anarchy, overlooked the fact that states were still legislators, judges and executive powers all in one, and mistakenly believed that a provisional condition did not have to be left in favour of a full public lawful condition (see Cavallar 2011: 64–84). Yet he also called them "important men" (Peace 8: 355), indicating that that their attempts, though ultimately deficient from the perspective of practical philosophy, were valuable in the development of the right of nations.

Secondly and more importantly, Hegel polemicized against abstract thinking, attacking philosophers who pretended that "no state or constitution had ever existed" and that one had to start from scratch with "projects, investigations, and proofs" (Hegel 1821: 6). Right should not be abstracted from the reality of political life, and Kant was apparently criticized for overlooking the insight that right comes into existence "because this is useful for people's needs" (Hegel 1821: § 209 addition). Hegel assumed that Kant's cosmopolitanism was not rooted, and he offered a philosophy of history that attempted to provide this context (especially Hegel 1956: 417–62). Hegel's explicit and famous example of abstract and uprooted thinking was the *terreur* during the French Revolution in 1793: "This period was an upheaval, an agitation, an intolerance of everything particular. Since fanaticism wills an abstraction only, nothing articulated, it follows that, when distinctions appear, it finds them incompatible with its own indeterminacy and annuls them. For this reason, the people during the French

Revolution destroyed once more the institutions they had themselves created, since any institution whatever is antagonistic to the abstract self-consciousness of equality" (Hegel 1821: § 5 addition). Negative freedom aims at destroying anything that *is* simply because it cannot fulfil the requirements of what *should be*. The accusation of offering mere "abstract philosophy", raised polemically, among others, by Herder since the 1760ies against the Enlightenment philosophers in general (see Herder 1765: 16–23 and 1774: 5–11 and 89–90), is repeated here. However, I have argued in this book that Kant favoured an embedded cosmopolitanism and the cultivation of our faculty of judgement, which critically mediates between abstract ideas and concrete situations (see for instance chapter 6, section 2). Subsequent critics like Hegel apparently failed to see that. In a passage that was most likely directed against the "fanaticism" of the French revolutionaries, Kant advocated gradual reform and "evolution instead of revolution" (Conflict, 7: 93). At stake is also Kant's philosophy of history, which can be read – contra Hegel – as providing a context for the development of right (see chapter 3). Also under attack is Kant's distinction between politics and morality (see Peace, 8: 370–80) and his claim that the former should be subordinated to, and conform to, the latter. However, this bipolar view was again softened by Kant himself when he attempted a synthesis of morals and politics at the end of his essay (Peace, 8: 381–86), asserting that morality could and should include an element of prudence, caution and embeddedness (for a succinct analysis see Gerhardt 1995).

The problem of interpreting Hegel is even more intricate than in Rousseau's case, and revisionists have come up with various – often creative – solutions. One possibility is distinguishing between Hegel's lack of an explicit theory of cosmopolitanism and an implicit Hegelian theory, based on his dialectical concept of freedom through recognition and intersubjective engagements. This might lead to a cosmopolitan theory of mutual and expanding spheres of recognition ultimately covering the whole earth (cf. Brooks 2012: 81, Brincat 2009: 55–9). Another possibility is claiming that Hegel's notorious doctrines about absolute state sovereignty and the irrelevance of the individuals (for instance Hegel 1821: § 272 addition and §§ 257–9) do in fact not express his own opinion but denounced "an idealised view of the modern state" as expressed by Kant and others (Fine 2007: 35).

I am sympathetic to these kinds of interpretations, though the revisionists themselves freely admit that a substantial reworking of Hegel's system is indispensable (see for instance Brincat 2009: 50–1), and the interpretations sometimes seem forced or strained. Yet there is a possibility that Hegel cherished some form of cosmopolitanism "properly understood", along the lines of his dialectical thinking that a certain "point is of the highest importance and, if taken in its true sense, may rightly be regarded as" a valid insight (Hegel 1821: § 272 on the separation of powers). Hegel apparently distorted Kant's philosophy, but the tendency to misrepresent one's philosophical predecessors seems to be typical of almost all major philosophers, and Kant himself is a splendid case in point (see chapter 5, section 4). Be that as it may, it is obvious that subsequent generations of German readers up to 1945 understood Hegel in a fairly un-dialectical way as an anti-cosmopolitan proponent of statism, of absolute state sovereignty and nationalism (see Cavallar 1992: 219–221, 235–40, 445–9 with examples). Anti-cosmopolitans in Germany had found one of their figureheads.

Johann Friedrich Herbart (1776–1841) is considered one of the founders of modern educational science. He was the second successor of Kant's chair at the University of Königsberg, and Kant's influence is obvious. Though Herbart frequently criticized Kant, he is usually considered a Kantian. Herbart's philosophical work started in the 1790ies with a reflection on the French Revolution; his *Umriss pädagogischer Vorlesungen* (1835) was a succinct summary of his mature pedagogical thought (for an introduction see Benner 1993, Coriand 1998, English 2013: 4–54, Matthes and Heinze 2003, Patry 2004). The goals of education are determined by moral philosophy and revolve around the concepts of virtue, inner freedom, morality, and self-legislation (Herbart 1835: 13–5). Since the goal is "moral formation", the means are stimulating moral insight in students with the help of discontinuity, especially moral dilemmas, and the aesthetic representation of the world (an obvious borrowing from Schiller). Herbart paid particular attention to what he called "pedagogical tact", the application of general and abstract theoretical concepts to a concrete teacher-student situation, which requires professionalism, judgement and deliberation (Patry 2004). Influenced by early German nationalism, and disappointed by the French Revolution, Herbart defended the Prussian monarchy and a form of patriotism that tended to coincide with nationalism, especially after the humiliation of 1806 (Herbart 1814: 259–68, Herbart 1986: 28–9, 219–30, Benner 1993: 185–97). Any reference to cosmopolitan education or cosmopolitan society had disappeared. In its stead, there was a focus on the individual and his "voluntary obedience" to the monarch, the state and society (which coincided with the former; cf. Herbart 1986: 220 and Herbart 1814: 262 and 267).

Almost all intellectuals writing after Kant shared his belief in the importance of formation (*Bildung*). Yet the generic trend was moving beyond Kant's moral philosophy. In particular, the writers discussed strove to abandon Kant's notorious dichotomies, such as the difference between duty and inclination, between faith and reason, theoretical and practical reason, or the distinction between the phenomenal and the noumenal world. These critical distinctions were usually given up in favour of a holistic view. Novalis might serve as an excellent example. In terms of cosmopolitan education, or ethical didactics in general, two trends can be discerned. The first trend was the eclipse of any kind of ethical didactics in the name of freedom. This was the early romantic or idealist response to Kant. In the words of Friedrich Schlegel, "humanity cannot be inoculated, and virtue cannot be taught or learned, other than through friendship and love with capable and genuine people, and other than through contact with ourselves, with the divine [mit den Göttern] within us" (Schlegel 1799: 44–45, translated in Beiser 2003: 105). This amounts to the triumph of uprooted, pure autonomy over qualified embeddedness. The early romantics were convinced that self-realization should be the product of inner freedom, not of educational, social or political arrangements, since otherwise this very freedom would be impaired or annihilated (cf. Beiser 2003: 105). I have tried to show in this book that this approach was not endorsed by Kant: he aimed at a theory of embedded cosmopolitan education and denied that teachers had to choose between freedom or education, between autonomy or formation (see especially chapters 6 and 7).

The second trend, diametrically opposed to the first, falls back on a traditional concept of education as indoctrination. In its most extreme form, the creation or making of virtuous citizens is the goal. A case in point might be Fichte's *Addresses to the German Nation*, where the explicit aim is producing a political form of virtue for all social classes and an ethical community (that ultimately coincides with the totality of the German nation). Fichte apparently has the early romantics in mind when he attacks traditional educators for quickly admitting defeat that they cannot influence the free will of the pupil, and "precisely in this acknowledgement and in this reckoning on the pupil's free will lies the first error of the existing education, and the clear admission of its impotence and futility" (Fichte 1808: 23). By contrast, the new education strives to cultivate and form the will. I believe that the crucial passages can be read in two ways. The first interpretation would stress Fichte's closeness to Kant, in particular to his concepts of virtue or the "strength of soul" (Anthropology, 7: 293), of moral training and moral character, defined as "the aptitude (*Fertigkeit*) of acting according to maxims [...] of humanity (*Menschheit*)" (LP, 9: 481; see chapters 6 and 7). In other words, Fichte would distance himself from the perceived inadequateness of the early romantics' concept of formation. Drawing on educational reformer Johann Heinrich Pestalozzi, Fichte in particular wanted to foster the pupil's capacity to form images or "pre-figurations" (*Vorbilder*) of states of affairs that are ideas of reason (Fichte 1808: 25). This coincided with Kant's idea of an ethical commonwealth, while adding the thought that forming these concepts was an act of self-determination (cf. James 2011: 188). Yet the passages could also be read as promoting a kind of education that, in the words of Fichte himself, "completely annihilates freedom of will, producing strict necessity in decisions and the impossibility of the opposite in the will" (Fichte 1808: 23). Fichte seems to work with another binary opposition: either you "merely appeal" to the student or pupil or "you fashion him such that he cannot will anything save what you want him to will" (ibid. 23–4). In short, Fichte seems to give up the idea of freedom qua autonomy in the name of a kind of virtue that can be taught and implemented successfully. According to this second interpretation, Fichte's production of virtue would ultimately lead to "the suppression of human freedom rather than its realization" (James 2011: 188; see also 195–207).

Many early romantics and Hegel, born around 1770, developed a concept of the highest good that was completely immanent (Beiser 2005b: 42–4). Here was a clear break with the Christian tradition, to which Kant still belonged (see chapter 2 and Cavallar 2015). The early romantics and Hegel were part of a younger generation that was still religious, but attracted to Spinozism and pantheism, usually rejecting the doctrines of Christian theism. As a consequence, there was no room for any form of theistic cosmopolitanism in the style of Kant. Most went beyond critical philosophy and its crucial distinctions: Fichte and Hegel, for instance, did not offer a mere hypothetical account of history, but claimed objective knowledge (see also James 2011: 168–87).

In terms of nationalism and cosmopolitanism, there was a subtle change: Kant had held that each nation or political community should and could contribute to the highest political good. He passed no judgement in his published writings on which nation had contributed "more than others". Perhaps he had feared that judgements of this kind might lead to a wrong mode of thinking or *Denkungsart*, to a kind of competition and rivalry who was better. Philosophers like the late Schiller, Fichte and Hegel dropped this restraint. There was only a short step from Fichte's speeches in 1806 to full-blown nationalism: the political community or state was transformed from a means to an end (the highest good) to an end in itself. The conditional (the state, the nation) in Kant's account was perceived by these nationalists as something unconditional and absolute, and the ethical community coincided with the totality of the German nation. In other words, Rousseau the politician ultimately triumphed over Rousseau the moral philosopher (see chapters 4 and 5). Still, a nuanced assessment of these authors is required. Up to and around 1806, cosmopolitanism was not simply rejected, but authors like Fichte and Hegel developed complex, perhaps dialectical doctrines – which were only *interpreted* as hostile towards cosmopolitanism later on. This difference between what they themselves wrote and what subsequent interpreters turned them into should not be lost sight of.

Since Hegel, the camps of cosmopolitans and anti-cosmopolitans have been firmly set up. Lee Harris's attack on Martha Nussbaum's cosmopolitan theory at the beginning of this century is a case in point. Harris exclusively focuses on

Nussbaum, ignoring the impressive diversity of cosmopolitan traditions since the eighteenth century (see among others Albrecht 2005 and Cavallar 2011). He describes – and misconstrues – cosmopolitanism as the naïve belief in enlightened rationality, in the power of education, in Kantian moral autonomy, and in a mechanistic understanding of human communities that should be transformed into giant anthills which work like clockworks (Harris 2003: 52–59). Cosmopolitan education is seen as seriously flawed because cosmopolitanism itself is an "illusion" (the title of Lee Harris' essay). According to Harris, it is not wrong to teach the younger generation to be patriotic; cosmopolitan education inevitably takes place at the expense of patriotic education; Nussbaum's approach is traced back to the naïve Enlightenment belief in the blessings of a wholesale re-education of the masses; cosmopolitanism, far from being universal, is just another sectarian ideology. Harris implicitly equates patriotism with "natural" and "concrete", whereas cosmopolitanism is seen as "artificial" and "abstract". These equations are not plausible, as Jeremy Waldron has convincingly shown in one of his articles (Waldron 2003: 24–5 and 27–39).

Critics of cosmopolitan education claim that it tends to weaken commitments to local identities, and especially loyalty to one's country. Thus – they assert – we have to choose between cosmopolitan education and patriotic education; endorsing the former weakens the latter, and the other way round. Cosmopolitans often counter with the concentric-circles imagery, which goes back to the Greek philosopher Theophrastus in the fourth century B. C. and was particularly popular in the age of Enlightenment (Heater 2002: 44–52). The Stoics suggested that we should perceive ourselves as surrounded by several concentric circles: the first one is the self, the next one's family, then one's neighbours, fellow-countrymen, and so on. The last circle would be the human race as a whole. Nussbaum concludes: "To be a citizen of the world, one does not, the Stoics stress, need to give up local affiliations, which can frequently be a source of great richness in life" (Nussbaum 1997a: 60; see also Nussbaum 1996: 9 and 141–3). However, people should also and at the same time develop an understanding of humanity "wherever they encounter it" (Nussbaum 1996: 9). This image raises the familiar problem how we should weigh and assess priorities. For the moment, let me just emphasize that cosmopolitans use the imagery to rebut the claim that cosmopolitans wind up being bloodless rationalists and egoists who pretend to love "everyone" in order not to have to love anyone at all, strangers who are at home nowhere in the world. As I have argued in this book, this is a stock argument of eighteenth-century cosmopolitans such as Kant. Philosophically speaking, we run into the problem if these concentric circles are not sometimes in conflict with each other and if they are, how to assess hierarchies and priorities – this takes us back to the role of judgments (see also below).

8.2 Kant's cosmopolitanism as a historical phenomenon: metaphysics, history, contingency

In his major work on ethics, *The Metaphysics of Morals*, Kant asserted that "metaphysical first principles" are indispensable for any ethics or legal philosophy. He criticized moral philosophers – like those of common sense – who started with "pathological or pure aesthetic or even moral *feeling*" (MM, 6: 377; see also MM, 6: 375 and Groundwork, 4: 410). Defending metaphysics is at odds with scepticism, and even some Kantians attempt to avoid them (see for instance Rawls 1985 and Sandkühler 2013: 397). The problem is the following: since "[t]houghts without content are empty" (KrV, A 51/B 75), any form of metaphysics seems to be uncritical by Kant's own standards and no longer possible. Yet Kant apparently tried to establish a form of new, practical metaphysics (see for instance KrV, A 776 f./B804 f.) which at the same time accepted the limits of knowledge.

Kant's intricate arguments concerning the problems of critical metaphysics are beyond the scope of this conclusion. I will only offer a short paragraph on how Kantian criticism and Kantian metaphysics might not be incompatible. I also want to note in passing that the "new Kant" of my introduction is the philosopher of practical metaphysics – far removed from analytical philosophy, empiricism or neo-Kantianism. A useful starting point for a brief discussion is attempting to define the term "metaphysical". In some passages it coincides with "rational", because in ethics empirical determining factors (such as self-interest) are excluded (the next two paragraphs follow Flikschuh 2003: 50–112, Flikschuh 2010, Höffe 1990: 90–125, Höffe 2001: 119–46, Höffe 2013 and Louden 2000). What matters is the "ground of an obligation" (Groundwork, 4: 389), and only this element is beyond experience, non-empirical and thus metaphysical. Kant claims to offer systematic knowledge *a priori* based on principles, which cannot replace, but also cannot be replaced by, evidence-based judgement, empirical knowledge about humans, or prudence. There is a second meaning of "metaphysical". Kant develops a substantive practical metaphysics that is beyond experience, but differs from traditional, rationalist metaphysics with his claim that we can have no theoretical knowledge about them. He acknowledges "the theoretical non-vindicability of his substantive metaphysical presuppositions" and admits that the ontological claims about "humanity" and "rational nature in general" are conditional, are "practically necessary presuppositions" (Flikschuh 2010: 113, 130 and 131).

In a second step, it can be conceded that what Kant terms applied moral philosophy or moral anthropology is not pure or a priori, since it is applied to the fact of human existence. This is, for instance, evident in the case of cosmopolitan right, where the a priori principle of "universal hospitality" is combined with empirical facts such as limited space on earth or the commercial interests of humans (cf. Peace, 8: 357–9). Yet this "combination" is done in a way that the a priori elements are normatively prior. In cosmopolitan right, this implies the priority of a thin concept of justice, namely the universal principle of right (cf. MM, 6: 230). Anthropological elements are part and parcel of Kant's practical philosophy, but it is important to distinguish in which step of the argument they appear, and whether they touch the "ground of an obligation" and the principle of generalizability (for elaborate arguments see Höffe 1990: 106–9, Höffe 2001: 19–23, Louden 2000: 167–82). Kant argued for modest and carefully limited practical metaphysics. I suppose that he was successful on the most abstract level of universal principles; the more his analysis "moves down" into the realm of applied anthropology, the more it is apparently fraught with a "racial, ethnic, religious, and sexist prejudices" (Louden 2000: 182).

Duncan Ivison summarizes Hunter's historicist interpretation of Kant the following way (see Introduction): "Kant's metaphysics needs to be treated as a contingent historical form, the product of a specific regional set of intellectual practices and institutions, as opposed to a valid claim about the structure of human understanding" (Ivison 2010: 43). Yet the author correctly continues that "we must be careful to avoid something like the genetic fallacy here" (ibid.). If historians manage to situate a certain philosophy or "web of beliefs" in its cultural context and construct a critical genealogy, this does not undermine their possible validity. Historical reflection often attempts to undermine seemingly obvious assumptions or doctrines, but this reflection itself may in turn be based on invalid normative or ideological webs of belief. For instance, the claim mentioned above that Kant's practical metaphysics is simply a "product of" something contingent may have constructed a causal relationship that cannot be verified (and may therefore amount to a metaphysical claim). The assertion that Kant's metaphysics is historically contingent rather than "a valid claim about the structure of human understanding" might be another example of our tendency to construct binary oppositions. Perhaps Kant has the final say, not necessarily with his own practical metaphysics (though its more abstract part does have a high degree of plausibility, I assume), but with the insight that metaphysics cannot be avoided in the first place because they are "always already" there. And those who claim that they do post-metaphysical philosophy may be Kant's "indifferentists" who "always unavoidably fall back into metaphysical assertions, which they yet professed so much to despise" (KrV, A X; cf. MM, 6: 230 and 355). If this analysis is correct, then the post-metaphysical, non-foundational, constructivist approaches of neo-Kantians are fraught with insurmountable difficulties, since they try to avoid Kant's transcendental idealism, in particular his transcendental account of freedom (see Flikschuh 2003 and Sutch 2000 for a discussion).

There have been persistent suspicions of strands of intercultural, postcolonial, postmodern, deconstructivist or realist philosophies that for all their talk of freedom, equality and critical reflection, cosmopolitan theories are prone to accept – perhaps unconsciously – Western ways of thinking and standards of science – in short, that one still winds up with a form of sophisticated cultural imperialism. These "hermeneutics of suspicion" (see Ricœur 1981: 63–100, Gadamer 1984 and below) are sometimes backed up with the theory that even – or especially – moral discourses are about power, difference, manipulation and conflict. When philosopher Paul Feyerabend taught in Berkeley after the Higher Education Act of 1964 was passed and representatives of minorities entered the university, he made the following experience. "Now there was much talk of liberation, of racial equality – but what did it mean? Did it mean the equality of these traditions and the traditions of the white man? It did not. Equality meant that the members of different races and cultures now had the wonderful chance to participate in the white man's manias, they had the chance to participate in his science, his technology, his medicine, his politics. These were the thoughts that went through my head as I looked at my audience and they made me recoil in revulsion and terror from the task I was supposed to perform. For the task – this now became clear to me – was that of a very refined, very sophisticated slavedriver. And a slavedriver I did not want to be" (Feyerabend 1993: 263 and 264). Feyerabend's reflections have to be qualified: in the meantime, many Western universities have become more culturally diverse, also among faculty members; students are not only passive victims; university instructors could always follow the motto of the Enlightenment that in the first place, young people should learn to think for themselves rather than (exclusively) studying modern science (cf. Enlightenment, 8: 35, LP, 9: 450). Essential is Feyerabend's – the instructor's – own self-critical attitude. The claim that cosmopolitan theories are "nothing but" a form of sophisticated cultural imperialism *may* be true, but it might also be a gross distortion, fairly one-sided, or only partially true.

"A crucial question here is whether the debunking of supposedly universal political forms (such as we find in Kant) invalidates the very idea of global justice itself. It is one thing to say a *particular* constitutional form is universal or not; it's another to deny there are any universals whatsoever. Every argument has its origins in some particular cultural form, but does that mean there are no claims or values that can be vindicated across cultures? What would the structure of a conception of global justice be that took plurality and history seriously?" (Ivison 2010: 34). Duncan Ivison raises the proper questions. It is one thing to say that a particular form of morals is, in spite of claims to the contrary, not universal. It is another thing to rule that "any universals whatsoever" and thus qualified moral universalism is impossible. It seems that many contemporary intellectuals have even ruled out the possibility of a formal understanding of morality "across cultures".

A common criticism of Kant's philosophy is that first, it is "unhistorical" like the eighteenth century in general, and that secondly, the very concept of cognitions a priori is incompatible with any approach that takes into account the historical dimension. The claim that the Enlightenment philosophy was unhistorical is in all likelihood a myth and a prejudice that is refuted by impressive historical evidence (see especially Cassirer 1932, Louden 2007, Rohbeck 1987 and Sommer 2006). In terms of the second criticism, I want to emphasize that key Kantian concepts like perfectibility, vocation, education and formation imply a historical dimension. It is obvious that Kant had no problem with asserting the apriority of concepts and the moral law while at the same time conceding that they have to become fully present for the individuals, trained, cultivated and applied in different contexts and historical circumstances. Human faculties and our predispositions are in need of cultivation (a standard theme of many previous chapters). This is a process occasioned by experience, but, according to Kant, this does not "compromise the apriority of the cognitions that depend solely on their use. In this way, it is perfectly consistent to hold of certain principles that they are *a priori* and that our knowledge of them is conditioned by a historical process that has conditioned the acquisition of the faculties that enable us to cognize them *a priori*" (Wood 1998: 31; see also Langthaler 2014: I, 183). Allen Wood even goes on to claim that Kant endorsed a form of historical materialism that is actually close to Marx. I suppose that this goes too far; in my opinion, Kant was close to what may be called an embedded understanding of human reason, an understanding that can, for instance, be found in the writings of the Scottish Enlightenment (see Cavallar 2002: 236–53). This approach is aware of the historical dimension of our theoretical and practical reasoning, but refuses to see it as fully determined by history, society, economics or culture along the lines of what Bevir has called "radical historicism" (see the end of chapter 1, section 5). I call my own position, and that of Kant, critical historicism, which is critical towards historicism's key tenets themselves, and avoids ontological assertions implied in hard determinism.

I do not want to claim here that Kant's philosophy is flawless or unassailable. What I want to emphasize is my suspicion that philosophical positions cannot avoid recourse to at least some minimal concepts a priori and metaphysical assumptions, and that contemporary attempts to get rid of "the old metaphysical baggage" (Fine 2008: 4) may be naïve.

8.3 Kant's legacy and the new cosmopolitanism

Robert Fine defines the new cosmopolitanism as the intellectual and international movement since 1989 that emphasizes global governance, human rights, a form of world citizenship, peaceful relations among states and is usually wary of nationalism, the realist approach to international relations, and uncontrolled economic globalization (see Fine 2007: X-XII, 1–4). Authors emphasize diverse aspects, but some themes keep reappearing. For instance, cosmopolitanism is perceived as "a set of dispositions centred on openness to foreign others and cultures", as "a new form of subjectivity coterminous with globalization" (Saito 2010: 334). There is often an emphasis on attitudes, openness, and cultural cosmopolitanism. Leonard Waks, for instance, gives cosmopolitan education a cultural twist, holding that it includes "drawing from *diverse* cultural values and practices" and that education "should thus make available rich multicultural resources and contacts" (Waks 2010: 253).

Kant seems to be omnipresent in contemporary cosmopolitan discourses. This can be done with a simple test: on which page in the monograph or article on cosmopolitanism is Kant mentioned for the first time? Here are a few examples. Jacques Derrida mentions Kant on the first pages of his book (Derrida 2001: 11), Esther Wohlgemut on the first page (there is also the vague phrase "in a Kantian sense", see Wohlgemut 2009: 1), Bo Earle on the second page (there is an extensive interpretation of Kant's "Idea"; Earle 2005: 210), Robert Fine in the third sentence of his preface (the book includes one chapter on Kant and Hegel; see Fine 2007: IX and 22–9). In Seyla Benhabib's *The Rights of Others*, Kant immediately shows up on the second page (Benhabib 2004: 2), in *Another Cosmopolitanism*, in the "Introduction" (Benhabib 2006: 3).

Even if Kant is usually the key reference point of the new cosmopolitanism, it often remains unclear what exactly Kant's contribution is or what he stands for. There are frequent references to "the Kantian perspective", "the Kantian legacy", "the Kantian tradition" or cosmopolitanism "in a Kantian sense", yet there is no consensus what these exactly entail. Robert Fine, for instance, claims that the new cosmopolitanism is rooted in the tradition of natural law, and that Kant is the most prominent representative of that tradition (cf. Fine 2007: XI). Few contemporary cosmopolitans would agree on this point, and argue instead that the new cosmopolitanism is really new, distinct from the past (Ulrich

Beck would be a case in point; see Beck 2006 and Beck and Grande 2007). In the following paragraphs, I will try to clarify this point: what is Kant's legacy? I am going to argue in the following paragraphs that Kant's legacy should be seen in his critical epistemology, in particular the power of transcendental arguments, in his search for a shared conception of thin morality, in his attempt to combine patriotism with cosmopolitanism and his ensuing qualified statist cosmopolitanism, and in his strict separation of moral and juridical forms of cosmopolitanism.

The first aspect of this legacy is Kant's critical epistemology, in particular the power of transcendental arguments. I have argued in the previous section that attacks on Kant's practical metaphysics as simply a "product of" something contingent should be exposed to the same kind of critical scrutiny as those metaphysics themselves. For instance, these charges often construct causal relationships that cannot be verified (and may therefore amount to a metaphysical claim). Along these lines, the assertion that Kant's metaphysics is historically contingent rather than "a valid claim about the structure of human understanding" may just be another example of our tendency to construct binary oppositions; and any claim about historical contingency has to rely on strong epistemological presuppositions. A similar kind of reasoning can be applied to certain forms of criticism of cosmopolitanism. Mathias Thaler, for instance, summarizes anti-cosmopolitan reasoning in an essay on Chantal Mouffe: "Most objections raised against cosmopolitanism, be they of the postcolonial, anti-globalization, or realist variety, share a deep discontent with formal appeals to universals" (Thaler 2010: 786). Moral universalism is rejected because it is debunked as nothing but a disguise, a mask – with naked power politics behind them: "In doing so, each critique employs a 'hermeneutics of suspicion' [...] that seeks to reconstruct the traces of power behind allegedly neutral references to world citizenship. Hence, it is vital for the critics of cosmopolitanism to detect evidence for their charge of the manipulative use of universals: if they managed to show conclusively that specific interests drive the actors who make use of universals, then it could be argued that cosmopolitan approaches are fundamentally flawed in their claim against certain localized actors, such as states within a Westphalian system of equal sovereignty" (Thaler 2010: 786). An anti-cosmopolitan critique of this sort runs into familiar problems: the applied hermeneutics of suspicion may be epistemologically unfounded; the connection between universalism, rhetoric, and naked interests may be nothing but a piece of rhetoric itself, merely asserting a connection rather than offering convincing evidence. The charge of manipulation presupposes some knowledge about the agent's intentions, her insincerity or ruthlessness – a knowledge that is difficult to establish. In short, all too often a fair and impartial assessment would have to conclude *"non liquet"*, that is, one should simply refuse to pronounce a verdict because the case is not clear (cf. KrV, B 770–1 and 8: 227).

This kind of critical thinking should equally apply to cosmopolitan and anti-cosmopolitan theories. I will try to illustrate this with an example. In her excellent study *Embedded Cosmopolitanism*, Toni Erskine contrasts "embedded" and "impartialist" cosmopolitanisms, and deliberately tries to avoid impartiality as the basis of her cosmopolitan theory (cf. Erskine 2008: 3–6 and 245). Erskine attempts to find a middle ground, beyond the conventional assumptions that genuine cosmopolitanism has to be impartialist, while communitarianism is always embedded, parochial, and state- or community-centered. Erskine criticizes Michael Walzer's communitarian political philosophy, claiming that he wavers between a universalist and a particularist perspective, between a "thin" and a "thick" framework (cf. ibid. 142–9). Her criticism culminates in the claim that Walzer is perhaps inconsistent: "A possibility that cannot be overlooked is that Walzer's attempt to enter discussions of transnational justice and obligation from an embedded perspective relies on covert appeals to the abstract and impartialist reasoning that he claims to reject" (ibid. 145). I suppose this is a sound objection, yet it might at the same time apply to Erskine as well. Erskine seems to wind up with an impartial defence of a theory which eagerly tries to be anti-impartialist. I get the impression that Erskine wants to do justice to those communitarian or embedded positions which ruthlessly attack impartial cosmopolitanism as mistaken. What is the motive behind this eagerness to do justice to positions one may not agree with? Is it not a sense of fairness and a wish to become a fairly impartial judge in a debate? In other words, Erskine does what Habermas or Apel have called *performativer Selbstwiderspruch:* I argue against impartiality, but in the process of arguing I rely on the very impartiality I try to debunk. Critical thinking aims at testing theories for their logical consistency and inner coherence. The underlying assumption is that the formal principles we explicitly or implicitly (cannot avoid to) rely on (consistency, coherence, impartiality, universalizability) are the one and only basis of a cosmopolitan philosophy that deserves this name – a philosophy that Kant called *"weltbürgerlich"* or *"in sensu cosmopolitico"* (see the discussion in Cheneval 2002: 407–11, 423–33).

Teaching critical thinking or thinking skills has become one of the educational issues debated over the last years (see for instance Winch 2006 and Johnson and Siegel 2010). Kant repeatedly stressed that one key educational aim should be that young people learn to think for themselves (especially LP, 9: 450). This goal is often in conflict with the interests of the political community. A fine example is the tension between patriotic education and teaching critical reflection. Kathleen Knight Abowitz and Joseph Wegwert have studied how a mid-western high school in the U. S. commemorated Veteran's Day in November

2003 (Abowitz and Wegwert 2007). There were three different activities for most social studies students, a slide show, a talk by veterans, and an assembly. The surprising element is the emphasis on emotions and simple messages and the absence of critical thinking, judgement or reflection during the day. Messages such as the claim that Vietnam soldiers were not allowed to "do their jobs" because of "politics", "we're losing good people over there [in Iraq] but what they're doing is right" or "Respect your flag: forget the politics" (ibid. 65 and 54) were communicated without critical debate. In particular, the lunch-time assembly in the large auditorium suggested that the wars fought by the U. S. armed forced since World War II have defended individual freedoms. These forms of propaganda, the authors comment, "are quite typical of patriotic displays, where emotional performances and sentimental expressions serve to simplify and selectively filter our meanings towards loyalty and praise rather than analysis and critique" (ibid. 57). The Veteran's Day thus turned into an example of "sentimental political education" with the goal of identifying emotionally with the country's history, foreign policy, and political institutions while discouraging civic engagement ("forget politics"). I have no intention to criticize the U. S. here, since I suppose that similar events take place in many schools all over the world (though they are rarely as well documented as is the case here). The essential point is that celebrations of this sort are very close to manipulation and propaganda. Kant would not necessarily argue that patriotic education should be replaced by cosmopolitan education, which is suggested by the authors (cf. Abowitz and Wegwert 2007: 69–72). Yet he would definitely have claimed that at the very least patriotic expressions should be supplemented by critical thinking, the maxim of the Enlightenment, in short, by the three maxims of enlarged thinking – though some might argue that this cognitive orientation is already cosmopolitanism, if only a very thin version of cognitive cosmopolitanism.

Secondly, Kant is indispensable for any contemporary search for a shared conception of thin morality. Attacks on moral universalism – and thus also on conceptions of cosmopolitan morality or justice – from realist, historicist, relativist or postmodern perspectives have become widespread. Edward Hallett Carr, for instance, claimed that morality was relative, that doctrines of international morality were merely "the product of dominant nations or groups of nations" looking for justifications (Carr 2001: 187; cf. 19, 75). More radical was Carl Schmitt, who denounced cosmopolitanism as "a banner under which powerful nations conduct wars against their enemies and portray them as enemies of humanity itself" (Fine 2003: 611), and combined this with an all-out attack on the alleged hypocrisy of the Allies in the two world wars. As I have argued above, the causal connection between power and morality is open to debate. Be that as it may, there is another dimension: the criticism makes the implicit assumption that genuine morality should not be the outcome of power; that hypocrisy and a moral disposition are incompatible; that might does not make right. In addition, Schmitt's moral judgement can in turn be challenged. Fine, for instance, calls Schmitt's criticism the "hypocritical critique of hypocrisy" (Fine 2003: 611). Chantal Mouffe is another case in point. Like Schmitt, she assumes that cosmopolitan theories are naïve and dangerous at best, and that a cosmopolitan democracy, if ever established, "could only signify the world hegemony of a dominant power that would have been able to impose its conception of the world on the entire planet and which, identifying its interests with those of humanity, would treat any disagreement as an illegitimate challenge to its 'rational' leadership" (Mouffe 2005: 107). Yet her distinction between politics and morality, her criticism of the "moralization" of politics in modern liberalism – where "'we'/'they' opposition constitutive of politics is now constructed according to moral categories of 'good' versus 'evil'" (Mouffe 2005: 75) -, and her endorsement of multipolarity as a normative goal has to take recourse to a thin conception of morality at the very least (for a full argument see Thaler 2010). Implicit normative assumptions and claims are "always already there", even in the criticism of thinkers as radical as Mouffe.

Kant focuses on a thin concept of morality in his search for a supreme moral principle, whose central features are universalizability, impartiality, internal consistency, and autonomy or self-legislation (see also Cavallar 2002: 46–59). He does not deny the distinction between good and evil, but rejects the simplistic judgement that "we" are the good ones and "they" are evil. His main argument is epistemological: no one can know for sure about one's inner disposition or that of others. What we do know is that we are prone to be lenient with ourselves – and, by extension, perhaps with members of our own group – and harsh with others (cf. Groundwork, 4: 407, 424). Hilary Putnam once wrote, "We can only hope to produce a more rational *conception* of rationality or a better *conception* of morality if we operate from *within* our tradition" (Putnam 1981: 216). Attempts to develop a coherent concept of morality that deserves to be called "cosmopolitan" will always have to remain rooted in one's culture, tradition and history. Humans cannot step "outside" their traditions, but they aren't enslaved by them either. Relativist positions of the sort that "every tradition is as rational or as moral as every other" (Rorty 1991: 202) are self-contradictory: they assume the God's-eye view they claim to reject. A relativist statement of this kind could only be made from a perspective that was beyond every tradition, from which it could make this comparison and pass this judgement about equal rationality or morality. Entering into conversations with members of different communities or traditions is not impossible. Our shared concept of thin morality will make communication and disputes possible, our divergent thick concepts of the good will make conversation difficult, and a never-ending enterprise that requires vigilance, critical thinking, and compassion.

There is another key difference between Kant and the new cosmopolitans. They usually argue pragmatically for cosmopolitanism along the following lines: accelerating economic, cultural and political interdependence and globalization since 1989 require, or have even made inevitable, a cosmopolitan ethics, perspective, or vision (see for instance Beck 2006: 2, 5–6, 18–20 and passim, Abowitz and Wegwert 2007: 69, Brown 2009: 1 and 3, Nussbaum 2010: 79–80, Roth 2007: 10–4). Kant, by contrast, would consider this a supplementary consideration. Put bluntly, his famous remark that the "community of the nations of the earth has now gone so far that a violation of right on *one* place of the earth is felt in *all*" (Peace, 8: 360) belongs to his philosophy of history, not to his ethics (see my interpretations in chapters 2 and 3). Historical phenomena such as intensified communication and interdependence do explain why a cosmopolitan ethics is nowadays more useful than in the past, but they do not offer a justification in a strict sense. A sceptic might argue that these phenomena should be interpreted in a different way, or that more traditional forms of ethics are still useful, more viable, or flexible enough to adapt to new conditions. She might also claim that obligations towards people with whom we have closer ties such as neighbours and compatriots "trump obligations to strangers as a matter of principle" (Kleingeld 2012: 184). A proper justification would have to refer to concepts of inner and external freedom, obligation, imperfect duties, imputation, and responsibility that are no longer located in the sphere of historical phenomena but in the realm of a priori practical metaphysics.

Kant differs from the new cosmopolitans in another respect. Sometimes inspired by Hannah Arendt, the latter tend to focus on the process of judgement and examples, which are preferred over principles (see for instance Arendt 2003: 167 and Todd 2009: 138–51; see also Fleischacker 1999, Louden 1992 and 2010). This emphasis has its limitations. Examples are necessary, but not sufficient (Louden 1992: 303 and Louden 2010: 78). Judgements presuppose the "general rule" or the attempt to find and apply it and turn it into a concrete, context-sensitive maxim, which combines determining and reflective judgement. For Kant, casuistry is always rule-directed, and the "casuistic questions" in the *Doctrine of Virtue* are supposed to help the learner to understand her moral predisposition or consciousness or the unconditional quality of the categorical imperative (see Schüssler 2012, Keienburg 2011: 160–3, Jollimore 2006: 370–2 and 382). It does make sense to emphasize the cultivation of moral judgements, and "to make the difficulties of judgment itself a central part of any cosmopolitan outlook" (Todd 2009: 139), but one should not overlook the aspect that judgements usually are – implicitly or explicitly – based on norms, and that they in turn should be based on formal principles which have passed the test of universalizability. The search for these principles, and not the cultivation of judgements alone, is the proper goal of cosmopolitan ethical didactics.

Kant's third legacy is his attempt to combine patriotism with cosmopolitanism. Many new cosmopolitans have strong sympathies for what may be called uprooted cosmopolitanism: the vagabond, the philosophical traveller "nowhere at home" with shifting identities is often conceived as the true cosmopolitan. According to Julia Kristeva, for example, the cosmopolitan's attitude is "temporary, moveable, changing ... it knows neither root nor soil, it is travelling, foreign" (Kristeva 1991: 39). Poststructuralist and postmodern understandings of shifting, flexible and adaptable identities were alien to Kant and his contemporaries. What they endorsed were more conventional, namely embedded forms of cosmopolitanism that did not sever their ties with some variants of patriotism, with people identifying with the local and the embedded, while also conceiving themselves in terms of universal norms and global identities (see Kleingeld 2012: 13–39 and 183–187). In recent years, there have been attempts to see civic patriotism and thin moral cosmopolitanism as compatible (see for instance Bowden 2003, Ypi 2008 and 2010 and Kleingeld 2012: 183–199). Recently Martha Nussbaum has abandoned her more radical version of moral cosmopolitanism of the 1990ies and moved towards the position of critics such as Kwame Anthony Appiah. Now she argues for "a globally sensitive patriotism", claiming that particularistic forms of attachment are not just derivative (Nussbaum 2008; see also Nussbaum 2002). Cosmopolitan-minded critics might still point at possible negative consequences linked with the traditional citizenship as identity-concept, with its emphasis on narrow moral commitments, affective bonds, loyalty, and identity. As a civic humanist, Rousseau endorsed this traditional concept (see chapter 4). Defenders of civic patriotism like Nussbaum retort by distinguishing between "purified" and "malign" forms of patriotism, a moral form of patriotism and hostile nationalism (Nussbaum 2008: 83 and 92). Nussbaum claims that patriotic sentiment can educate citizens to broaden their minds, and gradually foster feelings of compassion and love towards non-citizens. These ideas go at least back to Rousseau; some of them are also endorsed by Kant. Kant's theory of cosmopolitanism leaves "room for permissible forms of patriotism" (Kleingeld 2006: 490 and chapter 7).

Another aspect of Kant's legacy is a logical consequence of his cosmopolitan patriotism: statist cosmopolitanism. This form of cosmopolitanism "defends the normative relevance of political communities for the pursuit of cosmopolitan justice" (Ypi 2008: 48; see also Ypi 2010 and Mikalsen 2012). In recent years, philosophers and political scientists have formulated serious doubts concerning some forms of cosmopolitanism. For instance, Costas Douzinas is highly critical of what he terms contemporary "military humanitarianism", the proneness of Western powers to moralize politics, to use the "moral trump card" of human rights, and to assume the role of saviours, rescuing "Third World victims from their evil compatriots" in the name of cosmopolitanism and universal morality (Dozinas 2007: 11, 7, 58–66; see also Mouffe 2005). "As the scope of the human rights language expands and most political and social claims and counter-claims are expressed in it, the protection afforded by clearly formulated prohibitions of international law becomes weakened" (Dozinas 2007: 60). Jürgen Habermas could be a case in point. Drawing on Kant (see chapter 3), he has argued for the priority of cosmopolitan law understood as the right of each human "that [...] bypasses the collective subjects of international law and directly establishes the legal status of the individual subjects by granting them unmediated membership in the association of free and equal world citizens" (Habermas 1998: 181). State sovereignty is of instrumental value only. This in turn implies that the international community has a duty to intervene in cases of gross human rights abuses (Mikalsen 2012: 118 and 124). Kjartan Mikalsen has called Habermas and some other contemporary cosmopolitans like Brian Barry, Charles Beitz or Fernando Tesón "anti-statist cosmopolitans" who tend to overemphasize normative individualism, ascribe only derivative significance to state sovereignty, and argue for an international system that discriminates against illiberal states. In some cases, this has led to a tendency to abuse the concept of "humanity" and to support U. S. or Western exceptionalism. Where the goal is hegemonic control, the rhetoric clads it as the defence or spread of "universal values" to promote a cosmopolitan world order (see Mikalsen 2012: 76–8 and 81–5, Dozinas 2007: 58–66).

The Kantian position is an antidote to this radical form of moral cosmopolitanism. It does not blur the distinctions between moral and juridical forms of cosmopolitanism. It asserts non-intervention as a basic norm of international law. It postulates that states are moral persons, even if a people should bring upon itself "great troubles [...] by its lawlessness" (Peace, 8: 346). This does not invalidate the principle of political self-determination, as Kant pointed out with implicit reference to revolutionary France in 1795. The Kantian position entails "that state sovereignty is not only compatible with, but essential to the recognition of individuals as units of ultimate concern and that respect for the rights of persons therefore requires respect for sovereignty in the international realm" (Mikalsen 2012: 24; see also 79–80). It argues for the "complementarity of state sovereignty and individual freedom" (ibid. 91). If states are juridical persons, they have a right to make mistakes, but they also have a duty to reform themselves towards a more rightful republican constitution. The right of intervention only applies to states which have actually reverted to the state of nature – an example would be serious and continued violations of human rights such as genocide (Mikalsen 2012: 95–101). Cosmopolitan right as conceived by Kant complements the law of nations, but does not trump it (see chapter 3).

Finally, Kant's cosmopolitanism does not blur the distinction between moral and juridical forms of cosmopolitanism (see chapter 2). Consider the following interpretation of Kant's practical philosophy by the Kantian Christine Korsgaard: "[...] I must make your ends and reasons mine, and I must choose mine in such a way that they can be yours. But this just is reciprocity. Generalised to the Kingdom of Ends, my own ends must be the possible objects of universal legislation, subject to the vote of all. And this is how I realise my autonomy" (Korsgaard 1996: 193). The interpretation is unconvincing, for various reasons, which I cannot discuss at length here (for a succinct argument, see Flikschuh 2003: 12–112 and 2010). Korsgaard fuses the conception of political autonomy as co-legislation in a republic – where it can be realised – with the concept of moral autonomy as self-legislation, which can be completely independent of the "vote of all". The democratic form of government is not necessarily identical with the republican one or the "spirit of republicanism" (see chapter 7, section 1). Whereas Korsgaard introduces a democratic element ("the vote of all") into the concept of the Kingdom of Ends, Kant insisted that the idea of God as the head of the moral commonwealth cannot be eliminated if the highest good is conceived as the necessary and synthetic relation of morality and deserved happiness – only a divine being that is morally good, omniscient and at the same time all-powerful to realise this kingdom can be thought of as up to this task. Korsgaard can be read as a representative of the secularist camp, attempting to avoid Kant's practical metaphysics (see chapter 2, section 2 and chapter 8, section 2 above) and offering a politicized reading of the highest good and the Kingdom of Ends. This is a watered-down version of moral cosmopolitanism combined with elements of political cosmopolitanism. Kant's "project" is different: promoting the Kingdom of Ends is a bottom-up procedure, and the juridical commonwealth is the "womb" that makes working on the moral commonwealth possible.

Kant shares some features with the new cosmopolitanism, namely qualified normative individualism, a form of world citizenship, the emphasis on peaceful relations among states and the reform of international relations, and the rejection of the realist approach to international relations and of nationalism. Yet there are also differences. Kant has a different understanding of world citizenship, accepts rooted forms of allegiance, he holds that (civic) patriotism is compatible with moral and juridical cosmopolitanism, and he does not endorse contemporary versions of cosmopolitanism as a way of life with shifting and blurred identities. He does not overemphasize normative individualism, and, like Rousseau, ascribes significance to state sovereignty. In Kant's philosophy, there is a clear separation of right (*Recht*) and ethics (see chapters 3 and 7), and there is no room for a "moralization of politics", that is, the suspension of rightful (*rechtliche*) norms – even if they are "only to a small degree in conformity with right" -in the name of a higher cosmopolitan morality (Peace, 8: 373 note; see also TP, 8: 292–3, Peace, 8: 383, MM, 6: 372). Kant does not argue for an international system that discriminates against non-republican or illiberal states since he subscribes to the principle of political self-determination. He asserts non-intervention as a basic norm of international law, as he postulates that states establishing rightful conditions should be considered juridical persons.

8.4 Kant's didactics, contemporary discourses, and cultural developments

The heart of Kant's moral theory is the transformation of one's comportment of mind or *Gesinnung*, cultivating one's moral dispositions, making use of one's freedom in a proper way, promoting the highest good and becoming worthy of happiness, in short, reaching one's vocation: "The final destiny of the human race is moral perfection, so far as it is accomplished through human freedom", which is called "the inner *principium* of the world" (Collins, 27: 470; see also chapter 6). Kant defends the strong claim that humans all over the world share the same formal cognitive structures a priori, also in moral terms – Kant calls this our moral predisposition (see for instance MM 6: 376). This shared capacity (which is in need of actualization) makes possible a global public sphere, which encompasses a legal and moral dimension and is outlined by Kant as the idea of a world-wide legal community (the society of states) and the more challenging idea of a world-wide moral community (the ethical commonwealth; see chapter 3). I have argued in a previous chapter that Kant's moral educational theory is cosmopolitan in character (see chapter 6). Moral self-legislation and self-motivation ultimately aim at a cosmopolitan conduct of thought (*Denkungsart*) and a cosmopolitan comportment of mind or disposition (*Gesinnung*). Here I want to show that many key elements of Kant's didactics are at odds with contemporary education theories, even if they sometimes claim to be Kantian or related to Kantian principles in their approach.

At the end of the first critique, Kant formulated the hope that other intellectuals would contribute their part to make the "footpath" outlined in that book "into a highway" (KrV, A 855/B 883). I assume that some have actually followed Kant's path; I consider one case in point Max Horkheimer (1895–1973), German philosopher, sociologist and member of the "Frankfurt School", who assumed in his speech "The concept of education" (1952) that many of the students he addressed would not only be interested in the financial and social benefits of university education – Kant's prudence -, but also in studying as an opportunity to "develop human predispositions (*Anlagen*)", to reach one's "own vocation" (Horkheimer 1952: 409; see also Lahner 2011: 88 – 115). Kantian (and Wilhelm von Humboldt's) elements are obvious. The umbrella term of these goals is again formation or *Bildung*. Yet all in all, this is a forgotten tradition. More than 200 years after Kant's death, cosmopolitan education as envisioned by him is more unlikely than ever, for various reasons. For one thing, Kant's footpath has remained virtually undetected. For instance, many publications on Kant's cosmopolitanism still focus on his political philosophy, especially cosmopolitan right, ignoring Kant's unique approach to cosmopolitan formation (see for instance Todd 2009 or Kleingeld 2012). In addition, there are people who see the footpath, but claim – for various reasons – that it should not be taken, let alone broadened into a highway.

Kant's didactics are at odds with many trends in contemporary educational culture of Western societies, which emphasises success and usefulness and usually focuses on competences, skills and their evaluation. Lars Løvlie argues that educationists hostile to transcendental thinking sell short the ideas of moral freedom and autonomy: "That the Kantian approach is nearly absent in today's educational discourse can be explained by the inability of going beyond a taxonomy that translates the general aims of education into the particular pieces of knowledge or skills that can be taught and tested in the classroom. There is the professional inability to think abstractly and look beyond the restricted vocabulary of the social sciences" (Løvlie 2012: 119). The attempt to avoid any form of "metaphysics" has led to a tendency to rely on the empirical approach of the social sciences; they in turn can hardly provide educational aims apart from economic or social usefulness. So the focus is on learning outcomes, on measuring them, on means-end-thinking (see Hardarson 2012: 224).

In line with this empiricist approach, some cosmopolitan educational theories subscribe to a sentimental rather than a cognitive version (Jollimore and Barrios 2006). Strong sentimentalists assert that works of literature operate, and should operate, directly on the readers' sentiments, whereas (weak) cognitivists like Martha Nussbaum claim that normative truths are discovered in a fundamentally cognitive process. Postmodern philosopher Richard Rorty, for instance, is all in favour of the "cosmopolitan utopias" of philosophers like Kant, but holds that cosmopolitan moral education should focus on "manipulating our feelings rather than [...] increasing our knowledge". He denies that there could be something like "moral knowledge" and favours "sad and sentimental stories" to promote a cosmopolitan disposition (Rorty 1998: 173 and 172; see also Jollimore and Barrios 2006: 365 – 70). Representatives of the cognitivist camp usually claim that confronting our biases, engaging with another culture, or understanding "the other" presupposes the capacity for enlarged thinking (Nussbaum 1996: 10, Williams 2003: 237–9, Jollimore and Barrios 2006: 364 and 379). Nussbaum calls this ability to assume another point of view the "narrative imagination" (Nussbaum 1997a: 10). Kant firmly sides with the cognitivists against the sentimentalist account of morals. He presents a sophisticated account of the cultivation of the enlarged way of thinking and holds that if one "begins with pathological or pure aesthetic or even moral *feeling* (with what is subjectively rather than objectively practical); if, that is, one begins with the matter of the will, the *end*, instead of with the form of the will, the *law*, in order to determine duties on this basis, then there will indeed be no *metaphysical first principles* of the doctrine of virtue, since feeling, whatever may arouse it, always belongs to the *order of nature*" (MM, 6: 377). Moral philosophy cannot do without some minimal form of metaphysics (see section 2 above). Melissa Williams has enumerated three conditions which correspond with what Kant has to say on the issue: First, the capacity for enlarged thinking develops through exercise. We need training to make critical moral judgements. Second, we have to encounter diversity to make this exercise – we need perspectives different from our own. Third, the form of this encounter would be dialogue, "a mutual engagement among diverse perspectives that are *immediately present* in individuals' lives" (Williams 2003: 237). Strong sentimentalists, by contrast, can only accept the moral dispositions and judgements they find. They could attempt to manipulate their students (see below) but would have to abstain from critical and rational debate and dialogue.

"Autonomy" has become a catchword of some contemporary educational theories, yet it is obvious that these references often have little to do with what Kant understood as autonomy (see the excellent discussion in Hinske 1980: 67–85 on maturity and minority, *Unmündigkeit*). Genuine autonomy as self-legislation is usually lost in favour of a superficial concept where autonomy coincides with "what an agent wants to do", the freedom from external constraint (this is Kant's juridical or external freedom), liberal personal autonomy (individual competence to assess and define the good life) or a watered-down understanding, where it is related to any spontaneous activity of the mind (see for instance Ruitenberg 2011: 28 and Hand 2006: 535–9 and the useful discussion in Flikschuh 2010: 119–21 and 133–4). Put polemically, today there is a tendency to assume that most of us are already autonomous, whereas Kant held that full moral autonomy is a goal that can only be approximated in a long process of hard work. A symptomatic example in this respect is the head-on attack of Michael Hand on autonomy, the cornerstone of Kant's ethics (Hand 2006: 541–44). He concludes that this idea must be rejected as an aim of education (ibid. 544), and speaks up in favour of utilitarianism, at least implicitly:

"What makes a principle morally defensible is not its universal form, but the tendency of the actions it enjoins to advance the cause of human happiness or flourishing" (ibid. 543). What Hand in fact attacks is a caricature of Kant's concept of autonomy, loosely based on a few passages from the *Groundwork* – as if Kant had written nothing else in ethics -, and its watered-down version (cf. ibid. 535–6). Hand rejects the categorical imperative on the grounds that it alone – the principle of universality – cannot motivate people. Yet this is a psychological claim, a piece of dogmatic metaphysics by Kant's standards and ignorant of Kant's own elaborate theory of moral motivation (see chapter 6).

A similar eclipse of individual autonomy can be observed in an essay on cosmopolitan education by Hiro Saito, who emphasises the efficiency of the proposed actor-network theory. Words like "freedom" or "autonomy" do not appear in the text, but concepts like "disposition" and "action". In one passage, the author compares the new cosmopolitans with "marionettes", since they are connected with many other actors globally and thus become "more actionable". "Left on their own, their capacity to take actions and effect changes in the world diminishes" (Saito 2010: 335). The individual seems to have almost vanished and been replaced by a web of connections and activities with others. Saito's emphasis on the community is not the problem, but here it seems to be developed at the expense of the individual's possible autonomy.

In his dissertation on cosmopolitan education, Matthew Hayden already expresses a highly un-Kantian attitude in the title: "forging moral beings". The picture is that of the artist (educator) forming an object of art (the pupil) rather than helping her to become an agent herself. Consequently, political topics such as political freedom are left out in the study (see Hayden 2012: 43). While he claims that cosmopolitanism asserts the importance of "individual autonomy", this is apparently understood in a superficial way as the freedom from external constraint (cf. 184). Apart from this generic reference, the ideas of freedom and autonomy are non-existent – in a way reminiscent of Fichte in 1808. Even Martha Nussbaum, in her passionate plea for the humanities and cosmopolitan education, refers to "producing" suitable and cosmopolitan-minded citizens (cf. Nussbaum 2010: 29, 44, 45, 72 and 93). More outspoken is Richard Rorty when advocating what he calls "sentimental education". Since he considers Kant's notions of autonomy and moral obligation a myth, Rorty holds that moral educators should concentrate on nothing but "manipulating sentiments" (Rorty 1998: 176; cf. 172 and 179).

What distinguishes Kant from these authors is his comprehensive concept of reason (*Vernunft*) that he shares with the philosophical tradition up to Wittgenstein, not the reductionist conception of some contemporary authors, where reason coincides with understanding (*Verstand*) or prudence (see Kobusch 2012).

According to Kant, human autonomy and thus dignity is not some absolute inner value all humans possess (this is rather the doctrine of other forms of moral cosmopolitanism), but refers to sublimity (*Erhabenheit*), the prerogative of humans over the rest of nature because they are beings capable of self-legislation, autonomy or "internal lawgiving" and moral freedom, who in turn should respect this potential or capacity in all other rational agents and should develop it in themselves (MM, 6: 436; cf. Sensen 2009). Autonomy is not something given, but a task. Moral formation is distinct from the training of a dog or the manipulation of subjects in a totalitarian or despotic state. Kantian cosmopolitan education is education for moral freedom: educators cannot and should not directly influence, manipulate or cause anything in their pupils, because the ultimate goal is that these students themselves become moral beings and adopt a moral disposition (see chapter 6 for more).

Klas Roth has pointed out that the limitations of educational scientists described above correspond with worldwide trends, for instance, with current policy texts in the European Union which encourage people to develop their skills and competences to become efficacious and useful members of consumer societies, thus turning these members into additional consumer or market commodities. Enlightened or mature citizens who are helped to dare to think for themselves, who are helped to cultivate their predispositions and acquire a moral character are a subordinate end – if at all (cf. Roth 2012: 214–6). Criticism of this sort can be found Kant: in the Collins lecture, Kant attacked an understanding of education as a mere "empirical system" based on "custom", with norms simply "borrowed from experience" (Collins, 27: 253). He argued for the primacy of moral cultivation over the perfection of natural capacities, identical with today's skills: "moral goodness consists in the perfection of the will, not the capacities. Yet a good will needs the completeness and capacity of all powers to carry out everything willed by the will" (Collins, 27: 266). The second sentence makes it clear that capacities are subordinate, but not irrelevant. Skilfulness, prudence, and judgement refined by experience are also important, but they are not ends in themselves. They are part and parcel of a proportionate development of one's personality or character, but they should not be taken for the whole thing.

In all likelihood, education in modern societies is going to be progressively adapted "to the demands of the labour market" (Hirtt 2011: 171). Martha Nussbaum has warned that if current trends continue, "nations all over the world will soon be producing generations of useful machines, rather than complete citizens" (Nussbaum 2010: 2). In the long run, the future of democracy will be in peril. She claims that educational systems all over the world have embarked on one-sided teaching of competences that are economically useful, while at the same time "discarding skills that are needed to keep democracies alive" (ibid.). For Nussbaum, these skills overlap with, or even coincide with, cosmopolitan dispositions: the capacity to think for oneself, the expanded way of thinking, and the willingness to cultivate one's moral or narrative imagination. With a new emphasis on skills and competences useful for future jobs and the growth of low skilled jobs there will be little room for lofty ideals such as civic education, critical reflection, or moral cosmopolitanism.

This trend criticized by Nussbaum and others is apparently worldwide; the *Programme for International Student Assessment* (PISA), organized by an institution interested in economic progress and skills that are economically useful, is symptomatic. It goes without saying that Kant would also have criticized this trend. He warns educational reformers that they "must furthermore reflect especially on the development of humanity, and see to it that humanity becomes not merely skilful but also moral" (LP, 9: 449). Nowadays "useful" skills suffice; perhaps "social skills" are added since there is an awareness that they might come in handy as people occasionally do have to interact with each other. As mentioned above, Kant even differs from Nussbaum: at stake is not only democracy or the republic, but the idea of formation. *Bildung* is not only of instrumental value because it helps to avoid the decline of democracy, as Nussbaum argues. It is – to use a famous Kantian phrase – an end in itself, since it helps humans to approach their vocation, which goes beyond their economic or social usefulness. At the end of some of his lectures on ethics, Kant expressed his faith and hope that "after the lapse of many centuries" the human species might reach its vocation or final destiny, "the highest moral perfection" (Collins, 27: 471). With the complexity of the task at hand as Kant described it – divergent educational goals, the attainment of the proportionate cultivation of our predispositions, the inevitable longevity of the development, and the constant threat of war and evil – Kant's reference to "many centuries" was probably a realistic assessment. It seems to me that more than two hundred years after Kant's death, there has not been significant progress for the better in the crucial area of ethical didactics. In addition, I believe that Kant's diagnosis that we live "in a time of disciplinary training, culture, and civilization, but not by any means in a time of moralization" (LP, 9: 451) is still valid.

Rather than jumping to the facile and whiggish conclusion that Kant's cosmopolitanism merely anticipates contemporary forms of cosmopolitanism, this book has emphasized possible differences and the uniqueness of Kant's cosmopolitan theory, even by late eighteenth century standards. Kant's crucial contribution to contemporary cosmopolitan discourses was seen in the embedded, dynamic and pedagogical dimensions. His omnipresence in contemporary cosmopolitan discourses clouds the fact that little is known about his own complex cosmopolitan theory, its historical origins and his legacy. I hope this book has contributed to filling this gap.

Bibliography

Abizadeh, Arash (2005). "Was Fichte an Ethnic Nationalist? On Cultural Nationalism and its Double", *History of Political Thought*, 26, 334–59.

Abowitz, Kathleen Knight and Joseph Wegwert (2007). "Veteran's Day in a U. S. Public High School: Lessons for nationalistic Loyalty", in: Roth and Burbules, *Notions*, 51–75.

Achenwall, Gottfried and Johann Stephan Pütter (1750/1995). *Anfangsgründe des Naturrechts (Elementa iuris naturae)*, ed. and translated by Jan Schröder. Frankfurt am Main and Leipzig: Insel.

Adam, Ulrich (2006). *The Political Economy of J. H. G. Justi*. Oxford: Peter Lang.

Adorno, Theodor W. (1982). *Negative Dialektik*, 3rd edition, Frankfurt am Main: Suhrkamp.

Aksu, Esref (ed., 2008). *Early Notions of Global Governance. Selected Eighteenth-Century Proposals for "Perpetual Peace"*, Cardiff, Wales University Press.

Albert, Mathias, and Sascha Dickel (2006). "Educating Globality: Zum Lernfeld ‚Internationale Beziehungen/Globalisierung' im Gymnasium", *Zeitschrift für Internationale Beziehungen*, 13, 2, 261–74.

Albada, Michael (2012). "Fichte the fascist? The misappropriation of a republican philosopher in Weimar, Germany 1918–1933", in: *www.stanford.edu/.../Albada_Hum_2012.pdf*, visited September 6, 2013.

Albrecht, Andrea, 2005. *Kosmopolitismus. Weltbürgerdiskurse in Literatur, Philosophie und Publizistik um 1800*. Berlin and New York: de Gruyter.

Alexy, Robert et al., eds. (2002), *Neukantianismus und Rechtsphilosophie*. Baden-Baden: Nomos.

Allison, Henry E. (2009). "Teleology and history in Kant: the critical foundations of Kant's philosophy of history", in Rorty and Schmidt, *Kant's Idea*, 24–45.

Almeida, Guido Antônio de (2012). "Critique, Deduction, and the Fact of Reason", in: Rauscher and Perez, *Kant in Brazil*, 127–54.

Ameriks, Karl (2006). *Kant and the Historical Turn: Philosophy as Critical Interpretation*, Oxford: Clarendon Press.

Ameriks, Karl (2008). "The End of the Critiques: Kant's Moral 'Creationism'", in: Muchnik, *Rethinking Kant*, vol. 1, 165–90.

Ameriks, Karl and Otfried Höffe, eds. (2009), *Kant's Moral and Legal Philosophy*, translated by Nicholas Walker, Cambridge: Cambridge University Press.

Ameriks, Karl (2013). "Kant's Ambivalent Cosmopolitanism", in: Bacin et al., eds., *Kant und die Philosophie in weltbürgerlicher Absicht*, vol. 1, 55–72.

Anders, Günther (1980). *Die Antiquiertheit des Menschen*, vol. II, München: Beck.

Anderson-Gold, Sharon (2001a). *Cosmopolitanism and human rights*, Cardiff: Wales University Press.

Anderson-Gold, Sharon (2001b). *Unnecessary Evil. History and Moral Progress in the Philosophy of Immanuel Kant*, Albany: State University of New York Press.

Anderson-Gold, Sharon (2010), "Kant's Cosmopolitan Peace", in: Muchnik, *Rethinking Kant*, vol. 2, 205–21.

Anderson-Gold, Sharon and Pablo Muchnik, eds. (2010). *Kant's Anatomy of Evil*, Cambridge: Cambridge University Press.

Appiah, Kwame Anthony (1996). "Cosmopolitan Patriots", in: Nussbaum, *For Love of Country?*, 21–9.

Appiah, Kwame Anthony (1997). "Cosmopolitan Patriots", *Critical Inquiry*, 23, 3, 617–39.
Appiah, Kwame Anthony (2007). *Cosmopolitanism: Ethics in a world of strangers*, New York, Norton.
Archibugi, Daniele (2003). "Cosmopolitical Democracy", in Archibugi, Daniele (ed.), *Debating Cosmopolitics*. London: Verso, 1–15.
Archibugi, Daniele (2004). "Cosmopolitan Democracy and its Critics: A Review", *European Journal of International Relations*, 10, 3, 437–73.
Archibugi, Daniele and David Held, eds. (1995). *Cosmopolitan Democracy. An Agenda for a New World Order*. Cambridge: Polity Press.
Arendt, Hannah (2003). *Responsibility and Judgment*, edited by Jerome Kohn, New York: Schocken Books.
Armitage, David (2006). "Hobbes and the foundations of modern international thought", in: Annabel Brett and James Tully with Holly Hamilton Bleakley (eds.), *Rethinking the Foundations of Modern Political Thought*. Cambridge: Cambridge University Press, 219–35.
Asbach, Olaf (2000). "Staatsrecht und Völkerrecht bei Jean-Jacques Rousseau. Zur Frage der völkerrechtlichen Vollendung des *Contrat social*", in: Brandt und Herb, *Vom Gesellschaftsvertrag*, 241–69.
Baker, Bernadette (2001). "(Ap)pointing the Canon: Rousseau's Émile, Visions of the State, and Education", *Educational Theory*, 51, 1, 1–43.
Baker, Gideon, ed. (2013). *Hospitality and World Politics*. Basingstoke: Palgrave Macmillan.
Barnard, F. M. (1988). *Self-Direction and Political Legitimacy: Rousseau and Herder*. Oxford: Clarendon Press.
Bartelson, Jens (2009). *Visions of World Community*, Cambridge: Cambridge University Press 2009.
Basedow, Johann Bernhard (1768). *Vorstellung an Menschenfreunde und vermögende Männer über Schulen, Studien und ihren Einfluß in die öffentliche Wohlfahrt*, Hamburg.
Basedow, Johann Bernhard (1775). *Für Cosmopoliten Etwas zu lesen, zu denken und zu thun*, Leipzig.
Basedow, Johann Bernhard (1776). *Erstes Stück des Philanthropischen Archivs*, Dessau.
Basedow, Johann Bernhard (1777). *Practische Philosophie für alle Stände*, Copenhagen und Leipzig, 1758; 2nd revised edition, Dessau and Leipzig.
Basedow, Johann Bernhard (1909). *Elementarwerk. Ein geordneter Vorrath aller nöthigen Erkenntniß*, 4 vols., Dessau and Leipzig 1774. Ausgabe Theodor Fritzsch, 3 vols., Leipzig.
Basedow, Johann Bernhard (1965). *Ausgewählte pädagogische Schriften*, ed. Albert Reble, Paderborn: Ferdinand Schöningh.
Beardsworth, Richard (2011). *Cosmopolitanism and International Relations Theory*, Cambridge: Polity Press.
Beck, Lewis White (1979). "Kant on Education", in: J. D. Browning, ed., *Education in the 18th Century*, New York: Garland, 10–24.
Beck, Ulrich (2006). *The Cosmopolitan Vision*, translated Ciaran Cronin, Cambridge: Polity Press.
Beck, Ulrich and Edgar Grande (2007). *Cosmopolitan Europe*, Cambridge, Cambridge University Press.
Beckenridge, Carol A., Homi K. Bhabha and Dipesh Chakrabarty, eds. (2002), *Cosmopolitanism*, Durham, NC and London: Duke University Press.

Beiser, Frederick (2002). *German Idealism. The Struggle against Subjectivism, 1781–1801.* Cambridge, Mass.: Harvard University Press.
Beiser, Frederick (2003). *The Romantic Imperative. The Concept of Early German Romanticism.* Cambridge, Mass.: Harvard University Press.
Beiser, Frederick (2005). *Schiller as Philosopher. A Re-Examination.* Oxford: Clarendon Press.
Beiser, Frederick (2005b). *Hegel.* New York: Routledge.
Beiser, Frederick (2011). *The German Historicist Tradition.* Oxford: Oxford University Press.
Bell, Madison Smart (2007). *Toussaint Louverture. A Biography.* New York: Pantheon.
Benhabib, Seyla (2004). *The Rights of Others. Aliens, Residents, and Citizens,* Cambridge, Cambridge University Press.
Benhabib, Seyla (2006). *Another Cosmopolitanism. With Commentaries by Jeremy Waldron, Bonnie Honig, and Will Kymlicka,* edited by Robert Post, Oxford.
Benner, Dietrich (1993). *Die Pädagogik Herbarts. Eine problemgeschichtliche Einführung in die Systematik neuzeitlicher Pädagogik,* Weinheim und München: Juventa Verlag.
Benner, Dietrich (2003). *Wilhelm von Humboldts Bildungstheorie,* 3. Aufl. Weinheim and Munich: Juventa.
Bernasconi, Robert (2010). "The Place of Race in Kant's *Physical Geography* and in the Writings of the 1790s", in: Muchnik, *Rethinking Kant volume 2,* 274–90.
Bevir, Mark (2012). "Post-Analytic Historicism", *Journal of the History of Ideas,* 73, 4, 657–665.
Bielefeldt, Heiner (2001). *Kants Symbolik. Ein Schlüssel zur kritischen Freiheitsphilosophie,* Freiburg and München: Karl Alber.
Bielefeldt, Heiner (2004). "Verrechtlichung als Reformprozess. Kants Konstruktion der Rechtsentwicklung", in: Nagl and Langthaler, *Recht,* 73–84.
Bielefeldt, Heiner (2008). "Menschenrechte als interkulturelle Lerngeschichte", in: Hans Jörg Sandkühler, ed., *Philosophie, wozu?* Frankfurt am Main: Suhrkamp, 289–301.
Bittner, Rüdiger (2009). "Philosophy helps history", in: Rorty and Schmidt, *Kant's Idea,* 231–49.
Blackburn, Robin (2006). "Haiti, Slavery, and the Age of Democratic Revolution", *William and Mary Quarterly,* 63(4), 633–74.
Blesenkemper, Klaus (1987). *"Publice age" – Studien zum Öffentlichkeitsbegriff bei Kant,* Frankfurt am Main: Haag und Herchen.
Bohatec, Josef (1938). *Die Religionsphilosophie Kants in der "Religion innerhalb der Grenzen der bloßen Vernunft". Mit besonderer Berücksichtigung ihrer theologisch-dogmatischen Quellen,* Hamburg: Hoffmann und Campe.
Bohman, James (1997). "The Public Spheres of the World Citizen", in James Bohman and Matthias Lutz-Bachmann (eds.), *Perpetual Peace. Essays on Kant's Cosmopolitan Ideal,* Cambridge, Mass. and London: MIT Press, 179–200.
Bohman, James (2004). "Republican Cosmopolitanism", *The Journal of Political Philosophy* 12, 3, 336–52.
Bohman, James (2010). "Die Republik der Menschheit", in: Lutz-Bachmann et al., eds., *Kosmopolitanismus. Zur Geschichte und Zukunft eines umstrittenen Ideals.* Frankfurt am Main: Velbrück Wissenschaft 2010, 306–36.
Bolle, Rainer (2012). *Jean-Jacques Rousseau. Das Prinzip der Vervollkommnung des Menschen durch Eduktion und die Frage nach dem Zusammenhang von Freiheit, Glück und Identität.* 3. Auflage, Münster, New York, München, Berlin: Waxmann.

Bollenbeck, Georg (2007). *Friedrich Schiller: der unterschätzte Theoretiker*, Köln und Wien: Böhlau.
Bollnow, Otto Friedrich (1982). "Die Pädagogik des Barock", in: Georg S. Seidel, ed., *Orientierungen zum pädagogischen Handeln, Festschrift für Elfriede Höhn*, Göttingen, Toronto, Zürich: Hogrefe, 9–33.
Borries, Kurt (1928). *Kant als Politiker. Zur Staats- und Gesellschaftslehre des Kritizismus*. Reprint Aalen: Scientia 1973.
Boyd, Richard (2004). "Pity's Pathologies Portrayed. Rousseau and the Limits of Democratic Compassion", *Political Theory*, 32, 4, 519–46.
Bowden, Brett (2003), "Nationalism and Cosmopolitanism: Irreconcilable Differences or Possible Bedfellows?", *National Identities*, 5, 3, 235–49.
Brandt, Reinhard (2003). "The Guiding Idea of Kant's Anthropology and the Vocation of the Human Being", in: Jacobs and Kain, *Essays*, 85–104.
Brandt, Reinhard (2009). *Die Bestimmung des Menschen bei Kant*, second edition, Hamburg: Meiner.
Brandt, Reinhard und Karlfriedrich Herb (2000). *Vom Gesellschaftsvertrag oder Prinzipien des Staatsrechts*. Berlin: Akademie Verlag.
Breun, Richard (2002). "Kants ethische Didaktik und Methodenlehre", *Vierteljahrschrift für wissenschaftliche Pädagogik*, 78, 77–90.
Brincat, Shannon (2009). "Hegel's Gesture Towards Radical Cosmopolitanism", *Journal of Critical Globalisation Studies*, 1, 47–65.
Brock, Gillian and Harry Brighouse, eds. (2005). *The Political Philosophy of Cosmopolitanism*, Cambridge: Cambridge University Press.
Brockmöller, Annette (1997). *Die Entstehung der Rechtstheorie im 19. Jahrhundert in Deutschland*. Baden-Baden: Nomos Verlagsgesellschaft.
Brooks, Thom (2012). "Between Statism and Cosmopolitanism: Hegel and the Possibility of Global Justice", in Andrew Buchwalter, ed., *Hegel and Global Justice*, 65–83.
Brown, Garrett Wallace (2009). *Grounding Cosmopolitanism From Kant to the Idea of a Cosmopolitan Constitution*. Edinburgh: Edinburgh University Press.
Brown, Garrett Wallace (2010). "The Laws of Hospitality, Asylum Seekers and Cosmopolitan Right. A Kantian Response to Jacques Derrida", *European Journal of Political Theory*, 9, 3, 1–20
Brown, Garrett Wallace and David Held (2010). *The Cosmopolitanism Reader*. Cambridge: Polity Press.
Buchanan, Allen (2007). *Justice, Legitimacy, and Self-Determination. Moral Foundations for International Law*, Oxford: Oxford University Press.
Budelacci, Orlando (2003). *Kants Friedensprogramm. Das politische Denken im Kontext der praktischen Philosophie*. Athena: Oberhausen.
Busch, Hans Jürgen, and Axel Horstmann (1976). "Kosmopolit, Kosmopolitismus", in: Joachim Ritter (ed), *Historisches Wörterbuch der Philosophie*, vol. 4, 1155–67.
Busch, Hans Jürgen, and Ulrich Dierse (1985). "Patriot, Patriotismus", in: Joachim Ritter (ed), *Historisches Wörterbuch der Philosophie*, vol. 7, 207–17.
Byrd, Sharon, and Joachim Hruschka (2008). "From the State of Nature to the Juridical State of States", *Law and Philosophy*, 27, 599–641.
Byrd, Sharon and Joachim Hruschka (2010). *Kant's Doctrine of Right. A Commentary*, Cambridge, Cambridge University Press.

Caranti, Luigi, ed. (2006). *Kant's Perpetual Peace: New Interpretive Essays*, Rome: Luiss University Press.
Carr, Edward Hallett (2001). *The Twenty Years' Crisis, 1919–1939: An Introduction to Study International Relations*, New York: Palgrave.
Cassirer, Ernst (1932). *The Philosophy of the Enlightenment*, Boston: Beacon Press 1951.
Cassirer, Ernst (1939). *Rousseau, Kant, Goethe*, edited by Rainer A. Bast. Hamburg: Meiner 1991.
Cassirer, Heinz Walter (1988). *Grace and Law: St. Paul, Kant, and the Hebrew Prophets*. Grand Rapids: Eerdmans Publishing Co.
Caswell, Matthew (2006). "Kant's Conception of the Highest Good, the *Gesinnung*, and the Theory of Radical Evil", *Kant-Studien* 97, 184–209.
Cavallar, Georg (1992). *Pax Kantiana. Systematisch-historische Untersuchung des Entwurfs 'Zum ewigen Frieden' (1795) von Immanuel Kant*. Wien, Köln, Weimar: Böhlau.
Cavallar, Georg (1999). *Kant and the Theory and Practice of International Right*. Cardiff: University of Wales Press.
Cavallar, Georg (2002). *The Rights of Strangers: Theories of international hospitality, the global community, and political justice since Vitoria*. Aldershot: Ashgate.
Cavallar, Georg (2004). "The law of nations in the Age of Enlightenment: moral and legal principles", *Annual Review of Law and Ethics*, 12, 213–229.
Cavallar, Georg (2005). "Sphären und Grenzen der Freiheit: Dimensionen des Politischen in der Pädagogik", in: Lutz Koch and Christian Schönherr (eds.), *Kant – Pädagogik und Politik*, Würzburg: Ergon, 61–79.
Cavallar, Georg (2006). *Die europäische Union – Von der Utopie zur Friedens- und Wertegemeinschaft*, Wien: Lit.
Cavallar, Georg (2007). "Zwischen Integration und Abgrenzung: das Fremdenrecht als Teil der Europa-Ideen", in: Markus Kremer and Hans-Richard Reuter (eds), *Macht und Moral – Politisches Denken im 17. und 18. Jahrhundert*, Stuttgart: Kohlhammer, 143–60.
Cavallar, Georg (2011). *Imperfect cosmopolis: studies in the history of international legal theory and cosmopolitan ideas*, Cardiff: University of Wales Press.
Cavallar, Georg (2012a). "Jean-Jacques Rousseau (1712–1778)", in: Bardo Fassbender and Anne Peters, eds., *The Oxford Handbook of the History of International Law*, Oxford: Oxford University Press, 1114–7.
Cavallar, Georg (2012b). "From Francisco de Vitoria to Alfred Verdross. The Right to Preach the Gospel, the Right of Hospitality, and the International Community", in: Matthias Lutz-Bachmann (ed.), *Recht zwischen Philosophie, Theologie und Jurisprudenz. Beiträge zur Begriffsgeschichte von Vitoria bis Suárez*. Stttgart: frommann-holzboog, 1–35.
Cavallar, Georg (2013). "From Hospitality to the Right of Immigration in the Law of Nations, 1750–1850", in: Gideon Baker, ed., *Hospitality and World Politics*, Basingstoke: Palgrave Macmillan, 68–95.
Cavallar, Georg (2015). "Between cosmopolis and apology: Kant's dynamic and embedded religious cosmopolitanism", *Interdisciplinary Journal for Religion and Transformation in Contemporary Society* (in preparation).
Cavallar, Georg (2016). "Dynamic cosmopolitanism: a brief sketch with a special emphasis on Kant", in: Lorena Cebolla, ed., *Lectures on Cosmopolitanism and International Right: Between Ideals and Reality* (in preparation).
Césaire, Aimé (2008). *Toussaint Louverture: la Révolution Française et le problème colonial*. Paris: Éd. Présence Africaine.

Cheneval, Francis (2002). *Philosophie in weltbürgerlicher Bedeutung. Über die Entstehung und die philosophischen Grundlagen des supranationalen und kosmopolitischen Denkens der Moderne*, Basel: Schwabe.
Cheneval, Francis (2003). "Education nationale, education cosmopolitique: regards sur Rousseau et Kant ", in: Jean-Marc Ferry et Boris Libois (eds.), *Pour une éducation postnationale*, Bruxelles, Editions de l'Université de Bruxelles, 55–65.

Cheneval, Francis (2004). "Der kosmopolitische Republikanismus erläutert am Beispiel Anacharsis Cloots", *Zeitschrift für philosophische Forschung*, 58, 3, 373–96.
Chhachhi, Amrita (2006). "Postscript: Tensions and Absences in the Debate on Global Justice and Cosmopolitanism", *Development and Change*, 37, 6, 1329–1334.
Cladis, Mark S. (2007). *Public Vision – Private Lives. Rousseau, Religion, and 21st-Century Democracy*, New York: Columbia University Press.
Cohen, Alix (2009). *Kant and the Human Sciences. Biology, Anthropology and History*, Houndmills, Basingstoke: Macmillan Press.
Cohen, Alix (2012). "Enabling the Realization of Humanity. The Anthropological Dimension of Education", in: Roth and Surprenant, eds., *Kant and Education*, 152–62.
Cohler, Anne M. (1970). *Rousseau and Nationalism*. New York: Basic Books.
Cooper, Laurence D. (1999). *Rousseau, Nature, and the Problem of the Good Life*. University Park, PA: Pennsylvania State University Press.
Coriand, Rotraud and Michael Winkler, eds. (1998). *Der Herbartianismus – die vergessene Wissenschaftsgeschichte*. Weinheim: Studien-Verlag.
Courtney, Cecil P. (2006). "The Art of Compilation and the Communication of Knowledge: the Colonial World in Enlightenment Encyclopaedic Histories: The Example of Raynal's Histoire philosophique des deux Indes", in: Lüsebrink, *Europa der Aufklärung*, 39–50.
Cowen, Tyler, *Creative Destruction. How Globalization is Changing the World's Cultures* (Princeton and Oxford, 2002).
D'Alessandro, Giuseppe (1999). "Die Wiederkehr eines Leitworts. Die ‚Bestimmung des Menschen' als theologische, anthropologische und geschichtsphilosophische Frage der deutschen Spätaufklärung", in: Hinske, *Die Bestimmung des Menschen*, 21–47.
Dall'Agnol, Darlei (2012). "On the Faktum of Reason", in: Rauscher and Perez, *Kant in Brazil*, 109–26.
Dame, Frederick William (1997). *Jean-Jacques Rousseau on Adult Education and Revolution. Paradigma of Radical, Pedagogical Thought*. Frankfurt am Main et al.: Peter Lang.
Dean, Richard (2006). *The Value of Humanity in Kant's Moral Theory*, Oxford: Clarendon Press.
Dean, Richard (2012). "Moral Education and the Ideal of Humanity", in: Roth and Surprenant, eds., *Kant and Education*, 139–51.
Defoe, Daniel (1719). *Robinson Crusoe*. Bristol: Purnell Books, 1974.
Denis, Lara (2005). "Autonomy and the Highest Good", *Kantian Review*, 10, 33–59.
Denis, Lara (2011). "A Kantian conception of human flourishing", in: Jost and Wuerth, *Perfecting Virtue*, 164–93.
Dent, Nicholas (2005). *Rousseau*, London and New York, Routledge.
Derrida, Jacques (2000). *Of Hospitality*. Stanford CA: Stanford University Press.
Derrida, Jacques (2001). *On Cosmopolitanism and Forgiveness*. Transl. Mark Dooley and Michael Hughes, London and New York: Routledge.

Dewey John (1970). *German Philosophy and Politics* [1915, revised edition 1942], Freeport: Books for Libraries Press.
Dexter, Helen (2008). "The 'New War' on Terror, Cosmopolitanism and the 'Just War' Revival", *Government and Opposition*, 43, 1, 55–78.
DiCenso, James J. (2012). *Kant's Religion within the Boundaries of Mere Reason: A Commentary*. Cambridge: Cambridge University Press, 2012.
DiCenso, James J. (2013). "The Concept of *Urbild* in Kant's Philosophy of Religion", *Kant-Studien*, 104, 100–32.
Diderot, Denise (1780). "Extracts from the *Histoire des Deux Indes*", in: *Political Writings*. Ed. and transl. John Hope Mason and Robert Wokler. Cambridge: Cambridge University Press, 1992, 165–214.
Dieterich, Konrad (2009). *Kant und Rousseau* [1847], reprint Whitefish: Kessinger Publishing.
Dingwerth, Klaus and Philipp Pattberg (2006). 'Global governance as a perspective on world politics', *Global Governance*, 12, 185–203.
Dobson, Andrew, "Thick Cosmopolitanism", *Political Studies*, 54 (2006), 165–84.
Donald, James (2007). "Internationalisation, Diversity and the Humanities Curriculum: Cosmopolitanism and Multiculturalism Revisited", *Journal of Philosophy of Education*, 41, 3, 289–308.
Dorsett, Shaunnagh and Ian Hunter, eds. (2010). *Law and Politics in British Colonial Thought: Transpositions of Empire*, Houndmills: Plagrave/Macmillan.
Douzinas, Costas (2007). *Human Rights and Empire: The Political Philosophy of Cosmopolitanism*, Abingdon and New York: Routledge-Cavendish, 2007.
Dubois, Laurent (2005). *Avengers of the New World: The Story of the Haitian Revolution*. Cambridge, Mass.: Belknap Press.
Easley, Eric S. (2004). *The War over Perpetual Peace: An Exploration into the History of a Foundational International Relations Text*, Houndmills: Palgrave.
Earle, Bo (2005). "World legislation. The form and function of a romantic cosmopolitanism", *European Romantic Review*, 16, 2, 209–220.
Eberl, Oliver and Peter Niesen, eds. (2011). *Immanuel Kant, Zum ewigen Frieden und Auszüge aus der Rechtslehre*. Berlin: Suhrkamp.
Ehlers, Nils (2004). *Der Widerspruch zwischen Mensch und Bürger bei Rousseau*. Cuvillier, Göttingen.
English, Andrea R. (2013). *Discontinuity in Learning: Dewey, Herbart, and Education as Transformation*. Cambridge: Cambridge University Press.
Engstrom, Stephen (2009). *The Form of Practical Knowledge: A Study of the Categorical Imperative*. Cambridge, MA and London: Harvard University Press.
Erskine, Toni (2008). *Embedded Cosmopolitanism. Duties to Strangers and Enemies in a World of 'Dislocated Communities'*, Oxford: Oxford University Press.
Essen, G. und M. Striet, eds. (2005). *Kant und die Theologie*, Darmstadt.
Falduto, Antonino (2014). *The Faculties of the Human Mind and the Case of Moral Feeling in Kant's Philosophy*, Berlin and New York: de Gruyter.
Fassbender, Bardo and Anne Peters, eds. (2012). *The Oxford Handbook of the History of International Law*, Oxford: Oxford University Press.
Fetscher, Iring (1980). *Rousseaus politische Philosophie. Zur Geschichte des demokratischen Freiheitsbegriffs*, third edition, Frankfurt am Main, Suhrkamp.
Fetscher, Iring (2006). "Republicanism and popular sovereignty", in: Goldie and Wokler, eds., *The Cambridge History*, 573–97.

Feyerabend, Paul (1993). *Against Method*. 3rd edition, London: Verso.
Fichte, Johann Gottlieb (1792). *Attempt at a Critique of All Revelation*, ed. Allen Wood, translated Garrett Green, Cambridge: Cambridge University Press 2010.
Fichte, Johann Gottlieb (1797). *Foundations of Natural Right*, ed. Frederick Neuhouser, translated by Michael Baur, Cambridge: Cambridge University Press 2000.
Fichte, Johann Gottlieb (1800). *Die Bestimmung des Menschen*, ed. Horst D. Brandt, Hamburg: Felix Meiner 2000.
Fichte, Johann Gottlieb (1808). *Addresses to the German Nation*, ed. Gregory Moore, Cambridge: Cambridge University Press 2008.
Fidler, David P. (1996). "Desperately Clinging to Grotian and Kantian Sheep: Rousseau's Attempted Escape from the State of War", in: Ian Clark and Iver B. Neumann (eds.), *Classical Theories of International Relations*, Houndmills: Macmillan Press, 120–41.
Fine, Robert (2003). "Kant's theory of cosmopolitanism and Hegel's critique", *Philosophy and Social Criticism*, 29, 6, 609–30.
Fine, Robert (2007). *Cosmopolitanism*, London and New York: Routledge.
Fine, Robert (2009). "Cosmopolitanism and human rights: Radicalism in a global age", *Metaphilosophy*, 40, 1, 8–23.
Fine, Robert and Robin Cohen (2002). "Four Cosmopolitanism Moments", in Steven Vertovec and Cohen, Robin (eds), *Conceiving Cosmopolitanism: Theory, Context, and Practice*, Oxford: Oxford University Press, 137–62.
Firestone, Chris L. and Stephen Palmquist, eds. (2006), *Kant and the new philosophy of religion*, Bloomington, Indiana: Indiana University Press.
Fischer, Norbert, ed. (2004). *Kants Metaphysik und Religionsphilosophie*. Hamburg: Meiner.
Fischer, Norbert und Maximilian Forschner, eds. (2010). *Die Gottesfrage in der Philosophie Immanuel Kants*. Freiburg, Basel, Wien: Herder.
Fleischacker, Samuel (1996). "Values behind the Market: Kant's Response to the *Wealth of Nations*", *History of Political Thought*, 17, 379–407.
Fleischacker, Samuel (1999). *A Third Concept of Liberty: Judgment and Freedom in Kant and Adam Smith*, Princeton: Princeton University Press.
Flikschuh, Katrin (2003). *Kant and modern political philosophy*, Cambridge: Cambridge University Press.
Flikschuh, Katrin (2010). "Kant's kingdom of ends: metaphysical, not political", in: Timmermann, Jens, (ed.) *Kant's Groundwork of the Metaphysics of Morals. A Critical Guide*, Cambridge: Cambridge University Press, 119–39.
Förster, Eckart (1998). "Die Wandlungen in Kants Gotteslehre", *Zeitschrift für philosophische Forschung*, 52, 3, 341–62.
Förster, Eckart (2000). *Kant's Final Synthesis. An Essay on the Opus postumum*. Cambridge: Harvard University Press.
Förster, Eckart (2009). "The hidden plan of nature", in Rorty and Schmidt, *Kant's Idea*, 187–99.
Formosa, Paul (2007). "Kant on the Radical Evil of Human Nature", *The Philosophical Forum*, 38, 3, 221–45.
Formosa, Paul (2010). "Kant on the Highest Moral-Physical Good: The Social Aspect of Kant's Moral Philosophy", *Kantian Review*, 15, 1, 1–36.
Formosa, Paul (2012). "From Discipline to Autonomy. Kant's Theory of Moral Development", in: Roth and Surprenant, *Kant and Education*, 163–76.

Forschner, Maximilian (2010). "Im Westen nichts Neues? Bemerkungen zu neuerer Rousseauliteratur", in: *Philosophische Rundschau* 57, 14–32.
Friedman, Marilyn (2000). "Educating for World Citizenship", *Ethics*, 110, 586–601.
Gadamer, Hans-Georg (1984). "The Hermeneutics of Suspicion", *Man and World*, 17, 313–23.
Gawlina, Manfred (2004). "Kant, ein Atheist? Ein Strawson-Schüler liest das *Opus postmum*", *Kant-Studien*, 95, 235–7.
Gebhardt, Mareike (2012). "Von Göttern und Engeln. Die Republik zwischen Ideal und Utopie bei Kant und Rousseau", in: Herb and Scherl, eds., *Rousseaus Zauber*, 19–31.
Geismann, Georg (2009). "Sittlichkeit – Religion – Geschichte", in: *Kant und kein Ende Band 1. Studien zur Moral-, Religions- und Geschichtsphilosophie*. Würzburg: Königshausen und Neumann, 11–118.
Geismann, Georg (2010). *Kant und kein Ende Band 2. Studien zur Rechtsphilosophie*. Würzburg: Königshausen und Neumann.
Geismann, Georg (2012). *Kant und kein Ende Band 3. Pax Kantiana oder Der Rechtsweg zum Weltfrieden*. Würzburg: Königshausen und Neumann.
Gerhardt, Volker (1995). *Immanuel Kants Entwurf "Zum ewigen Frieden". Eine Theorie der Politik*, Darmstadt: Wissenschaftliche Buchgesellschaft.
Gerhardt, Volker, ed. (2005). *Kant im Streit der Fakultäten*. Berlin and New York: Walter de Gruyter.
Gerlach, Stefan (2010). *Wie ist Freiheit möglich? Eine Untersuchung über das Lösungspotenzial zum Determinismusproblem in Kants Kritik der reinen Vernunft*. Tübingen: Francke.
Gessmann, Martin (2013). "Das Urgestein der Moderne. Neue Literatur zur Rousseaus 300. Geburtstag", *Philosophische Rundschau* 60, 1, 1–34
Giri, Ananta Kumar (2006). "Cosmopolitanism and Beyond: Towards a Multiverse of Transformations", *Development and Change*, 37, 6, 1277–1292.
Goldie, Mark (2006). "The English system of liberty", in: Goldie and Wokler, *The Cambridge History*, 40–78.
Goldie, Mark and Robert Wokler, eds. (2006). *The Cambridge History of Eighteenth-Century Political Thought*. Cambridge: Cambridge University Press 2006.
Goldstein, Jürgen (2010). "Die Höllenfahrt der Selbsterkenntnis und der Weg zur Vergötterung bei Hamann und Kant", *Kant-Studien*, 101, 189–216.
Golmohamad, Muna (2009). "Education for World Citizenship: Beyond national allegiance" Copyright Journal compilation © 2009 Philosophy of Education Society of Australasia, *Educational Philosophy and Theory*, 41, 4, 466–486.
González, Ana Marta (2011). *Culture as Mediation: Kant on Nature, Culture and Morality*, Hildesheim: Georg Olms.
Goy, Ina (2010). "Immanuel Kant on the Moral Feeling of Respect", in: Muchnik, Pablo, *Rethinking Kant Volume 2*, 156–79.
Grenberg, Jeanine (2005). *Kant and the Ethics of Humility. A Story of Dependence, Corruption, and Virtue*. Cambridge: Cambridge University Press.
Großmann, Michael (2003). *Wertrationalität und notwendige Bildung. Immanuel Kants praktische Philosophie in ihrer Bedeutung für eine heutige pädagogische Ethik*. Frankfurt am Main: Peter Lang.
Gunesch, Konrad (2004). "Education for cosmopolitanism", *Journal of Research in International Education*, 3, 251–75.

Guyer, Paul (2000). *Kant on Freedom, Law, and Happiness*. Cambridge: Cambridge University Press.
Guyer, Paul, ed. (2003). *Kant's Critique of the Power of Judgement: Critical Essays*, New York.
Guyer, Paul (2005). *Kant's System of Nature and Freedom. Selected Essays*, Oxford: Oxford University Press 2005
Guyer, Paul, ed. (2006), *The Cambridge companion to Kant and modern philosophy*, Cambridge, New York: Cambridge University Press.
Guyer, Paul (2006). "Kant's ambitions in the third *Critique*", in: Paul Guyer, ed. (2006), *The Cambridge companion to Kant and modern philosophy*, Cambridge, New York: Cambridge University Press, 538–87.
Guyer, Paul (2009). "The crooked timber of mankind", in Rorty and Schmidt, *Kant's Idea*, 129–149.
Guyer, Paul (2010). "Moral feelings in the Metaphysics of Morals", in: Denis, *Metaphysics*, 130–51.
Guyer, Paul (2011). "Kantian perfectionism", in: Jost and Wuerth, *Perfecting Virtue*, 194–214.
Guyer, Paul (2012). "Examples of Moral Possibility", in: Roth and Surprenant, eds., *Kant and Education*, 126–38.
Habermas, Jürgen (1997). "Kant's Idea of Perpetual Peace, with the Benefit of Two Hundred Years' Hindsight", in: James Bohman and Matthias Lutz-Bachmann (eds.), *Perpetual Peace. Essays on Kant's Cosmopolitan Ideal*. Cambridge, Mass. and London: MIT Press, 113–153.
Habermas, Jürgen (1998). *The Inclusion of the Other. Studies in Political Theory*, translated and edited Ciaran Cronin, Cambridge, Mass.: MIT Press.
Haase, Marco (2004), *Grundnorm – Gemeinwille – Geist. Der Grund des Rechts nach Kelsen, Kant und Hegel*, Tübingen: Mohr.
Häntsch, Carola (2008). "The World Citizen from the Perspective of Alien Reason: Notes on Kant's Category of the *Weltbürger* according to Josef Simon", in: Rebecka Lettevall and My Klockar Linder (eds.), *The Idea of Kosmopolis. History, philosophy and politics of world citizenship*, Huddinge: Södertörns högskola, 51–63.
Halldenius, Lena (2010). "Building Blocks of a Republican Cosmopolitanism", *European Journal of Political Philosophy*, 9, 1, 12–30.
Hand, Michael (2006). "Against Autonomy as an Educational Aim", *Oxford Review of Education*, 32, 4, 535–50.
Hand, Michael (2011). "Patriotism in schools", *Impact*, 19, 1–40.
Hansen, David T. (2008). "Curriculum and the idea of cosmopolitan inheritance", *Journal of Curriculum Studies*, 40, 3, 289–312.
Hansen, David T. (2009). "Education Viewed Through a Cosmopolitan Prism", *Philosophy of Education, 2008*, 206–214.
Hansen, David T. (2010). "Walking with Diogenes: Cosmopolitan Accents in Philosophy and Education", *Philosophy of Education 2009*. Urbana, Illinois: University of Illinois, 1–13.
Hardarson, Atli (2012). "Why the Aims of Education Cannot Be Settled", *Journal of Philosophy of Education*, 46, 223–35.
Harris, Lee (2003). "The Cosmopolitan Illusion", *Policy Review*, 118, 45–59.
Hayden, Matthew J. (2012). *Cosmopolitan Education and Moral Education: Forging Moral Beings Under Conditions of Global Uncertainty*, dissertation Columbia University.
Hayden, Patrick (2005). *Cosmopolitan Global Politics*, Aldershot, Ashgate.

Heater, Derek (1996). *World Citizenship and Government: Cosmopolitan Ideas in the History of Western Political Thought*, Basingstoke, UK.
Heater, Derek (2002). *World Citizenship: Cosmopolitan Thinking and its Opponents*, London and New York.
Hebeis Michael (1996). *Karl Anton von Martini (1726–1800). Leben und Werk*. Frankfurt am Main et al.: Lang.
Hedrick, Todd (2008). "Race, Difference, and Anthropology in Kant's Cosmopolitanism", *Journal of the History of Philosophy* 46, 245–268.
Hegel, Georg Wilhelm Friedrich (1821). *Outlines of the Philosophy of Right*, trans. T. M. Knox, ed. Stephen Houlgate, Oxford: Oxford University Press 2008.
Hegel, Georg Wilhelm Friedrich (1956). *The Philosophy of History*, Toronto and London: Dover Publications.
Heinz, Marion und Christian Krijnen, eds. (2007), *Kant im Neukantianismus. Fortschritt oder Rückschritt? Studien und Materialien zum Neukantianismus*, Würzburg: Königshausen und Neumann.
Held, David (2010). *Cosmopolitanism. Ideals and Realities*. Cambridge: Polity Press.
Hentig, Hartmut von (2003). *Rousseau oder Die wohlgeordnete Freiheit*, München.
Herb, Karlfriedrich (2012). "Schweigende Mehrheit oder frohes Fest? Ambivalenzen des Öffentlichkeitsbegriffs bei Rousseau", in: Herb and Scherl, eds., *Rousseaus Zauber*, 93–100.
Herb, Karlfriedrich and Magdalena Scherl, eds. (2012). *Rousseaus Zauber. Lesarten der Politischen Philosophie*, Würzburg: Königshausen und Neumann.
Herbart, Johann Friedrich (1814). "Über den freywilligen Gehorsam als Grundzug des ächten Bürgersinnes in Monarchien", in: Karl Kehrbach, Otto Flügel and Theodor Fritzsch, eds., *Johann Friedrich Herbarts Sämtliche Werke*, 19 vols., Langensalza 1887–1912, vol. 3, 259–68.
Herbart, Johann Friedrich (1835). *Umriss pädagogischer Vorlesungen*, hrsgeg. Von Eva Matthes und Carsten Heinze, Darmstadt: Wissenschaftliche Buchgesellschaft 2003, 9–103.
Herbart, Johann Friedrich (1986). *Systematische Pädagogik*, eingeleitet, ausgewählt und interpretiert von Dietrich Benner, Stuttgart: Klett.
Herder, Johann Gottfried (1765). "How Philosophy Can Become More Universal and Useful for the Benefit of the People", in: *Philosophical Writings*, transl. and ed. Michael N. Forster, Cambridge: Cambridge University Press 2004, 3–29.
Herder, Johann Gottfried (1774). "Another Philosophy of History for the Education of Mankind", in: Herder, *Another Philosophy of History and Selected Political Writings*, ed. Ioannis D. Evrigenis and Daniel Pellerin, Indianapolis: Hackett 2004, 3–97.
Herder, Johann Gottfried von (2004). *Philosophical Writings*, transl. and ed. Michael N. Forster, Cambridge: Cambridge University Press.
Heuvel, Gerd van den (1986). "Cosmopolite, Cosmopoli(ti)sme", in: Rolf Reichardt and Eberhard Schmidt (eds), *Handbuch politisch-sozialer Grundbegriffe in Frankreich 1680–1820*, München, 41–55.
Heydt-Stevenson, Jillian and Jeffrey N. Cox (2005). "Introduction: Are those who are 'strangers nowhere in the world' at home anywhere: Thinking about Romantic cosmopolitanism", *European Romantic Review*, 16, 2, 129–140.
Hill, Lisa (2010). "Adam Smith's cosmopolitanism: The expanding circles of commercial strangership", *History of Political Thought*, 31, 3, 449–473.

Hill, Thomas E., (2000). *Respect, Pluralism, and Justice: Kantian Perspectives*. Oxford: Oxford University Press.
Hinske, Norbert (1980). *Kant als Herausforderung an die Gegenwart*. Freiburg and München: Alber.
Hinske, Norbert, ed. (1999). *Die Bestimmung des Menschen*, Aufklärung vol. 11, 1, Hamburg: Meiner.
Hirschmann, Albert (1981). *The Passions and the Interests: Political Arguments for Capitalism before its Triumph*, Princeton: Princeton University Press.
Hirtt, Nico (2011). "Education in the 'knowledge economy': consequences for democracy", in Luise Ludwig et al., eds., *Bildung in der Demokratie II*, Opladen and Farmington Hills, MI: Barbara Budrich, 167–76.
Höffe, Otfried (1990). *Kategorische Rechtsprinzipien. Ein Kontrapunkt der Moderne*. Frankfurt am Main: Suhrkamp.
Höffe, Otfried (2006). *Kant's cosmopolitan theory of law and peace*. Cambridge: Cambridge University Press.
Höffe, Otfried, ed. (2008a). *Kritik der Urteilskraft*, Berlin: Akademie-Verlag.
Höffe, Otfried (2008b). "Der Mensch als Endzweck", in: ibid., 289–308.
Höffe, Otfried (2008c). "Kants universaler Kosmopolitismus", in: Rohden et al., *Recht und Frieden*, vol. 1, 139–51.
Höffe, Otfried, ed. (2011). *Die Religion innerhalb der Grenzen der bloßen Vernunft*, Berlin: Akademie-Verlag.
Höffe, Otfried (2013). "Anthropology and Metaphysics in Kant's Categorical Imperative of Law", in Timmons and Baiasu, eds., *Kant on Practical Justification*, 110–24.
Hoesch, Matthias (2012). "Lässt Kants Völkerbund als Mitgliedsstaaten nur Republiken zu?", *Kant-Studien*, 103, 114–25.
Hoffmann, Stanley (2006). "Rousseau on War and Peace", in Scott, *Rousseau*, 24–52.
Honneth, Axel (2004). "Die Unhintergehbarkeit des Fortschritts. Kants Bestimmung des Verhältnisses von Moral und Geschichte", in: Nagl and Langthaler, *Recht*, pp. 85–98.
Hont, Istvan (2005). *Jealousy of Trade. International Competition and the Nation-State in Historical Perspective*. Cambridge, Mass.: Harvard University Press.
Hüning, Dieter, ed. (2009). *Naturrecht und Staatstheorie bei Samuel Pufendorf*. Baden-Baden: Nomos.
Huggler, Jorgen (2010). "Cosmopolitanism and Peace in Kant's Essay on 'Perpetual Peace'", *Studies in Philosophy and Education* 29, 129–40.
Humboldt, Wilhelm von (1792). "Ideen zu einem Versuch, die Gränzen der Wirksamkeit des Staats zu bestimmen", in: *Werke in fünf Bänden*, ed. Andreas Flitner and Klaus Giel, vol. 1, Darmstadt: Wissenschaftliche Buchgesellschaft 1960, 56–233.
Humboldt, Wilhelm von (1793). "Theorie der Bildung des Menschen", in: *Werke*, ed. Flitner and Giel, vol. 1, 234–40.
Humboldt, Wilhelm von (1960). *Werke in fünf Bänden*, ed. Andreas Flitner and Klaus Giel, vol. 1, Darmstadt: Wissenschaftliche Buchgesellschaft.
Hunter, Ian (2001). *Rival Enlightenments. Civil and Metaphysical Philosophy in Early Modern Germany*. Cambridge: Cambridge University Press.
Hunter, Ian (2010). "Global Justice and Regional Metaphysics: On the Critical History of the Law of Nature and Nations", in Dorsett and Hunter, eds., *Law and Politics*, 11–30.
Husain, Ed (2007). *The Islamist: Why I Joined Radical Islam in Britain, What I Saw Inside and Why I Left*, London: Penguin.

Ittersum, Martine Julia van (2006). *Profit and Principle. Hugo Grotius, Natural Rights Theories and the Rise of Dutch Power in the East Indies 1595–1615*. Leiden: Brill.

Ittersum, Martine Julia van (2010). "The wise man is never merely a private citizen: The Roman Stoa in Hugo Grotius' *De Jure Praedae* (1604–1608)," *History of European Ideas*, 36, 1–18.

Ivison, Duncan (2010). "Justice and Imperialism. On the Very Idea of a Universal Standard", in Dorsett and Hunter, eds., *Law and Politics*, 31–48.

Jackson, Liz (2007). "The Individualist? The autonomy of reason in Kant's philosophy and educational views", *Studies in Philosophy and Education*, 26, 4, 335–344.

Jacob, Margaret C. (2006). *Strangers Nowhere in the World: The Rise of Cosmopolitanism in Early Modern Europe*, Philadelphia: University of Pennsylvania Press.

Jacobs, Brian, and Patrick Kain, eds. (2003). *Essays on Kant's Anthropology*, Cambridge: Cambridge University Press.

James, David (2011). *Fichte's Social and Political Philosophy: Property and Virtue*, Cambridge: Cambridge University Press.

James, David (2013). "Fichte's Critical Reappraisal of Kant's Cosmopolitanism", in: Bacin et al., eds., *Kant und die Philosophie in weltbürgerlicher Absicht*, vol. 4, 707–18.

Jedan, Dieter und Christoph Lüth, eds. (2001). *Moral Philosophy and Education in the Enlightenment*, Bochum: Winkler.

Johnson, Stephen and Harvey Siegel (2010). *Teaching Thinking Skills*, 2nd edition, London: Continuum.

Johnston, James Scott (2006). "The education of the categorical imperative", *Studies in Philosophy and Education*, 25, 5, 385–402.

Johnston, James Scott (2007). "Moral Law and Moral Education: Defending Kantian Autonomy", *Journal of Philosophy of Education*, 41, 2, 233–45.

Johnston, James Scott (2012). "Kant as Moral Psychologist?", in: Roth and Surprenant, eds., *Kant and Education*, 177–92.

Jollimore, Troy and Sharon Barrios (2006). "Creating cosmopolitans: the case for literature", *Studies in Philosophy and Education*, 25, 5, 363–383.

Jonas, Mark E. (2010). "When Teachers Must Let Education Hurt: Rousseau and Nietzsche on Compassion and the Educational Value of Suffering", *Journal of Philosophy of Education*, 44, 1, 45–60.

Jost, Lawrence, and Julian Wuerth, eds. (2011). *Perfecting Virtue: New Essays on Kantian Ethics and Virtue Ethics*, Cambridge: Cambridge University Press.

Jost, Lawrence and Julian Wuerth (2011). "Introduction", in: *Perfecting Virtue*, 1–7.

Junga, Kristin (2011). *Wissen – Glauben – Bilden: ein bildungsphilosophischer Blick auf Kant, Schleiermacher und Wilhelm von Humboldt*, Paderborn: Schöningh.

Kater, Thomas (1999). *Politik, Recht, Geschichte. Zur Einheit der politischen Philosophie Immanuel Kants*. Würzburg: Königshausen und Neumann.

Kauder, Peter and Wolfgang Fischer (1999). *Immanuel Kant über Pädagogik. 7 Studien*, Hohengehren: Schneider.

Keienburg, Johannes (2011). *Immanuel Kant und die Öffentlichkeit der Vernunft*, Kantstudien Ergänzungshefte 164, Berlin and New York: de Gruyter.

Keil, Rainer (2009). *Freizügigkeit, Gerechtigkeit, demokratische Autonomie: Das Weltbürgerrecht nach Immanuel Kant als Masstab der Gerechtigkeit geltenden Aufenthalts-, Einwanderungs- und Flüchtlingsrechts*. Baden-Baden: Nomos.

Kelsen, Hans (1992). 'Reine Rechtslehre, "Labandismus" und Neukatianismus. Ein Brief an Renato Treves', in: Hans Kelsen and Renato Treves, *Formalismo giuridico e realità sociale*, ed. Stanley L. Paulson, Neapel and Rome: Edizioni Scientifiche Italiane, 55–8.

Kelsen, Hans (1928). *Die philosophischen Grundlagen der Naturrechtslehre und des Rechtspositivismus*, Berlin: Heise.

Kelsen, Hans (1960). *Reine Rechtslehre*, 2nd edition, Wien: Deuticke.

Kelsen, Hans, and Fritz Sander (1988). *Die Rolle des Neukantianismus in der Reinen Rechtslehre. Eine Debatte zwischen Sander und Kelsen*, ed. Stanley L. Paulson, Aalen: Scientia.

Kemp, Peter (2006). "Kant the Cosmopolitan", in: Hans Lenk and Reiner Wiehl (eds.), *Kant today – Kant aujourd'hui – Kant heute*, Berlin: Lit, 142–62.

Kemp, Ryan (2011). "The Contingency of Evil: Rethinking the Problem of Universal Evil in Kant's Religion", in: Thorndike, *Rethinking Kant: Volume 3*, 100–23.

Kersting, Wolfgang (1984). *Wohlgeordnete Freiheit. Immanuel Kants Rechts- und Staatsphilosophie*. New paperback edition Frankfurt am Main: Suhrkamp 1993.

Kersting, Wolfgang (2004). *Kant über Recht*. Paderborn: Mentis.

Kleingeld, Pauline (1995). *Fortschritt und Vernunft: Zur Geschichtsphilosophie Kants*. Würzburg: Königshausen und Neumann.

Kleingeld, Pauline (1999). "Six Varieties of Cosmopolitanism in Late Eighteenth-Century Germany", *Journal of the History of Ideas*, 60, 1, 505–24.

Kleingeld, Pauline (2004). "Approaching Perpetual Peace: Kant's Defence of a League of States and his Ideal of a World Federation", *European Journal of Philosophy*, 12, 304–325.

Kleingeld, Pauline (2006). "Kant's Cosmopolitan Patriotism", in: Sharon Byrd and Joachim Hruschka (eds), *Kant and Law* (Aldershot, Burlington: Ashgate), pp. 473–90.

Kleingeld, Pauline (2007). "Kant's Second Thoughts on Race", *The Philosophical Quarterly*, 57, 573–92.

Kleingeld, Pauline (2008). "Romantic Cosmopolitanism: Novalis's 'Christianity or Europe'", *Journal of the History of Philosophy*, 46, 2, 269–84.

Kleingeld, Pauline (2009). "Kant's changing cosmopolitanism", in: Rorty and Schmidt, *Kant's Idea for a Universal History*, 171–86.

Kleingeld, Pauline (2012). *Kant and Cosmopolitanism: The Philosophical Ideal of World Citizenship*, Cambridge: Cambridge University Press.

Kleingeld, Pauline, and Eric Brown (2002). "Cosmopolitanism", in: Edward N. Zalta (ed.), *The Stanford Encyclopedia of Philosophy*, at http://plato.stanford.edu/archives/fall2002/entries/cosmopolitanism, visited November 23, 2007.

Klemme, Heiner (1999). "Die Freiheit der Willkür und die Herrschaft des Bösen. Kants Lehre vom radikalen Bösen zwischen Moral, Religion und Recht", in: Heiner Klemme, Bernd Ludwig, Michael Pauen, Werner Stark, eds., *Aufklärung und Interpretation. Studien zu Kants Philosophie und ihrem Umkreis*, Würzburg: Königshausen und Neumann, 125–51.

Knippenberg, Joseph M. (1989). "Moving Beyond Fear: Rousseau and Kant on Cosmopolitan Education", *Journal of Politics*, 51, 4, 811–27.

Knippenberg, Joseph M. (1991). "From Kant to Marx: The Perils of Liberal Idealism", *The Political Science Reviewer*, 20, 101–43.

Knowles, Dudley (2004). *Hegel and the Philosophy of Right*, London and New York: Routledge.

Kobusch, Theo (2012). "Welt der Gründe oder Welt der Vernunft? Zur Einseitigkeit des Rationalismus", *Allgemeine Zeitschrift für Philosophie*, 37, 3, 243–64.
Koch, Lutz (2002). "Friedensidee und kosmopolitische Bildung", *Das Kind. Halbjahresschrift für Montessori-Pädagogik*, 31, 42–57.
Koch, Lutz (2003). *Kants ethische Didaktik*, Würzburg: Ergon.
Koch, Lutz (2013). "Kants kosmopolitische Erziehungsidee", Bacin, Stefano, Alfredo Ferrarin, Claudio La Rocca and Margit Ruffing, eds., *Kant und die Philosophie in weltbürgerlicher Absicht*, vol. 4, Berlin: de Gruyter, 720–28.
Koch, Lutz and Christian Schönherr, eds. (2005), *Kant – Pädagogik und Politik*. Ergon Verlag: Würzburg.
Korsgaard, Christine M. (1996). *Creating the Kingdom of Ends*, Cambridge: Cambridge University Press.
Korsgaard, Ove (2006). "Giving the Spirit a National Form: From Rousseau's advice to Poland to Habermas' advice to the European Union", *Educational Philosophy and Theory*, 38, 2, 231–46.
Kristeva, Julia (1991). *Strangers to Ourselves*, translated Leon S. Rudiez, New York: Columbia University Press.
Kuehn, Manfred (2001). *Kant. A Biography.* Cambridge: Cambridge University Press.
Ladenthin, Volker (2005). "Öffentlichkeit und Erzählung", in: Koch and Schönherr, eds., *Kant – Pädagogik und Politik*, 97–116.
Lahner, Alexander (2011). *Bildung und Aufklärung nach PISA. Theorie und Praxis außerschulischer politischer Jugendbildung*, Wiesbaden: Verlag für Sozialwissenschaften.
Langthaler, Rudolf (1991). *Kants Ethik als 'System der Zwecke'*, Berlin: de Gruyter.
Langthaler, Rudolf (2014). *Geschichte, Ethik und Religion im Anschluss an Kant. Philosophische Perspektiven ‚zwischen skeptischer Hoffnungslosigkeit und dogmatischem Trotz'*. Deutsche Zeitschrift für Philosophie, Sonderband 19, 2 vols., Berlin: de Gruyter.
Laursen, John Christian (2010). "Basedow, Johann Bernhard (1724–90)", in: Heiner F. Klemme and Manfred Kuehn, eds., *The Dictionary of Eighteenth-Century German Philosophers*, vol. 1, London and New York: Continuum.
Lazos, Efraín (2010). "Devils with with Understanding: Tensions in Kant's Idea of Society", in: Muchnik, *Rethinking Kant volume 2*, 182–204.
Lettevall, Rebecka (2008). "The Idea of *Kosmopolis*: Two Kinds of Cosmopolitanism", in Letteval and Linder, *Kosmopolis*, 13–30.
Lettevall, Rebecka (2009). "Turning golden coins into loose change: Philosophical, political and popular readings of Kant's *Zum ewigen Frieden*", *Jahrbuch für Recht und Ethik*, 17, 133–150.
Lettevall, Rebecka and My Klockar Linder, eds. (2008). *The Idea of Kosmopolis. History, philosophy and politics of world citizenship.* Huddinge: Södertörns högskola.
Lex, Nina (2014). "Exemplary Universality: Jean-Jacques Rousseau and Global Citizenship", in: Lettevall and Petrov, eds., *Cosmopolitanism*, 119–40.
Linden, Harry van der (1988). *Kantian Ethics and Socialism*. Indianapolis and Cambridge: Hackett Publishing.
Louden, Robert B. (1992). "Go-carts of Judgement: Exemplars in Kantian Moral Education", *Archiv für Geschichte der Philosophie*, 74, 303–22.

Louden, Robert B. (2000), *Kant's Impure Ethics. From Rational Beings to Human Beings*, Oxford: Oxford University Press.
Louden, Robert B. (2007), *The World We Want. How and Why the Ideals of the Enlightenment Still Elude Us*, Oxford: Oxford University Press.
Louden, Robert B. (2008). "Anthropology from a Kantian point of view: toward a cosmopolitan conception of human nature", in: Muchnik, *Rethinking Kant*, vol. 1, 88–108.
Louden, Robert B. (2010). "Making the law visible: the role of examples in Kant's ethics", in: Timmermann, *Kant's Groundwork*, 63–81.
Louden, Robert B. (2011), *Kant's Human Being: Essays on His Theory of Human Nature*, Oxford: Oxford University Press.
Louden, Robert B. (2012), "Not a Slow *Reform*, but a Swift *Revolution*': Kant and Basedow on the Need to Transform Education", in: Roth and Surprenant, eds., *Kant and Education*, 39–54.
Louden, Robert B. (2014). "Cosmopolitical Unity: The Final Destiny of the Human Species", in Alix Cohen, ed., *Kant's Lectures on Anthropology: A Critical Guide*, Cambridge: Cambridge University Press, 211–29.
Løvlie, Lars (1997). "The Uses of Example in Moral Education", *Journal of Philosophy of Education*, 31, 1, 409–25.
Løvlie, Lars (2012). "Kant's Invitation to Educational Thinking", in: Roth and Surprenant, eds., *Kant and Education*, 107–23.
Lüsebrink, Hans-Jürgen, ed. (2006). *Das Europa der Aufklärung und die außereuropäische koloniale Welt*. Göttingen: Wallstein.
Lutz-Bachmann, Matthias, Andreas Niederberger and Philipp Schink, eds. (2010), *Kosmopolitanismus. Zur Geschichte und Zukunft eines umstrittenen Ideals*, Frankfurt am Main: Velbrück Wissenschaft.
Makino, Eiji (2013). "Weltbürgertum und die Kritik an der postkolonialen Vernunft", in: Bacin et al., eds., *Kant und die Philosophie in weltbürgerlicher Absicht*, vol. 1, 321–38.
Maly, Sebastian (2012), *Kant über die symbolische Erkenntnis Gottes*, Berlin: de Gruyter.
Manthey, Jürgen (2005). *Königsberg. Geschichte einer Weltbürgerrepublik*, München, Wien: Carl Hanser Verlag.
Martens, Georg Friedrich von (1796). *Einleitung in das positive europäische Völkerrecht auf Verträge und Herkommen gegründet*. Göttingen: Johann Christian Dieterich.
Martini, Karl Anton Freiherr von (1791). *Erklärung der Lehrsätze über das allgemeine Staats- und Völkerrecht*. Reprint Aalen: Scientia 1969.
Matthes, Eva and Carsten Heinze (2003). "Interpretation", in: Herbart, Johann Friedrich (1835). *Umriss pädagogischer Vorlesungen*, ed. Eva Matthes and Carsten Heinze, Darmstadt: Wissenschaftliche Buchgesellschaft, 105–68.
Matuschek, Stefan (2009). "Kommentar", in: Friedrich Schiller, *Über die ästhetische Erziehung des Menschen in einer Reihe von Briefen*, kommentiert von Stefan Matuschek, Frankfurt am Main: Suhrkamp, 125–281.
McCarthy, Thomas (2009). *Race, Empire, and the Idea of Human Development*, Cambridge: Cambridge University Press.
McCarty, Luise Prior (2010). "Failing to Cosmopolitanize Diogenes in Montréal: A Peripatetic Excursion", *Philosophy of Education 2009*, Urbana, Illinois: University of Illinois, 14–7.
McConnell, Michael W. (1996). "Don't Neglect the Little Platoons", in: Nussbaum, *For Love of Country?*, 78–84.

McDonough, Kevin, and Walter Feinberg (eds., 2003). *Education and Citizenship in Liberal-democratic Societies. Teaching for Cosmopolitan Values and Collective Identities*, Oxford: Oxford University Press.
Meiers, Kurt (1969). *Der Religionsunterricht bei Johann Bernhard Basedow. Seine Bedeutung für die Gegenwart*, Dissertation Saarbrücken.
Meyer, Sabine (2005). "Der Rechtsfrieden als Prinzip moderner Friedenserziehung", in: Koch and Schönherr, eds., *Kant – Pädagogik und Politik*, 81–96.
Mendham, Matthew D. (2010). "Enlightened gentleness as soft indifference: Rousseau's critique of cultural modernization", *History of Political Thought*, 31, 4, 605–637.
Menke, Christoph, and Arnd Pollmann (2007). *Philosophie der Menschenrechte zur Einführung*, Hamburg.
Mertens, Thomas (2002). "Am Ausgang des Neukantianismus: Cassirer und Heidegger in Davos 1929", in: Alexy et al., *Neukantianismus und Rechtsphilosophie*, 523–40.
Menke, Christoph, and Arnd Pollmann (2007). *Philosophie der Menschenrechte zur Einführung*, Hamburg.
Michalson, Gordon E. (1999). *Kant and the Problem of God*. Oxford: Blackwell.
Mikalsen, Kjartan Koch (2012). *Justice Among States. Four essays*, Trondheim: Norwegian University of Science and Technology.
Milstein, Brian (2013). "Kantian Cosmopolitanism beyond 'Perpetual Peace': Commercium, Critique, and the Cosmopolitan Problematic", *European Journal of Philosophy*, 21, 1, 118–143.
Moellendorf, Darrel (2002). *Cosmopolitan Justice*, Boulder, Colorado: Westview Press.
Moland, Lydia L. (2011). *Hegel on Political Identity: Patriotism, Nationality, Cosmopolitanism*, Northwestern University Press, 2011.
Montesquieu, baron de, Charles de Secondat (1989). *The Spirit of the Laws* [1748], transl. and ed. by Anne M. Cohler, Basia Carolyn Miller and Harold Samuel Stone, Cambridge: Cambridge University Press.
Moran, Kate A. (2009). "Can Kant Have an Account of Moral Education?", *Journal of Philosophy of Education*, 43, 4, 471–84.
Moran, Kate A. (2011). "The Ethical Community as Ground of Moral Action: An Interpretation of the Highest Good", in: Thorndike, *Rethinking Kant: Volume 3*, 78–99.
Moran, Kate A. (2012). *Community and progress in Kant's moral philosophy*, Washington, DC: Catholic University of America Press.
Morgan, Diane (2009). "Trading Hospitality: Kant, Cosmopolitics and Commercium", *Paragraph*, 32, 105–122.
Mori, Massimo (2013). "Reine Vernunft und Weltbürgertum – Recht, Politik und Geschichte in Kants Kosmopolitismus", in: Bacin et al., eds., *Kant und die Philosophie in weltbürgerlicher Absicht*, vol. 1, 339–56.
Mouffe, Chantal (2005). *On the Political*, Routledge: London and New York.
Muchnik, Pablo (2008). "Competing Enlightenment Narratives: A case Study of Rorty's Anti-Kantianism", in: Muchnik, *Rethinking Kant*, vol. 1, 294–317.
Muchnik, Pablo (2009). *Kant's Theory of Evil. An Essay on the Dangers of Self-Love and the Aprioricity of History*, Lanham: Lexington Books.
Muchnik, Pablo (2010). *Rethinking Kant Volume 2*, Newcastle upon Tyne: Cambridge Scholars Publishings.

Munzel, Felicitas (1996). "Reason's Practical Idea of Perpetual Peace, Human Character, and the Pedagogical Function of the Republican Constitution", *Idealistic Studies*, 26, 101–34.
Munzel, G. Felicitas (1999). *Kant's Conception of Moral Character. The 'Critical' Link of Morality, Anthropology, and reflective Judgment*, Chicago and London: University of Chicago Press.
Munzel, G. Felicitas (2003). "Kant on Moral Education, or 'Enlightenment' and the Liberal Arts", *The Review of Metaphysics*, 57, 1, 43–73.
Munzel, G. Felicitas (2012). *Kant's Conception of Pedagogy. Toward Education for Freedom*. Evanston, Illinois: Northwestern University Press.
Murray, Patrick T. (1994). *The Development of German Aesthetic Theory from Kant to Schiller: A Philosophical Commentary in Schiller's 'Aesthetic Education of Man'*, Lewiston, Queenston, Lampeter.
Muthu, Sankar (2003). *Enlightenment against Empire*, Princeton: Princeton University Press.
Muthu, Sankar (2006). "Justice and Foreigners: Kant's Cosmopolitan Right", reprinted in Sharon Byrd and Joachim Hruschka (eds.), *Kant and Law*, Aldershot, Burlington: Ashgate, 449–71.
Nagl-Docekal, Herta and Rudolf Langthaler, eds. (2004). *Recht – Geschichte – Religion. Die Bedeutung Kants für die Gegenwart*. Berlin: Akademie-Verlag.
Nawrath, Thomas (2010). "The Moral Laboratory: On *Kant's* Notion of Pedagogy as a Science", *Studies in Philosophy and Education*, 29, 4, 365–377.
Neidleman, Jason (2012). "Rousseau's rediscovered communion des coeurs: Cosmopolitanism in the *Reveries of the solitary walker*", *Political Studies*, 60, 1, 76–94.
Neuhouser, Frederick (2008). *Rousseau's Theodicy of Self-Love. Evil, Rationality, and the Drive for Recognition*, Oxford: Oxford University Press.
Nour, Soraya (2012). "Kant and Kantian Themes in International Relations", in: Rauscher and Perez, *Kant in Brazil*, 246–70.
Novalis (Friedrich von Hardenberg; 1799). "Christianity or Europe. A Fragment", in: Frederick C. Beiser, ed., *The Early Political Writings of The German Romantics*, Cambridge: Cambridge University Press 1999, 59–79.
Nussbaum, Martha C. (1996), edited by Joshua Cohen. *For Love of Country?*, Boston: Beacon Press.
Nussbaum, Martha C. (1997a). *Cultivating Humanity. A Classical Defense of Reform in Liberal Education*, Cambridge, Mass., Harvard University Press.
Nussbaum, Martha C. (1997b). "Kant and Stoic Cosmopolitanism", *The Journal of Political Philosophy*, 5, 1, 1–25.
Nussbaum, Martha (2002). "Education for Citizenship in an Era of global Connection", *Studies in Philosophy and Education*, 21, 289–303.
Nussbaum, Martha C. (2008). "Toward a globally sensitive patriotism", *Daedalus*, 137, 3, 78–93.
Nussbaum, Martha C. (2010). *Not For Profit: Why Democracy Needs the Humanities*, Princeton and Oxford: Princeton University Press 2010.
O'Connell, Eoin (2008). "Motivation, Futility and the Highest Good in Kant's Practical Philosophy", in: Muchnik, ed., *Rethinking Kant*, vol. 1, 136–64.
Oelkers, Jürgen (2008). *Jean-Jacques Rousseau*, London, Cointinuum.
O'Neill, Daniel (2009). "Rethinking Burke and India", *History of Political Thought*, 30, 3, 492–523.

O'Neill, Daniel (2012). "Revisiting the Middle Way: *The Logic of the History of Ideas* after More Than a Decade", *Journal of the History of Ideas*, 73, 4, 583–92.
O'Neill, Onora (2013). "Cosmopolitanism Then and Now", in: Bacin et al., eds., *Kant und die Philosophie in weltbürgerlicher Absicht*, vol. 1, 357–68.
Onuf, Nicholas (2009). "Friendship and Hospitality: some conceptual preliminaries", *Journal of International Political Theory*, 5, 1–21.
Overhoff, Jürgen (2000). "Immanuel Kant, die philanthropische Pädagogik und die Erziehung zur religiösen Toleranz", in: Dina Emundts, ed., *Immanuel Kant und die Berliner Aufklärung*, Wiesbaden: Reichert, 133–47.
Overhoff, Jürgen (2004). *Die Frühgeschichte des Philanthropismus (1715–1771)*, Tübingen: Max Niemeyer.
Palmquist, Stephen R. (2000). *Kant's Critical Religion. Volume Two of Kant's System of Perspectives*. Aldershot: Ashgate.
Papastephanou, Mariana (2005). "Globalisation, Globalism and Cosmopolitanism as an Educational Ideal", *Educational Philosophy and Theory*, 37, 4, 533–51.
Pasternack, Lawrence (2011). "The Development and Scope of Kantian Belief: The Highest Good, The Practical Postulates and The Fact of Reason", *Kant-Studien*, 102, 290–315.
Patry, Jean-Luc (2004). "Der Pädagogische Takt – Brücke zwischen Theorie und Praxis. Ein Essay", in: Anton A. Bucher, ed., *Erziehung – Therapie – Sinn. Festschrift für Heinz Rothbucher*, Münster: Lit, 145–68.
Pauen, Michael (1999). "Teleologie und Geschichte in der ‚Kritik der Urteilskraft'", in: Heiner Klemme, Bernd Ludwig, Michael Pauen, Werner Stark, eds., *Aufklärung und Interpretation. Studien zu Kants Philosophie und ihrem Umkreis*, Würzburg: Königshausen und Neumann, 197–216.
Paulson, Stanley L. (2002). "Faktum/Wert-Distinktion: Zwei-Welten-Lehre und immanenter Sinn: Hans Kelsen als Neukantianer", in: Alexy et al., *Neukantianismus und Rechtsphilosophie*, 223–51.
Paulson, Stanley L. (2005). "Konstitutive und methodologische Formen. Zur Kantischen und neukantischen Folie der Rechtslehre Hans Kelsens", in: Heinz und Krijnen, *Kant im Neukantianismus*, 149–65.
Peltre, Monique (1999). "Kant et l'éducation. Un dialogue avec Jean-Jacques Rousseau", in: Monique Samuel-Scheyder and Philippe Alexandre, eds., *La Pensée pédagogique. Enjeux, continuité et rupture en Europe du XVIe au XXe siècle*, Berne: Haupt.
Perkins, Mary Anne, and Martin Liebscher, eds. (2006). *Nationalism versus Cosmopolitanism in German Thought and Culture, 1789–1914: Essays on the Emergence of Europe*, Lewiston: Edwin Mellen Press.
Peterson, Andrew (2011). *Civic Republicanism and Civic Education: The Education of Citizens*, Basingstoke: Palgrave MacMillan.
Pinkard, Terry (2002). *German Philosophy, 1760–1860. The Legacy of Idealism*, Cambridge: Cambridge University Press.
Pocock John Greville A. (1975). *The Machiavellian Moment: Florentine Political Thought and the Atlantic Republican Tradition*, Princeton: Princeton University Press.
Pollmann, Arnd (2011). "Der Kummer der Vernunft. Zu Kants Idee einer allgemeinen Geschichtsphilosophie in therapeutischer Absicht", *Kant-Studien*, 102, 69–88.
Popkin, Richard H. (1993). "The Philosophical Bases of Modern Racism' and 'Hume's Racism'", in: *The High Road to Pyrrhonism*, Indianapolis: 79–102 and 267–76.

Poulsen, Frank Ejby (2014). "Anacharsis Cloots and the Birth of Modern Cosmopolitanism", in: Lettevall and Petrov, eds., *Cosmopolitanism*, 87–118.

Putnam, Hilary (1981). *Reason, Truth and History*, Cambridge: Cambridge University Press.

Quadrio, Philip A. (2009). "Kant and Rousseau on the Critique of Philosophical Theology: The Primacy of Practical Reason", *Sophia* 48, 179–93.

Rauscher, Frederick, and Daniel Omar Perez, eds. (2012). *Kant in Brazil. North American Kant Society Studies in Philosophy volume 10*. Rochester: University of Rochester Press.

Rawls, John (1985). "Justice as Fairness: Political not Metaphysical", *Philosophy and Public Affairs*, 14, 3, 223–51.

Raynal, Guillaume-Thomas-Francois Abbé de (1780/2006). *A History of the Two Indies. A Translated Selection of Writings from Raynal's Histoire philosophique et politique des établissements des Européens dans les Deux Indes*, ed. Peter Jimack. Aldershot: Ashgate.

Reath, Andrews (2006). *Agency and Autonomy in Kant's Moral Theory*, Oxford: Clarendon Press.

Recki, Birgit (2001). *Ästhetik der Sitten. Die Affinität von ästhetischem Gefühl und praktischer Vernunft bei Kant*, Frankfurt am Main: Klostermann.

Recki, Birigt (2006). *Die Vernunft, ihre Natur, ihr Gefühl und der Fortschritt. Aufsätze zu Immanuel Kant*, Paderborn: mentis.

Reed, Jim (2006). "Before the Storm: Internationalism before German-ness", in Mary Anne Perkins and Martin Liebscher (eds), *Nationalism versus Cosmopolitanism in German Thought and Culture, 1789–1914: Essays on the Emergence of Europe*, Lewiston, 35–48.

Rehm, Michaela (2006). *Bürgerliches Glaubensbekenntnis. Moral und Religion in Rousseaus politischer Philosophie*, München: Wilhelm Fink.

Reich, Klaus (1936). "Rousseau und Kant", in: *Gesammelte Schriften*, Hamburg: Meiners 2001, 147–65.

Reichenbach, Roland (2007). *Philosophie der Bildung und Erziehung. Eine Einführung.* Kohlhammer: Stuttgart.

Reisert, Joseph R. (2012). "Kant and Rousseau on Moral Education", in: Roth and Surprenant, *Kant and Education*, 12–25.

Richter, Melvin (2006). "The comparative study of regimes and societies", in: Mark Goldie and Robert Wokler (eds.), *The Cambridge History of Eighteenth-Century Political Thought*. Cambridge: Cambridge University Press, 147–171.

Ripstein, Arthur (2009). *Force and Freedom: Kant's Legal and Political Philosophy*. Cambridge, Mass.: Harvard University Press

Rohbeck, Johannes (1987). *Die Fortschrittstheorie der Aufklärung. Französische und englische Geschichtsphilosophie in der zweiten Hälfte des 18. Jahrhunderts*, Frankfurt am Main, New York: Campus.

Rohden, Valério et al., eds. (2008a). *Recht und Frieden in der Philosophie Kants. Akten des X. Internationalen Kant-Kongresses. Band 1: Hauptvorträge*. Berlin, New York, NY: de Gruyter.

Rohden, Valério et al., eds. (2008b). *Recht und Frieden in der Philosophie Kants. Akten des X. Internationalen Kant-Kongresses. Band 4: Sektionen V-VII*. Berlin, New York, NY: de Gruyter.

Roosevelt, Grace G. (1990). *Reading Rousseau in the Nuclear Age*, Philadelphia: Temple University Press.

Rorty, Amélie Oksenberg and James Schmidt, eds. (2009). *Kant's Idea for a Universal History with a Cosmopolitan Aim. A Critical Guide*, Cambridge: Cambridge University Press.
Rorty, Richard (1991). *Objectivity, Relativism, and Truth. Philosophical Papers vol. 1*, Cambridge, Mass.: Cambridge University Press.
Rorty, Richard (1998). "Human Rights, Rationality, and Sentimentality", in: *Truth and Progress. Philosophical Papers, Volume 3*, Cambridge: Cambridge University Press, 167–85.
Rorty, Richard (2005). "Analytic Philosophy and Narrative Philosophy", in: Gerhardt, Volker, ed., *Kant im Streit der Fakultäten*. Berlin and New York: Walter de Gruyter, 269–85.
Rosenblatt, Helena (2008). "Rousseau, the anticosmopolitan?", *Daedalus*, 137, 3, 59–69.
Rossi, Philip J. (2005). The Social Authority of Reason: Kant's Critique, Radical Evil, and the Destiny of Humankind. Albany: State University of New York Press.
Rossi, Philip J. (2008). "Cosmopolitanism and the Interests of Reason: Hope as Social Framework for Human Action in History", in: Rohden et al., eds., *Recht und Frieden in der Philosophie Kants*, vol. 4, 65–75.
Roth, Klas (2007). "Cosmopolitan Learning", in: Klas Roth and Nicholas C. Burbules, eds., *Changing Notions of Citizenship Education in Contemporary Nation-states*, Rotterdam and Taipei: Sense Publishers, 10–29.
Roth, Klas and Chris Surprenant, eds. (2012), Kant and Education. Interpretations and Commentary, New York and London: Routledge.
Roth, Klas (2012). "Freedom and Autonomy in Knowledge-Based Societies", in: Roth and Surprenant, eds., Kant and Education, 214–25.
Rousseau, Jean-Jacques (1887/1991). "First Version of the 'Social Contract", in: *Rousseau on International Relations*, ed. Stanley Hoffmann and David P. Fidler. Oxford: Clarendon Press.
Rousseau, Jean-Jacques (1995). *The Confessions*, trans. Christopher Kelly, *The Collected Writings of Rousseau*, vol. 5. Hanover and London: University Press of New England.
Rousseau, Jean-Jacques (1997a). "Discourse on the Sciences and Arts or First Discourse", in: *The Discourses and Other Early Political Writings*, ed. and translated by Victor Gourevitch, Cambridge, Cambridge University Press, 1–28.
Rousseau, Jean-Jacques (1997b). "Discourse on Political Economy", in: *The Social Contract and other later political writings*, ed. and translated by Victor Gourevitch, Cambridge, Cambridge University Press, 3–38.
Rousseau, Jean-Jacques (1997c). "From Of the Social Contract or Essay about the Form of a Republic (Known as the Geneva Manuscript)", in: *The Social Contract and other later political writings*, ed. and translated by Victor Gourevitch, Cambridge, Cambridge University Press, 153–61.
Rousseau, Jean-Jacques (1997d). "Considerations on the Government of Poland and on its projected Reformation", in: *The Social Contract and other later political writings*, ed. and translated by Victor Gourevitch, Cambridge, Cambridge University Press, 177–260.
Rousseau, Jean-Jacques (1997e). "Discourse on the Origin and Foundations of Inequality Among Men or Second Discourse", in: *The Discourses and Other Early Political Writings*, ed. and translated by Victor Gourevitch, Cambridge, Cambridge University Press, 113–222.
Rousseau, Jean-Jacques (1997f). "Of the Social Contract", in: *The Social Contract and other later political writings*, ed. and translated by Victor Gourevitch, Cambridge, Cambridge University Press, 39–152.

Rousseau, Jean-Jacques (2007). *Emile*, Teddington, Echo Library.
Rousseau, Jean-Jacques (2008). "'Abstract' and 'Judgment' of the Abbé de Saint-Pierre's Project for Perpetual Peace", in: Esref Aksu, ed., *Early Notions of Global Governance. Selected Eighteenth-Century Proposals for 'Perpetual Peace'*, Cardiff: Wales University Press, 95–131.
Ruitenberg, Claudia W. (2011). "The Empty Chair: Education in an Ethic of Hospitality", in: Robert Kunzman, ed., *Philosophy of Education 2011*, Urbana, Illinois, 28–36.
Saito, Hiro (2010). "Actor-network theory of cosmopolitan education", *Journal of Curriculum Studies*, 42, 3, 333–51.
Sala, Giovanni B. (2004). "Das Reich Gottes auf Erden. Kants Lehre von der Kirche als ‚ethischem gemeinen Wesen'", in: Fischer, *Metaphysik*, 225–64.
Sandkühler, Hans Jörg (2013). "Moral, Recht und Staat in weltbürgerlicher Perspektive. Überlegungen im Anschluss an Kant", in: Bacin et al., eds., *Kant und die Philosophie in weltbürgerlicher Absicht*, vol. 1, 387–406.
Schalowski, Stefan (2010). *Erziehung, Selbstbestimmung und Zwang bei Immanuel Kant und Jean-Jacques Rousseau. Zwei Philosophen mit identischen Ideen?* Munich: GRIN Verlag.
Scheffler, Samuel (2001). "Conceptions of Cosmopolitanism", in: *Boundaries and Allegiances*, Oxford, Oxford University Press, 111–30.
Schiller, Friedrich (1795). *Über die ästhetische Erziehung des Menschen in einer Reihe von Briefen*, kommentiert von Stefan Matuschek, Frankfurt am Main: Suhrkamp 2009.
Schiller, Friedrich (2006). *Aesthetical and philosophical Essays*, Project Gutenberg EBook.
Schlegel, Friedrich (1799). "Über die Philosophie", in: Schlegel, Friedrich, *Kritische Friedrich Schlegel Ausgabe*, ed. Ernst Behler, Jean Jacques Anstett, and Hans Eichner. Munich: Schöningh 1975, vol. VIII, 41–62.
Schneewind, Jerome B. (2009). "Good out of evil: Kant and the idea of unsocial sociability", in: Rorty and Schmidt, *Kant's Idea*, 94–111.
Schneider, Barbara (2005). *Jean-Jacques Rousseaus Konzeption der "Sophie". Ein hermeneutisches Projekt*, Bonn, Universitätsdruckerei.
Schröder, Jan (1995). "Gottfried Achenwall, Johann Stephan Pütter und die ‚Elementa Iuris Naturae.'" In: Achenwall and Pütter, *Anfangsgründe des Naturrechts*, 331–351.
Schröder, Jan (2001). *Recht als Wissenschaft. Geschichte der juristischen Methode vom Humanismus bis zur historischen Schule (1500–1850*, München: Beck.
Schröder, Jan (2008). "The Concept of (Natural) Law in the Doctrine of Law and Natural Law of the Early Modern Era", in: Lorraine Daston and Michael Stolleis (eds.), *Natural Law and Laws of Nature in Early Modern Europe*. Aldershot: Ashgate, 57–71.
Schröder, Jan (2010). *Rechtswissenschaft in der Neuzeit. Geschichte, Theorie, Methode. Ausgewählte Aufsätze 1976–2009*. Ed. Thomas Finkenauer, Claes Peterson, and Michael Stolleis. Tübingen: Mohr Siebeck.
Schönecker, Dieter, Alexander Cotter, Magdalena Eckes, and Sebastian Maly (2010). "Kant über Menschenliebe als moralische Gemütsanlage", *Archiv für Geschichte der Philosophie*, 92, 133–75.
Schüssler, Rudolf (2012). "Kant und die Kasuistik: Fragen zur Tugendlehre", *Kant-Studien*, 103, 70–95.
Scott, John T., ed. (2006). *Jean-Jacques Rousseau. Critical Assessments of Leading Political Philosophers*, volume III: Political Principles and Institutions, London and New York, Routledge.

Scuccimarra, Luca (2006). *I confini del mondo. Storia del cosmopolitismo dall' Antichità al Settecento.* Bologna: Mulino.
Scuderi, Phillip (2012). "Rousseau, Kant, and the Pedagogy of Deception", in: Roth and Surprenant, *Kant and Education*, 26–38.
Scrivener, Michael (2007). *The Cosmopolitan Ideal in the Age of Revolution and Reaction, 1776–1832*, London: Pickering and Chatto.
Sellars, John (2007). "Stoic Cosmopolitanism and Zeno's Republic", *History of Political Thought*, 28, 1, 1–29.
Sensen, Oliver (2009). "Kant's Conception of Human Dignity", *Kant-Studien*, 100, 309–31.
Silber, John R. (1959). "Kant's Conception of the Highest Good as Immanent and Transcendent", *The Philosophical Review*, 68, 469–92.
Simons, Penelope (2003). "The Emergence of the Idea of the Individualized State in the International Legal System", *Journal of the History of International Law*, 5, 293–336.
Skinner, Quentin (1998). *Liberty Before Liberalism*, Cambridge: Cambridge University Press.
Smith, Adam (1776/1976). *An Inquiry into the Nature and Causes of the Wealth of Nations.* Ed. R. H. Campbell, A. S. Skinner, and W. B. Todd. Oxford: Clarendon Press.
Smith, Adam (1762–3, 1766/1978). *Lectures on Jurisprudence.* Ed. R. L. Meek, D. D. Raphael, and P. G. Stein. Oxford: Clarendon Press, 1–558.
Sommer, Andreas Urs (2001). "Sinnstiftung durch Individualgeschichte. Johann Joachim Spaldings *Bestimmung des Menschen*", *Zeitschrift für neuere Theologiegeschichte*, 8, 163–200.
Sommer, Andreas Urs (2006). *Sinnstiftung durch Geschichte? Zur Entstehung spekulativ-universalistischer Geschichtsphilosophie zwischen Bayle und Kant*, Basel: Schwabe.
Sommer, Andreas Urs (2007). "Neuerscheinungen zu Kants Religionsphilosophie", *Philosophische Rundschau*, 54, 31–53.
Spaemann, Robert (2008). *Rousseau. Mensch oder Bürger. Das Dilemma der Moderne*, Stuttgart: Klett-Cotta.
Spankeren, Malte van (2011). "Johann Joachim Spalding und der Berliner Gesangbuchstreit (1781)", *Zeitschrift für neuere Theologiegeschichte*, 18, 191–211.
Städtler, Michael, ed. (2005). *Kants ‚ethisches Gemeinwesen'. Die Religionsschrift zwischen Vernunftkritik und praktischer Philosophie*, Berlin: Akademie Verlag.
Stapelbroek, Koen, 2008. "Universal Society, Commerce and the Rights of Neutral Trade: Martin Hübner, Emer de Vattel and Ferdinando Galiani", in: Petter Korkman and Virpi Mäkinen (eds.), *Universalism in International Law and Political Philosophy*. Helsinki: Helsinki Collegium for Advanced Studies, 63–87.
Starobinski, Jean (1988). *Jean-Jacques Rousseau. Transparency and Obstruction*, Chicago and London, University of Chicago Press.
Streck, Danilo R. (2006). *Erziehung für einen neuen Gesellschaftsvertrag*, Oberhausen, Athena.
Stroud, Scott R. (2005). "Rhetoric and Moral Progress in Kant's Ethical Community", *Philosophy and Rhetoric*, 38, 4, 328–354.
Stroud, Scott R. (2008). "Ritual and Performative Force in Kant's Ethical Community", in: Rohden et al., eds., *Recht und Frieden in der Philosophie Kants*, vol. 4, 143–55.
Sturm, Thomas (2009). *Kant und die Wissenschaft vom Menschen*, Paderborn: mentis.
Surprenant, Chris W. (2010). "Kant's contribution to moral education: the relevance of catechistics", *Journal of Moral Education*, 39, 165–74.

Sutch, Peter (2000). "Kantians and Cosmopolitanism: O'Neill and Cosmopolitan Universalism", *Kantian Review*, 4, 98–120.
Swanton, Christine (2011). "Kant's impartial virtues of love", in: Jost and Wuerth, *Perfecting Virtue*, 241–59.
Sweet, Kristi (2010). "The Moral Import of the Critique of Judgment", in: Muchnik, *Rethinking Kant volume 2*, 222–37.
Tan, Kok-Chor (2004). *Justice without Borders: Cosmopolitanism, Nationalism and Patriotism*, Cambridge: Cambridge University Press.
Terra, Ricardo (2013). "Hat die kantische Vernunft eine Hautfarbe?", in: Bacin et al., eds., *Kant und die Philosophie in weltbürgerlicher Absicht*, vol. 1, 431–47.
Thiede, Werner, ed. (2004). *Glauben aus eigener Vernunft? Kants Religionsphilosophie und die Theologie*, Göttingen: Vandenhoeck und Ruprecht.
Thielking, Sigrid (2000). *Weltbürgertum. Kosmopolitische Ideen in Literatur und politischer Publizistik seit dem 18. Jahrhundert*, München.
Thompson, Kevin (2008). "Sovereignty, Hospitality, and Commerce: Kant and Cosmopolitan Right", *Jahrbuch für Recht und Ethik* 16, 305–19.
Tintemann, Ute, ed. (2012). *Wilhelm von Humboldt: Universalität und Individualität*, München und Paderborn: Fink 2012.
Todd, Hedrick (2008). "Race, Difference, and Anthropology in Kant's Cosmopolitanism", *Journal of the History of Philosophy* 46, 245–268.
Todd, Sharon (2009). *Toward an Imperfect Education. Facing Humanity, Rethinking Cosmopolitanism*, Boulder and London: Paradigm Publishers.
Thaler, Mathias (2010). "The illusion of purity: Chantal Mouffe's realist critique of cosmopolitanism", *Philosophy and Social Criticism*, 36, 7, 785–800.
Thorndike, Oliver (2008). "Understanding Kant's claim that 'Morality cannot be without Anthropology'", in: Muchnik, ed., *Rethinking Kant vol. 1*, 109–35.
Thorndike, Oliver (2011). *Rethinking Kant: Volume 3*, Newcastle upon Tyne: Cambridge Scholars Publishing.
Timmermann, Jens (2003). *Sittengesetz und Freiheit. Untersuchungen zu Immanuel Kants Theorie des freien Willens*, Berlin, New York: de Gruyter.
Timmermann, Jens (2007). *Kant's Groundwork of the Metaphysics of Morals. A Commentary*, Cambridge: Cambridge University Press.
Timmermann, Jens, ed. (2010). *Kant's Groundwork of the Metaphysics of Morals. A Critical Guide*, Cambridge: Cambridge University Press.
Timmons, Mark and Sorin Baiasu, eds. (2013). *Kant on Practical Justification: Interpretive Essays*, Oxford: Oxford University Press.
Todd, Sharon (2009). *Toward an Imperfect Education. Facing Humanity, Rethinking Cosmopolitanism*, Boulder and London: Paradigm Publishers.
Todorov, Tzvetan (2001). *Frail Happiness. An Essay on Rousseau*, University Park, Pennsylvania State University Press.
Uleman, Jennifer K. (2010). *An Introduction to Kant's Moral Philosophy*, Cambridge: Cambridge University Press.
Usher, Robin and Richard Edwards (1994). *Postmodernism and Education. Different voices, different worlds*, London and New York: Routledge, 1994.
Vattel, Emer de (1758/2008). *The Law of Nations, Or, Principles of the Law of Nature, Applied to the Conduct and Affairs of Nations and Sovereigns*, ed. B. Kapossy and R. Whatmore. Indianapolis: Liberty Fund.

Vertovec, Steven and Robin Cohen, eds. (2002). *Conceiving Cosmopolitanism: Theory, Context, and Practice.* Oxford: Oxford University Press.

Viroli, Maurizio (2003). *For Love of Country. An Essay on Patriotism and Nationalism*, Oxford: Clarendon Press.

Vitoria, Francisco de (1528/1991). "On civil Power", in: *Political Writings.* Ed. Anthony Padgen and Jeremy Lawrance, Cambridge: Cambridge University Press, 1–44.

Wain, Kenneth (2011). *On Rousseau: An Introduction to his Radical Thinking on Education and Politics*, Rotterdam: Sense Publishers.

Waks, Leonard J. (2008). "Cosmopolitanism and Citizen Education", in: *Global Citizenship Education: Philosophy, Theory and Pedagogy*, eds. Michael A. Peters, Alan Britton, and Harry Blee, Rotterdam: Sense Publishers, 203–20.

Waks, Leonard J. (2009), "Reason and Culture in Cosmopolitan Education", *Educational Theory*, 59, 589–604.

Waks, Leonard J. (2010). "Cosmopolitan Education and Its Discontents", *Philosophy of Education 2009*, Urbana, Illinois: University of Illinois, 253–62.

Waldron, Jeremy (2003). "Teaching Cosmopolitan Right", in McDonough and Feinberg (eds.), *Education and Citizenship*, pp. 23–55.

Ward, Robert (1795). *An Enquiry into the Foundation and History of the Law of Nations in Europe from the Time of the Greeks and the Romans to the Age of Grotius*, 2 volumes. London: Allen and Unwin.

Warda, Arthur (1922). *Immanuel Kants Bücher.* Berlin: Breslauer.

Weisskopf, Traugott (1970). *Immanuel Kant und die Pädagogik. Beiträge zu einer Monographie*, Zürich: Editio Academica.

White, Richard (2008). "Rousseau and the Education of Compassion", *Journal of Philosophy of Education*, 42, 1, 35–48.

Willaschek, Marcus (2005). "Recht ohne Ethik? Kant über die Gründe, das Recht nicht zu brechen", in: Gerhardt, Volker, ed. (2005). *Kant im Streit der Fakultäten.* Berlin and New York: Walter de Gruyter, 198–204.

Williams, Alfred Tuttle (2009). *The Concept of Equality in the Writings of Rousseau, Bentham, and Kant.* 1907. Reprint. Whitefish: Kessinger Publishing.

Williams, Melissa S. (2003). "Citizenship as Identity, Citizenship as Shared Fate, and the Functions of Multicultural Education", in: McDonough and Feinberg (eds.), *Education and Citizenship*, 208–47.

Wilson, Holly L. (2006). *Kant's Pragmatic Anthropology. Its Origin, Meaning, and Critical Significance.* Albany: State University of New York Press.

Wilson, Holly L. (2013). "Is Kant's Worldly Concept of Philosophy really 'Regional Philosophy'?", in: Bacin et al., eds., *Kant und die Philosophie in weltbürgerlicher Absicht*, vol. 1, 763–72.

Wimmer, Reiner (1990). *Kants kritische Religionsphilosophie.* Berlin, New York: de Gruyter.

Winch, Christopher (2006). *Education, Autonomy, and Critical Thinking*, London: Routledge.

Winter, Aloysius (2000). *Der andere Kant. Zur philosophischen Theologie Immanuel Kants*, Hildesheim, Zürich, New York.

Wohlgemut, Esther (2009). *Romantic Cosmopolitanism.* Houndmills, Basingstoke: Plagrave Macmillan.

Wood, Allen (1970). *Kant's Moral Religion.* Ithaca and London: Cornell University Press [reprint 2009].

Wood, Allen (1998). "Kant's Historical Materialism", in Jane Kneller and Sidney Axinn, eds., *Autonomy and Community: Readings in Contemporary Kantian Social Philosophy*, Albany, NY: SUNY Press, 15–38.
Wood, Allen (2008). *Kantian Ethics*. Cambridge: Cambridge University Press.
Wood, Allen (2009). "Kant's Fourth Proposition: the unsociable sociability of human nature", in: Rorty and Schmidt, *Kant's Idea*, 112–28.
Wood, Allen (2011a). "Kant and agent-oriented ethics", in: Jost and Wuerth, *Perfecting Virtue*, 58–91.
Wood, Allen (2011b). "Ethical Community, Church and Scripture", in Höffe, *Religion*, 131–50.
Wuerth, Julian (2011). "Moving beyond Kant's account of agency in the Grounding", in: Jost and Wuerth, *Perfecting Virtue*, 147–63.
Yonah, Yossi (1999). "'*Ubi Patria – Ibi Bene*': The Scope and Limits of Rousseau's Patriotic Education", *Studies in Philosophy and Education*, 18, 365–88.
Yovel, Yirmiyahu (1980). *Kant and the Philosophy of History*. Princeton: Princeton University Press.
Ypi, Lea L. (2008a). "Statist Cosmopolitanism", *Journal of Political Philosophy*, 16, 1, 48–71.
Ypi, Lea L. (2008b). "Political Membership in the Contractarian Defence of Cosmopolitanism", *The Review of Politics*, 70, 3, pp. 442–472.
Ypi, Lea L. (2010a). "Justice and Morality beyond Naive Cosmopolitanism", *Ethics and Global Politics*, 3, 3, pp. 171–192.
Ypi, Lea (2010b). "*Natura Daedala Rerum?* On the Justification of Historical Progress in Kant's Guranantee of Perpetual Peace", *Kantian Review*, 14 (2010), 118–48.
Zelle, Carsten (2005). "Über die ästhetische Erziehung des Menschen in einer Reihe von Briefen (1795) ", in: Matthias Luserke-Jaqui, ed., *Schiller-Handbuch. Leben – Werk – Wirkung*, Stuttgart, Weimar: Metzler 409–445.
Zembylas, Michalinos (2010). "The ethic of care in globalized societies: implications for citizenship education", *Ethics and Education*, 5, 3, 233–45.
Zöller, Günter (2011). "Between Rousseau and Freud: Kant on Cultural Uneasiness", in: Thorndike, Oliver (2011). *Rethinking Kant: Volume 3*, Newcastle upon Tyne: Cambridge Scholars Publishing, 52–77.

Subject index

Absolutism 143
Amour de soi-meme 79, 85
Amour-propre 77, 79, 81, 85, 112
Anarchy 66, 105
- International anarchy 50, 101, 155
Anthropology 5–9, 11, 14, 16, 23, 29, 59, 67, 74, 97, 101, 106–108, 110, 113, 115f., 118, 124f., 128f., 136–138, 142–145, 153, 158, 162
- practical anthropology 100, 115
A priori 7, 20, 39, 63, 93, 125, 142, 145, 161f., 164f., 170, 174
Archetype 38f.
Atheism, atheist 24
Autonomy/autonomous 3, 6, 7, 8, 9, 29, 43, 92, 93, 108, 113, 118–122, 125, 137, 139, 140, 158, 159, 160, 169, 173, 175–178

catechism 123, 127
Categorical imperative 6, 9, 26, 39, 41, 62, 84, 93, 99, 101, 108, 117, 119–121, 170, 177
Christianity, Christian 3, 17, 35f., 39, 56, 64, 103–105, 111, 149f., 153
Church, churches 3, 36, 39, 45, 96, 113, 138, 150
- Invisible church 28, 36, 39, 45, 150
Citizen 13, 16, 23, 27, 30, 35, 49, 51–55, 73, 77, 79, 81f., 85, 88, 90f., 96, 99, 101–104, 106, 110f., 113, 115, 117, 125–128, 134f., 138f., 142–144, 146, 150, 158, 160, 171f., 177f.
citoyen 17, 88, 94, 102, 106, 112
civilization 44, 59, 64, 89f., 102, 106–108, 113f., 138, 146, 150f., 179
Colonialism 11, 25, 52f., 56, 59–61, 69f., 130
Commerce 16, 50, 52–54, 60, 62–64, 66f., 69f., 78, 90
- spirit of commerce (Handelsgeist) 16, 50, 64–66, 73
Common human reason 121, 123, 132, 142

Commonwealth 13–15, 21f., 26–28, 35, 39, 44, 58, 69f., 73, 120, 125, 134f., 139, 143f., 173
- Ethical commonwealth 3, 6, 23, 28, 35, 38, 44–46, 69, 109, 112, 127, 133, 136, 142f., 158, 174
- Political commonwealth see republic, republicanism
- Religious commonwealth 28
communitarian 45, 88, 90, 102, 112, 167
Community, see commonwealth 2, 4, 12, 21, 22, 26
- Political community 28, 45, 52, 59, 79, 90, 103, 136, 159, 167
conscience 27, 58, 83, 88, 90, 103, 151
Constitution 18, 28, 42–45, 51f., 62, 101, 110, 133f., 136, 138, 155
- Constitutional patriotism 13, 139
- Republican constitution 16, 42, 74, 134, 136, 138, 141, 143–146, 172
Contingency 161, 166
contract 25, 53, 104, 106, 142
Cosmopolitanism 1–5, 10f., 13–19, 21–30, 36f., 47f., 52, 55, 64, 74–78, 80–82, 84, 86–94, 96, 99f., 102–105, 107, 109, 111–119, 124, 128, 130f., 134, 138–140, 143, 147–156, 159–161, 165–168, 170–173, 175, 177–179
- cognitive 23, 25, 26, 86, 128, 168
- commercial 5, 29, 51–5, 78
  - Kant's commercial cosmopolitanism 51–5, 51
- cultural 4, 26, 29, 78, 165
- dynamic 13–15, 109
- embedded 13–15, 17, 75, 76, 82, 131, 139, 156, 167
- legal/political 28, 29, 37, 64, 77, 80, 81, 82, 88, 96, 111, 151
- moral 4, 5, 11, 13, 17, 21, 25, 27, 30, 76, 77, 80, 81–82, 84, 86, 87, 88, 89, 99, 103, 104, 105–114, 118, 119, 134, 139, 143, 171, 172, 173, 178, 179,
  - Dynamic moral cosmopolitanism 105
- republican 17, 78–81, 84, 103, 104

– statist   52, 154, 166, 171 f.
– thick   5, 56, 61, 78, 167, 169
– types of cosmopolitanism   4, 15 f., 21, 23, 76
critical metaphysics   161
– Practical metaphysics   10, 28 f., 116, 161 f., 166, 170, 173
Critique   3, 5 f., 9 f., 25, 29, 37 f., 41, 54, 75, 94, 108 f., 155, 166, 168 f., 174
cultivation   14, 42, 69, 74, 85, 88, 107, 113, 117, 121, 124, 127, 131, 135, 138–141, 146, 148, 150, 152, 156, 164, 170 f., 176, 178 f.
Culture, cultural   4, 9, 12, 14, 16, 29 f., 42, 44, 64, 66, 72, 76, 78, 82, 88, 101, 105–108, 130, 145, 148–152, 163–165, 169, 175, 179

Decadence, decadent   78, 107, 110
Decline   61, 89 f., 106 f., 114, 179
Democracy   16, 49, 74, 169, 178 f.
Denkungsart, see way of thinking
Denomination, denominational   95, 100
Despair   7, 39 f., 110 f., 114
Despotism, despotic   13, 66, 72, 134, 136, 139, 143, 145, 153
Development, see also cultivation, formation
Didactics, didactical   95, 174 f.
– Ethical didactics   7–9, 14, 117, 121, 146, 158, 171, 179
discipline   42, 59, 110, 138 f.
Disposition (Gesinnung)   1 f., 4 f., 7, 15, 18 f., 24, 29–33, 35, 37, 40–47, 67, 70, 81, 83, 87, 92 f., 99, 101, 105, 107, 109 f., 112–116, 118–120, 125–128, 131–138, 145, 148, 150, 165, 169, 174–179
Dogmatism, dogmatic   19, 24, 26, 140, 177
Duty   21, 34, 38, 40, 42, 45, 53, 55, 57–60, 72, 74, 86 f., 89, 106, 109, 112, 114, 119 f., 125, 127, 134, 140, 142, 149, 157, 172
– Duty of the human race towards itself   44

economics, economical   64, 164
Education 4, 8–9, 12, 14–17, 19, 23, 31, 36, 40–43, 174–179, see also formation
– cosmopolitan education   3 f., 17 f., 41, 74–78, 81–87, 89, 92–95, 100–102, 108, 115–118, 124–32, 131, 134, 157 f., 160, 165, 168, 175, 177 f.
– cosmopolitical education   136–140
– moral education   3, 7 f., 15, 41 f., 77, 81, 83 f., 86, 94, 97, 99 f., 107, 109–112, 115–117, 119–132, 144, 175
– political education   84, 103, 113, 115, 168
– self-education   40 f., 43, 47, 138
Egoism   23, 79, 103, 128, 143, 145
– Logical egoism   23, 128, 143 f.
empirical   7, 8, 11, 14, 33, 37, 70, 97, 121, 122, 124, 139, 161, 162, 175, 178
End   6 f., 10, 13, 18, 21–23, 25, 27, 35–38, 40–42, 44, 53, 56 f., 61 f., 67, 72, 74, 87, 90 f., 102, 104, 107–111, 113 f., 117, 119 f., 131, 136, 139, 141, 147, 149 f., 152, 156, 159, 164, 173–176, 178 f.
– Final end (Endzweck)   9, 29, 32, 41 f., 105, 117, 152
– Ultimate end (letzter Zweck)   9, 14, 31, 41 f., 108, 124
Enlightenment 1, 8, 11, 12, 13, 15, 16, 17, 35, 39, 44, 48, 63, 66, 69, 74, 76, 93, 96 f., 98, 101, 108, 111, 116, 124, 134, 141, 142, 147, 149, 150, 156, 160, 163, 168
– Scottish Enlightenment   5, 164
Epistemology   6, 10, 95, 150
– Critical epistemology   1, 166
Eschatology, eschatological   35 f., 45
Eurocentrism, Eurocentric   10, 82
Europeanism   78, 114, 147
Europe, European   12, 62–64, 72 f., 83 f., 87, 89 f., 99, 114, 130, 147, 149–151
Evil   7, 14, 34, 39 f., 45 f., 50, 81, 83, 85, 107, 109, 112, 122, 124, 139, 142, 169, 172, 179
– Radical evil   7, 33, 45, 107, 109, 112 f.
Existence, existential   14 f., 22, 24, 31, 34, 37 f., 47, 73, 77, 105, 108, 119, 124, 152, 154 f., 162

Subject index

experience   10, 20, 24 f., 33, 90, 130 f., 134, 144, 161, 163 f., 178
exploitation   68, 83

Faith   22, 28, 35–37, 39 f., 44, 47, 70, 75, 86, 95, 99, 108, 111, 114, 150 f., 157, 179
Feeling   1, 6, 8, 66, 69, 72, 81, 85, 125, 135, 171, 175 f.
– Moral feeling   27, 72, 126, 129, 135, 149, 161, 176
Finiteness, finite   31, 33, 46
Foreigner, foreigners   17, 53, 59, 63, 67, 81, 94, 152 f.
Form   2 f., 5, 8, 12 f., 15, 17 f., 21–23, 26–30, 32, 35–37, 40–42, 44, 46 f., 51, 54, 60 f., 64, 67, 71, 76–81, 85–87, 89, 91, 93, 96, 104, 107 f., 111, 113, 116, 118–121, 123, 125–127, 131–134, 136–140, 143–145, 147, 149–151, 153–166, 168, 170–173, 175–179
– Form of government   19, 101, 133 f., 136, 139, 142–144, 146, 173
Formation (Bildung)   15–17, 41, 44, 74, 82, 84, 93, 97, 99, 101, 104, 107 f., 115 f., 118, 121 f., 125 f., 134, 136, 138, 144–146, 149, 151, 154, 157 f., 164, 175, 179
– Cosmopolitan formation   18, 74, 88, 93, 113, 115, 117 f., 124 f., 138, 143, 175
– Cosmopolitical formation   133, 141
– Moral formation   3, 9, 17–19, 41, 74, 93, 98 f., 108 f., 118, 120–122, 125 f., 133, 136, 138–141, 144–146, 157, 178
Freedom   1, 3 f., 7–9, 13–15, 18, 24 f., 27, 29, 31, 34, 36–38, 42, 44–46, 51, 54 f., 57, 60, 62, 65, 67, 70, 74, 78, 93, 96, 98, 101, 106, 108–110, 112, 114, 116, 118–120, 124, 126, 131, 136 f., 139–142, 144–146, 150–152, 154, 156–159, 163, 168, 170, 172, 174, 176 f.
– Moral freedom   4, 14, 29 f., 74, 108, 123–125, 132, 145 f., 175, 178
– Of choice   14, 27, 29, 46, 55, 74, 120, 124, 131, 144
– of the pen   142
– political freedom   4, 67, 69, 98, 113, 143, 145, 177

function   8, 16, 19, 30, 38, 58, 65, 70, 74, 123, 127, 133, 136, 138, 143 f.
– pedagogical function of the republican constitution   141

General   13, 20, 26, 50, 58, 64, 66 f., 69, 81, 86, 112, 119, 127, 143, 147, 156–158, 162, 164, 170, 175
– General will   77, 79–81, 143
Germany, German   2, 17, 62, 65, 72, 93, 149, 151, 153, 157
Germs (Keime)   13 f., 74, 101, 124, 137, 141
Global   3–5, 16, 21, 23, 27, 30 f., 35, 45, 49–54, 57, 67 f., 70, 74, 80, 82, 87, 98 f., 101, 118, 127, 133, 137, 141 f., 147, 151, 154, 163–165, 171, 174
globalization   13, 18, 67, 70, 90, 118, 165 f., 170
God   23 f., 28, 31, 33–38, 40, 43–47, 58, 83, 92, 95, 109, 112, 129 f., 133, 169, 173
– Kingdom of God   15, 21–23, 30, 35–37, 39, 46, 48 f., 99, 133
Good   9, 12, 15, 18, 21, 23, 32 f., 35 f., 38–42, 44 f., 47, 49, 53, 56, 61 f., 66–68, 70, 73, 77 f., 81–83, 85 f., 92, 98 f., 107, 109 f., 112, 114, 120, 122, 127 f., 133–136, 139, 146, 168 f., 173, 176, 178
grace   46
gradualism   12

Haiti   70
Happiness   6, 22 f., 28, 30–34, 36, 38–40, 43 f., 46 f., 55, 93, 98, 109, 120, 124, 138, 148, 173 f., 177
„hermeneutics of suspicion"   163
highest good   3, 6 f., 9, 11, 15, 21–23, 28–40, 42, 44–47, 49, 98 f., 105, 108 f., 114, 117, 124, 133, 144 f., 148, 159, 173 f.
– highest political good   21, 23, 32 f., 36–38, 40, 49 f., 99, 105, 133, 135, 141, 159
historicism   19 f., 62 f., 164
historiography   8, 20, 28, 134
– cosmopolitan historiography   28
History, historical   9, 18 f., 21, 23, 28, 30–33, 35 f., 39–43, 48 f., 61, 63, 65, 67–70, 74, 80, 87, 94, 98, 104, 106, 108–

110, 113, 116, 124, 129, 131, 140 f., 149 –
154, 161, 164, 168 f.
Homme   17, 78, 94, 102, 106, 112
hope   32, 35, 37 – 39, 70, 73, 86, 106, 110,
112 – 114, 146, 169, 174, 179 f.
Humanity (Menschheit)   3, 9, 12, 15, 26, 31,
40, 43, 68, 72, 74, 79 f., 84 – 86, 88,
90 – 92, 94, 96, 98 f., 101, 103, 105 – 107,
116 – 118, 126 f., 130 f., 136 – 138, 140 f.,
152 – 155, 158, 160 f., 168 f., 172, 179
Hypothetical imperative   41, 107, 120

Idea   4, 14 – 17, 19, 21 f., 25, 27 f., 30 – 34,
36 – 43, 47 – 51, 54, 56 – 61, 64 f., 67, 69,
74, 76, 78, 80 f., 83 f., 87, 93, 96, 98 –
101, 104 – 110, 113, 116, 121, 125 – 127,
129, 132, 138 – 143, 146 f., 150, 153 – 156,
158 f., 163, 165, 171, 173 – 177, 179
Ideal   3, 5, 12, 18, 23, 31, 35, 50, 55, 61, 65,
68, 73, 79, 99, 101, 109, 111, 118, 120 f.,
128, 130, 134, 140, 152 f., 179
Immanent   22, 30 – 32, 36 – 38, 45, 47, 148,
151, 159
impartiality   5, 72, 87, 89, 96, 131, 167, 169
Imperative   41, 62, 107, 119 f., 139
Imperialist school   56, 58 f.
– Society of states school   56, 58 f.
Individual   2, 4, 7 f., 10, 14, 16, 19, 27, 29 –
32, 34 – 36, 38, 40, 43, 45 – 47, 49, 51,
53 – 55, 57 f., 63, 67 – 69, 74, 77, 79 f.,
82, 85 f., 88, 93, 99, 101 – 104, 108 f.,
112, 116 f., 119 f., 124 – 126, 136 – 138,
140, 142, 146, 148, 150, 154, 156 f., 164,
168, 172, 176 f.
Individualism   19, 105, 126
– Normative individualism   72, 172 f.
indoctrination   121, 137, 140, 158
Integration, global   16, 50, 64 f., 67 f.
Interaction   6, 13, 53 f., 57, 61, 66 f., 69 f.,
73, 87, 121, 126, 141, 144, 154
interest   2 f., 5, 12, 19, 38, 40, 43, 56 f., 66,
68, 73, 77, 79, 81, 83, 94, 96, 98 f., 117,
123, 125, 127, 134, 136, 162, 166 f., 169
Isolationism, isolationist   60, 64

judge   52, 83, 89, 96, 123, 128 f., 154 f., 167
Judgement   1, 6 f., 9, 23 – 27, 41 f., 71, 74 f.,
111, 113, 120, 123, 125 – 128, 131, 141,
143 – 145, 156 f., 159, 161, 168 – 171, 176,
178
– Power of judgement   41, 108, 125, 127 f.,
144
justice   24, 29, 51 f., 55, 57, 66, 69, 75, 80,
82 f., 85 f., 88, 118 f., 142, 154 f., 162 –
164, 167 f., 171

Kingdom of ends   25, 27, 31, 39, 44, 120, 173
knowledge   3, 10, 17, 19, 24 f., 28 f., 32, 36,
46, 83 f., 86, 92 f., 105, 109, 113, 121 –
123, 126, 159, 161, 164, 166, 175

Law   2, 4, 6 – 8, 12 – 15, 19, 21, 27 f., 30 – 34,
39, 44 f., 53, 56, 58, 74, 76, 78 – 81, 93,
99, 108 – 110, 112, 115, 119 – 128, 130,
133 – 141, 144, 148 f., 155, 164 f., 172 –
174, 176
– Cosmopolitan law   15, 172
Legacy   13, 165 f., 171, 180
– Kant's legacy   165 f., 171
Legality   32, 37 f., 41 f., 107, 110, 120, 134 f.,
144
Legislation   29, 51 f., 54, 58, 79, 173
– Self-legislation   18 f., 25, 27, 30, 92, 111,
113, 115, 118 – 120, 124 f., 132 f., 137, 143,
157, 169, 173 f., 176, 178
Liberalism, liberal   169

maxim   10, 18, 23, 28, 45, 72, 81, 85, 89,
109, 115 – 121, 123, 126 – 131, 137, 142 f.,
158, 168, 170
metaphysics, metaphysical   9, 19, 24, 26,
29, 36, 54, 59, 74 f., 108, 123, 140, 150,
161 f., 166, 175 – 177
Method   3, 9, 15, 18, 42, 44, 94 f., 97, 101,
108, 110, 115, 121 – 123, 125, 129, 132,
140 f.
– Method of moral formation   122
Mode of thinking (Denkungsart)   111, 113,
136, 159
Morality   6 – 8, 14, 18 f., 22 – 24, 28, 30 – 32,
34, 36, 38, 40 – 47, 60 – 63, 72, 83, 88,
93, 98, 100 – 102, 106 – 114, 116 – 121,

123 f., 127 – 129, 131, 133, 135 – 138, 140 f., 144, 146, 150 – 152, 156 f., 164, 166, 168 f., 172 – 174
- Morality and religion, 99 – 100   47, 99, 150
Motivation   6, 18 f., 115, 118, 121, 123, 133, 137, 174
- Moral motivation   7 f., 73, 122, 177

Nationalism, nationalistic   16 f., 76 – 78, 88 f., 94, 97, 104, 147, 151, 153, 157, 159, 165, 171, 173
Nation states   52, 147
Nature   8 f., 11, 13 f., 16, 23, 28 – 36, 40 – 47, 58 f., 65, 81, 85, 90, 93, 97, 102, 106 f., 109 f., 112, 116, 119, 124, 138, 148 – 150, 162, 176, 178
- State of nature   45, 51, 55, 101, 106, 172
Neo-Kantianism   5 f., 161
Noumenon, noumenal   134

pacifism   82, 84
Paternalism, paternalistic   12, 26
Patriotism, patriotic   1, 13, 16, 66, 76 f., 79, 88 f., 96 f., 105, 111, 114, 137, 139 f., 147, 149 f., 157, 160, 166, 171, 173
- Civic patriotism   17, 77, 79 f., 91, 102, 143, 171
- Republican patriotism   2, 17, 78, 80, 82, 88 f., 103 f., 111, 136, 153
Peace   8, 15, 18, 21, 23, 27, 42 f., 49 – 51, 53 – 55, 59 f., 62 f., 65 f., 68 – 70, 73 f., 98, 110, 130, 133 – 136, 141 – 143, 146, 149, 151, 155 f., 162, 170, 172, 174
pedagogy   3 f., 7 – 9, 14 f., 18 f., 41, 74 f., 95, 97, 99, 107, 117, 119, 125 f., 133 f., 137, 145
Perfection   1, 6, 27, 31, 35, 93, 98, 101, 115, 117, 138 f., 148, 151, 174, 178 f.
Perfectionism
- Species perfectionism   101, 117
Phenomenon, phenomena   9, 63 f., 98, 100, 161
Philanthropismus   94, 97 f., 100
Philosophy   1 f., 5 – 11, 13, 15 – 18, 21 – 29, 31 – 33, 36 – 47, 49 f., 53 f., 56 – 59, 61 f., 65, 69, 73, 75 – 77, 79, 82, 88 – 90, 93 f., 96, 99 f., 102 f., 107 f., 110, 113 – 119, 124, 128, 131, 133, 140, 142, 147 f., 150 – 152, 154 – 157, 161 f., 164, 167, 170, 173, 175 f.
- Critical philosophy   3, 5, 22, 33, 42 f., 110, 159
- German philosophy   147
pity   79 – 83, 85 f.
Politics, political   18, 21, 44, 51, 57, 59, 73, 108, 111, 123, 126, 133, 137, 142 f., 147, 156, 163, 166, 168 f., 172, 174
Postulate   33 – 35, 37, 43 f., 101, 117, 172, 174
practical   1, 7 f., 10, 15, 20, 25, 27, 29 f., 37, 41, 47, 59, 95, 107 f., 116 f., 119 – 122, 124, 126 f., 140, 143, 155, 162, 164, 173, 176
pragmatism   146
Predisposition (Anlage)   14, 27, 30, 34, 46, 72, 74, 88, 93, 100 f., 107, 109 f., 115, 117 – 119, 121, 123 – 125, 127 f., 137, 139 – 141, 143, 150, 164, 170, 174 f., 178 f.
prejudice   8, 11, 66, 82 f., 86, 88, 144, 162, 164
Private   10, 26, 66, 96, 98, 104, 112, 134 f., 138, 143
Progress   14 f., 18 f., 25, 31 f., 36 f., 61, 94, 101, 106, 109, 113 f., 116, 125, 133, 139 – 141, 146, 148, 150 – 152, 154, 179
- Legal progress   31, 33, 39, 42
- Moral progress   32 f., 36 f., 70, 106, 109, 113, 140, 152
project   2 f., 7, 15, 73 f., 77, 100, 113, 115, 141, 155, 173
Propensity (Hang)   7, 45, 107, 112, 116, 127, 139
Providence   36, 40, 43 f., 46 f., 93, 110, 114, 138
prudence   12 – 14, 18, 41, 44, 101, 107 f., 117, 120 – 124, 129, 138 f., 146, 148, 150, 156, 161, 175, 177 f.
Public   6, 8, 29, 46, 50, 52, 54 f., 65, 69, 90, 98, 104, 112, 121, 134, 136, 138, 141 – 143, 145, 155
- Public opinion   143
- Public space   51
- Public sphere   52, 54, 70, 142 f., 174
- Public use of reason   134, 143
publicity   8, 141 f.

Pure   5–9, 13, 24 f., 30, 33, 35, 39, 54, 59, 63, 98 f., 108 f., 111, 114, 119, 121–123, 158, 161 f., 176
Purposiveness (Zweckmäßigkeit)   41, 109

Race   1, 4, 11 f., 21 f., 26–30, 32, 40–45, 47, 74, 82, 86, 88, 96, 99, 101, 108–110, 112, 115, 118 f., 125, 127, 130, 135, 140 f., 150–152, 160, 163, 174
Racism, racist   11, 130
Reason (Vernunft)   5 f., 8–10, 13–15, 21, 23–26, 29, 31, 33, 35–40, 46 f., 50, 52, 54, 60, 63, 69, 73, 81–83, 89, 93, 96, 98, 101, 103, 107, 112 f., 116, 120–128, 131, 139–143, 148 f., 154 f., 157 f., 164, 173, 175, 177
– Autocracy of reason   122, 140
– egoism of reason   23, 128, 130
– fact of reason   121
– practical reason   6, 9, 13, 25, 30, 32–34, 38, 40, 47, 59, 98, 119–121, 126, 148, 157
– primacy of practical reason   92
Reform   15, 17 f., 21, 27, 44, 74, 93–101, 106, 114–116, 133 f., 140, 142, 156, 172 f.
reformer   2, 94, 96, 98, 110, 154, 158, 179
Religion   4, 7, 9, 14 f., 17, 21 f., 28, 31–35, 37–40, 42, 44–48, 69, 95, 99 f., 102–104, 108–116, 118, 125, 127 f., 131, 135–137, 139, 146, 149, 153
Republican, republicanism 2, 13, 17, 19, 26, 52, 59, 67, 77–82, 84, 89, 101, 103 f., 110 f., 113, 116, 133–139, 142–146, 151–153, 173 f.
– Kantian republic   134, 144
– republican tradition 18, 133 f.
respect   8, 10, 25–27, 30, 44, 54, 56, 62, 66 f., 70, 72 f., 79, 81, 86, 89, 92 f., 100, 106, 109, 113, 115, 120, 123, 125 f., 135, 138, 144 f., 148, 151 f., 168, 170, 172, 176, 178
Revolution   27, 43, 73, 95, 97, 147 f., 156
– French Revolution   42, 44, 71, 110, 114, 147 f., 155–157
Right, rights   3–5, 8, 12 f., 16, 21, 25, 27, 29, 36 f., 43, 49–67, 69–74, 78, 83, 86, 90, 92, 104 f., 108 f., 113, 117, 135, 139, 142–145, 151, 154–156, 162, 165, 168–170, 172–175
– „Doctrine of Rights"   59
– Hospitality rights   12, 16, 49, 56 f., 59–62, 73
– Human rights   4, 27, 51, 149, 165, 172
– of nations (Völkerrecht) 16, 50–59, 63–65, 74, 76, 81, 105, 155, 168, 173
– of world citizens   15, 21, 49, 66
– public coercive rights   50
Romanticism, romantics   140

School   56–59, 94–98, 110, 130, 138, 167 f., 174
– Cosmopolitan school   56–60
Self-interest   4, 16, 50, 64 f., 67, 69 f., 73, 86, 96, 119, 124, 135, 145, 149, 161
Sin
– Original sin   7, 34, 45
Skill, skilfulness   30, 42, 118, 132, 137, 146, 167, 175, 178 f.
slavery   11, 67, 70–72
sociability, social   32, 42, 65, 67, 69, 78, 89
societas humani generis   30, 105
society   17, 23, 30, 36, 40, 45, 49, 53, 56–58, 62, 66 f., 73, 79, 81 f., 88, 90, 98, 102–105, 112, 115, 122, 133, 137–140, 142 f., 151 f., 157, 164, 174
– civil society   16, 28, 30, 41, 49, 51 f., 54, 70, 74, 105, 107, 113
– cosmopolitan society   14, 69, 107, 124 f., 157
Socratic   24, 123, 127, 145
– Semi-Socratic method   121, 126
Species   2, 7–10, 13–16, 23, 26, 30–32, 34 f., 38, 40–42, 47, 49, 69, 80 f., 85, 96, 100–102, 106 f., 109, 113, 115–117, 124 f., 127, 147 f., 150 f., 153 f., 179
Sphere   5, 25–27, 31–33, 36, 38, 43, 51, 54, 57, 60–62, 84, 110, 135, 141, 143 f., 154, 156, 170
Standpoint   23 f., 128
– Universal standpoint   24, 128
State   4 f., 18 f., 23, 27–29, 33, 37 f., 40, 42, 49–59, 62 f., 66, 73, 80 f., 87, 89, 96, 99, 101, 103–105, 109–112, 115, 117,

133 f., 136, 138, 141 f., 145–149, 151, 154–159, 165–167, 172–174, 178
– juridical state   27, 29, 50 f.
– of nations (Völkerstaat, civitas gentium) 50, 55
Stoic, stoicism   29, 33 f., 56, 69, 84, 90, 99, 102–104, 108, 127, 160
subject, subjective   13, 18, 26, 31, 51, 57, 60, 63, 108, 117, 120, 124, 126, 143, 172 f., 178
Sublime, sublimity   9, 104, 111
Symbol, symbolic   38 f.
synthetic   34, 43, 173

teleology, teleological   42 f., 47, 70, 99 f., 109, 111, 115 f.
theism   24, 36, 159
theology   9, 11, 22, 36 f., 43, 57, 59, 94, 99 f., 122 f.
theory   1–4, 6–8, 11 f., 16, 18 f., 22, 25–27, 36, 54, 58 f., 61, 65, 74–78, 80, 82, 99 f., 106, 109–111, 115–118, 132 f., 135, 137 f., 140, 147, 152, 154, 156, 158 f., 163, 167, 171, 174, 177, 179 f.
– educational theory   2, 4, 17 f., 93, 97, 100, 102, 115, 117 f., 120, 124, 132, 137, 139, 174
– four-stage theory   16, 50, 64–66
– international legal theory   16, 49, 53, 55, 57
thesis   9, 11, 34, 37, 47, 51 f., 59, 66, 80, 82, 88, 91, 103, 121, 145 f., 152
– doux-commerce thesis   65 f.
– identity thesis   88, 118
Thinking   5, 11, 19, 23 f., 26, 73 f., 87, 106, 111 f., 125–130, 132, 142 f., 153–156, 163, 167 f., 170, 175 f., 179
– Thinking for oneself   130, 143
– Way of thinking, see also mode of thinking
  – Enlarged way of thinking   24–26, 72, 100, 127, 129–131, 142–144, 176
Thought   1, 6, 11, 35, 54, 73, 77, 84, 90, 105, 112, 116, 122 f., 129 f., 141 f., 145, 151, 155, 157 f., 163, 173
tolerance   95 f., 98, 115 f.
totality   25, 31, 33, 48, 98, 158 f.

Trade   27, 52–57, 61, 68–70
– Free trade   5, 55 f., 73
  – Free-trade doctrine   55, 73
– World trade   51, 54, 73
transcendent   21–23, 30–33, 35, 37 f., 46, 48 f., 99, 133
Transcendental   4, 6, 11, 121, 144 f., 163, 166, 175
Turn   1, 10, 17 f., 23, 39, 42, 62, 64, 75 f., 79, 83, 88, 90 f., 95, 97, 101, 116, 118 f., 122, 126, 131, 137, 139, 142 f., 151, 162, 169–172, 175, 178
– Individualistic turn   51, 53

Understanding (Verstand)   3, 18, 21, 23, 34, 36, 40 f., 43, 52, 60, 72, 88, 96, 100, 105, 108, 118, 123, 126, 128, 130, 137, 145, 148 f., 160, 162, 164, 166, 171, 173, 176–178
Universalism   4 f., 10 f., 93, 149, 166
– Moral universalism   63, 82–84, 88, 130, 164, 166, 168
Universality, universal   7, 11, 24, 119, 127, 131, 144, 154, 177
utilitarianism   146, 176

Value   30, 41, 61, 92, 108, 116, 118, 126, 131 f., 149, 164 f., 172, 178 f.
– Cosmopolitan values   18, 116, 118, 126, 133, 137
Virtue   6, 19, 29–31, 33 f., 40, 42, 44–46, 53, 60 f., 63, 66 f., 74, 81–83, 85–88, 90, 92, 98–100, 109, 113, 115 f., 118, 121, 123, 129, 133, 135–141, 145, 155, 157–159, 170, 176
– civic virtue   79, 111, 134 f., 137
– political virtue   134, 136
vocation (Bestimmung)   1–3, 8–10, 12–15, 25, 29 f., 42, 47, 92, 97, 100–102, 105–109, 113, 115 f., 119, 124 f., 136–140, 147 f., 150–154, 164, 174 f., 179
– vocation of the species   150 f.

war   1, 50, 66, 68, 84, 89, 101, 107, 141, 153 f., 168, 179
Whiggish, Whig interpretation of history   3, 179

Index of names

Abowitz, Kathleen 167f., 170
Achenwall, Gottfried 58, 60, 62
Appiah, Kwame Anthony 5, 171
Arendt, Hannah 3, 75, 131, 170
Augustine 88

Basedow, Johann Bernhard 3f., 17, 36, 75, 92–102, 108, 110–112, 114f.
Beck, Lewis White 5, 7, 8, 119, 166, 170
Beck, Ulrich 5, 8, 87, 119, 166, 170
Beiser, Frederick 35f., 40, 134, 140, 148–150, 158f.
Bentham, Jeremy 68
Bevir, Mark 19f., 164
Burke, Edmund 71–73
Byrd, Sharon 8, 12, 26, 29, 50–55, 58, 127, 135

Cheneval, Francis 2, 11f., 22, 25–28, 30f., 36f., 41f., 44, 49–51, 58, 77f., 80, 127, 167
Coleridge, Samuel Taylor 76
Cramer, Johann Andreas 95f.
Crusoe, Robinson 129f., 138

Defoe, Daniel 129f.
Dewey, John 1, 5
Diderot, Denis 25, 60–63, 68, 70f., 78
Douzinas, Costas 171

Erskine, Tony 167

Feyerabend, Paul 163
Fichte, Johann Gottlieb 147, 151–154, 158f., 177
Fine, Robert 2, 154–156, 165, 168f.

Grotius, Hugo 56–59, 61, 69, 155

Habermas, Jürgen 3, 73, 167, 172
Hand, Michael 132, 176f.
Hastings, Warren 64, 71f.
Hayden, Matthew 3f., 177

Hegel, Georg Wilhelm Friedrich 147, 154–157, 159, 165
Herbart, Johann Friedrich 19, 147, 157
Herder, Johann Gottfried 130, 156
Hobbes, Thomas 57, 101
Horkheimer, Max 174f.
Hruschka, Joachim 8, 12, 26, 29, 50–55, 58, 127, 135
Humboldt, Wilhelm von 154, 175
Hume, David 63–65, 67–69, 83
Hunter, Ian 12, 19, 57, 162
Husain, Ed 130f.

Kelsen, Hans 6
Kleingeld, Pauline 1–5, 11–13, 23, 27, 32, 41f., 50f., 53, 55, 73, 111, 114, 130, 133, 139f., 149f., 170f., 175
Koch, Lutz 2, 9, 107, 111, 119, 121–123, 125–128, 140
Korsgaard, Christine 77, 173
Kristeva, Julia 171

Langthaler, Rudolf 6, 22, 29, 33, 164
Louden, Robert 2, 8, 11–14, 29, 31, 39, 44, 94, 97f., 100f., 105f., 108–110, 114, 117, 119, 124, 128, 131, 133, 141, 161f., 164, 170
Løvlie, Lars 128, 175
Luther, Martin 153

Martens, Georg Friedrich von 62–64
Martini, Karl Anton Freiherr von 58f., 62, 64
Montesquieu, Charles-Louis de Secondat 54, 63, 65f., 68, 72, 78, 83, 134, 136
Moran, Kate 2, 6f., 22, 31, 41, 105, 107, 135f., 138, 141, 144
Mouffe, Chantal 3, 166, 169, 172
Munzel, Felicitas 3f., 6, 9, 24, 40, 94, 96–98, 114, 118f., 121f., 125, 128f., 137, 139–141, 143–145

Norris, Henry   129
Novalis (Georg Philipp Friedrich Freiherr von Hardenberg)   147, 149–151, 157
Nussbaum, Martha   2, 5, 80, 88, 159f., 170f., 175–179

Pufendorf, Samuel   57–60, 62, 65, 69, 78, 155
Putnam, Hilary   169
Pütter, Johann Stephan   58, 60, 62

Raynal, Abbé de   60, 68, 70–72
Rorty, Richard   8f., 41, 65, 108, 114, 140, 169, 175, 177
Roth, Klas   2, 9, 121, 170, 178
Rousseau, Jean-Jacques   2–4, 13, 16–19, 36, 65–69, 75–95, 97, 100, 102–116, 118f., 128f., 133, 135–139, 143, 156, 159, 171, 173

Saint-Pierre, Abbé de   80, 84, 105, 147
Saito, Hiro   165, 177

Schiller, Friedrich von   147–149, 154, 157, 159
Schlegel, Friedrich   80, 158
Schmitt, Carl   168f.
Smith, Adam   5, 23, 55, 61, 63–65, 67–70, 73, 78, 128
Socrates   90, 121
Spalding, Johann Joachim   4, 14, 30, 36, 108, 124, 137

Todd, Sharon   2f., 74f., 117, 131, 147, 170, 175

Vattel, Emer de   24, 54, 58–60, 64, 69, 155
Vitoria, Francisco de   16, 49, 55–57, 59, 61f., 70, 72, 130

Walzer, Michael   167
Ward, Robert Plumer   61, 63f.
Wegwert, Joseph   167f., 170
Wolff, Christian   24f., 30, 58f., 62, 64
Wood, Allen   10, 12, 22f., 33, 40, 44–46, 55, 62, 69, 99, 112, 119, 128, 164

www.ingramcontent.com/pod-product-compliance
Lightning Source LLC
Chambersburg PA
CBHW050901160426
43194CB00011B/2244